'A number of textbooks have been published that examine organizational behaviour issues in sport. They are all highly instructive, but tend to do it in conventional ways by taking generic models of organizational theory, group dynamics and interpersonal relations, and inserting a few sport-related cases. This book is different because it first and foremost provides a detailed contextual frame that both connects sport to the world of business, and sets it apart from it. Within this strong sport-business framework it uses hardened theories of workplace behaviour to illuminate the ways sport works, and how it can ultimately work better. In taking this approach this book highlights the various individual, interpersonal and organizational behaviours that occur when delivering the sport product to its various stakeholders.

The book has three additional strengths:

- First, it is written by two highly experienced sport management academics: James Skinner is Director of the Institute for Sport Business, and Professor of Sport Business, in the London campus of Loughborough University in the UK. Bob Stewart is the Sport Management Program Director in the College of Sport and Exercise Science at Victoria University in Melbourne in Australia. Between them, James and Bob have 40 years of teaching and research experience. They have also published more than 20 books that examine the commercial, social and cultural development of sport. They have the ideal background for putting together a book that examines the complex behaviours of people working in sport setting, be they highly bureaucratized sport businesses, or informal community associations and clubs. They both write very clearly and concisely and bring prosaic theories and concepts to life by linking them to highly grounded cases and incidents. This fusion of theory and practice threads its way through the entire book, and places it in a league of its own.

- Second, the book has something for everyone. There are 21 succinctly written chapters together with more than 40 cases that cover everything you wanted to know about managing people in sport settings. Specific chapters are allocated to sport's special features, organizational design and structure, culture and climate, job analysis and selection, orientation and induction, rewards and incentives, training and development, personality, perception, motivation, emotions, attitudes and job satisfaction, group behaviour, team dynamics, interpersonal communication, safety and risk, stress and aggression, conflict, misbehaviour and dispute resolution, power and politics, bargaining and negotiation, and, finally, change and organizational realignment. The coverage is broad, but it is also deep.

- Finally, everything is superbly glued together by the overarching proposition that sport enterprises will only fulfil their potential if their staff – be they highly paid or volunteers – are managed in ways that enhance their technical skills, creative capabilities, and interpersonal sensitivities.

I unreservedly recommend this book to anyone who wants to find out how best to manage people working in the sport industry. Students and practitioners alike will find it a highly valuable resource that offers fresh insights at every turn of the page. Essential reading!'

Aaron Smith, Professor of Management, RMIT University, Australia

Organizational Behaviour in Sport

What makes a sport enterprise successful? How can managers working in sport improve organizational effectiveness through strategic behaviour management? This comprehensive and accessible textbook addresses these important questions and examines the theories that underpin organizational analysis in sport. Helping both students and practitioners to understand the different types of behaviour that occur within a sports enterprise, it also demonstrates how to develop ways of managing behaviour more effectively for the benefit of all stakeholders.

The book explores behaviour on individual, interpersonal, group and whole-organization levels, and presents an evidence-based framework for analysis built around key concepts such as:

- Change and culture
- Leadership
- Motivation, rewards and incentives
- Power and influence
- Conflict, disputes and grievances
- Equity, diversity and inclusion.

With international case studies, learning objectives, review questions and guides to further reading included in every chapter, no other textbook develops critical skills or an awareness of ethical issues in such detail and depth. *Organizational Behaviour in Sport* is essential reading for all students and practitioners working in sport, leisure or recreation management.

James Skinner is the Director of the Institute for Sport Business and Professor of Sport Business at Loughborough University London, UK. His primary research interests are in leadership, culture and change in sport.

Bob Stewart is a Professor of Sport Management in the College of Sport and Exercise Science at Victoria University, Australia. His primary research interests are in the field of sport policy, culture and the regulation of sport.

Foundations of Sport Management

Series Editor:
David Hassan, University of Ulster at Jordanstown, UK

Foundations of Sport Management is a discipline-defining series of texts on core and cutting-edge topics in sport management. Featuring some of the best known and most influential sport management scholars from around the world, each volume represents an authoritative, engaging and self-contained introduction to a key functional area or issue within contemporary sport management. Packed with useful features to aid teaching and learning, the series aims to bridge the gap between management theory and practice and to encourage critical thinking and reflection among students, academics and practitioners.

Also available in this series:

Managing Sport Business: An Introduction
David Hassan and Linda Trenberth

Managing Sport: Social and Cultural Perspectives
David Hassan and Jim Lusted

Managing High Performance Sport
Popi Sotiriadou and Veerle De Bosscher

Routledge Handbook of Sport and Corporate Social Responsibility
Kathy Babiak, Juan Luis Paramio-Salcines and Geoff Walters

Sport Governance: International Case Studies
Ian O'Boyle and Trish Bradbury

Research Methods for Sport Management
James Skinner, Allan Edwards and Ben Corbett

Leadership in Sport
Ian O'Boyle, Duncan Murray and Paul Cummins

Organizational Behaviour in Sport
James Skinner and Bob Stewart

Organizational Behaviour in Sport

James Skinner and
Bob Stewart

Routledge
Taylor & Francis Group

LONDON AND NEW YORK

First published 2017
by Routledge
2 Park Square, Milton Park, Abingdon, Oxon OX14 4RN

and by Routledge
711 Third Avenue, New York, NY 10017

Routledge is an imprint of the Taylor & Francis Group, an informa business

© 2017 James Skinner and Bob Stewart

British Library Cataloguing-in-Publication Data
A catalogue record for this book is available from the British Library

Library of Congress Cataloging in Publication Data
A catalog record for this book has been requested

ISBN: 978-0-415-67175-0 (hbk)
ISBN: 978-0-415-67176-7 (pbk)
ISBN: 978-0-203-13196-1 (ebk)

Typeset in Perpetua
by Saxon Graphics Ltd, Derby

Contents

CONTENTS

Illustrations

FIGURES

TABLES

Organizational behaviour in sport

Sport has an ambivalent status in Western societies. On one hand, it is a pivotal component of our popular culture; to many people sport is life, and the rest a shadow. On the other hand, it is sometimes viewed as ephemeral, anti-intellectual, and the 'toy department of life'. Be that as it may, it has now become a massive commercial enterprise, with huge global reach. And, like any large-scale business, it must be properly organized and managed to ensure its long-term sustainability. Sport is also a special sort of commercial enterprise, and while it has many of the generic features of so-called normal business, it has many distinguishing features, which include:

1   Its primary focus on athletic success.
2   Secondary importance of profits.
3   The need to collaborate with rival organizations to ensure an effective competition.
4   Use of partnerships to secure essential income flows.
5   Additional use of partnerships to engage in social causes.
6   Capacity to engender highly levels of commitment and loyalty.
7   The fact that the employees – that is, the players and athletes – are simultaneously the service deliverers and the products purchased by consumers.
8   Use of volunteers to complement the work of paid staff.
9   Use of highly targeted rules and regulations to manage player and athlete behaviour.
10 Saturation attention that media gives to the off-field lives of players and athletes.

Although there are textbooks that examine organizational behaviour issues in sport, most of them do it in very conventional ways. They take generic models of organizational theory, group dynamics and interpersonal relations, insert a few cases, give some examples from the world of sport and then claim that the book explains all there is to know about sport and its management. This approach is succinct and safe, but fails to locate sport management within an appropriate contextual frame, or to work within the special features of sport and the things that make it different from mainstream business.

This book is different because it begins by providing a detailed contextual frame that not only connects sport to the world of business, but also sets it apart from business. It then examines the theories that underpin the conventional organizational analysis and prioritizes those models that best explain and illuminate the ways sport works, and how it can, ultimately, work better. Moreover, given the strong person-centred focus of sport, where the role of sport managers is to assist others to deliver a performance to be watched by even more people, this book highlights the various individual, interpersonal and organizational behaviours that occur when delivering the sport product to its various stakeholders.

Our main concern is to assist readers to better understand the different types of behaviours that occur in sport organizations – both functional and dysfunctional – and use appropriate theory to help the reader to work out ways of managing the behaviours to secure the best possible outcomes for the club, league, event or whatever other sport activity is under scrutiny. To this end, the topics will not only have people-management issues front and centre, but also include cases that involve problems and opportunities that are central to the operation of sport enterprises. Some of these are purely fictional and for illustrative purposes, whereas others are based on specific sources, as indicated in the text. We believe this approach will: (1) give the book a unique edge over more conventional organizational development (OD) texts; and (2) ensure that it will appeal to people whose special interest is people-management in sport. This book is thus distinctive in terms of its structure, its topics and themes, its theoretical backdrop and its case analysis.

This book, which comprises 21 succinctly written chapters, is designed for people who want to become better managers of sports enterprises and the people in them, and additionally have the theory and evidence to back up their decisions, and inform their policies and strategies. To this end the following topics are addressed.

PART A: CONTEXTUAL, STRUCTURAL AND OPERATIONAL FEATURES OF SPORT ENTERPRISES

- Chapter 1. Sport's special features: What is it about sport that makes sport enterprises it different from normal commercial business? What are the implications of these 'special features' for the people-management capabilities of sport enterprise staff?
- Chapter 2. Design and structure: What are the design options for sport enterprises? Is there one best structure, or is structure dependent on the strategic and operational demands of specific sport enterprises?
- Chapter 3. Culture and climate: Is the culture and operational climate of sport enterprises all that important in the light of its taken-for-granted competitive ethos? In what ways can culture and climate vary between sport enterprises? Is there an ideal culture and climate for sport enterprises, and if there is, how can it be created?

PART B: JOB-TASK PROCESSES IN SPORT ENTERPRISES

- Chapter 4. Job analysis and selection: Why is job analysis such an important part of the staff recruitment process? How can the recruitment process be designed to ensure the selection of the most capable staff?
- Chapter 5. Orientation and induction: What makes the orientation and induction process so important for sport enterprises? What does the socialization/integration process involve, and how should it be organized? How might the socialization/integration

process be adapted to the needs of paid staff, on the one hand, and volunteer staff, on the other?

■ Chapter 6. Reward systems: What incentivizes people to work hard and be smart? What rewards do people seek implicitly in sport enterprises? Are there differences between paid staff and volunteer staff? Does the provision of incentives also need a counter-balancing array of threats and punishments?

■ Chapter 7. Training and development: What is the purpose of training and development? What are the key components of a training and development programme? What has to be done to ensure the effective delivery of a training programme in sport enterprises? How might the success (or failure) of a training programme be determined?

PART C: EMPLOYEE TRAITS, DISPOSITIONS AND BEHAVIOURS

■ Chapter 8. Personality: What is personality, and what is meant by the term 'personality trait'? To what extent does personality shape behaviour? Does personality matter when appointing staff to jobs in sport-related workplaces? Is personality a predictor of job performance?

■ Chapter 9. Perceptions: What is perception and how does it work? What do the principles of perception tell us about the propensity of people to perceive the same social phenomena in different ways? What are perceptual sets and how might they lead to perceptual error? What are some perceptual errors, and how can they undermine the effective management of sport enterprises?

■ Chapter 10. Motivation: Why do some people invest enormous energy into work and others not so much? What drives people to work hard or not so hard in different sport environments? What is the difference between intrinsic motivation and extrinsic motivation, and how can they applied to motivational issues in sport enterprises? Do temperament and personality have roles to play in motivating staff in sport enterprise settings?

■ Chapter 11. Attitudes, emotions and job satisfaction: What is meant by the concept of job satisfaction? When examining the conduct of staff in sport enterprises, what emotional states are associated with different levels of job satisfaction? In sport, what factors lead to job satisfaction, on the one hand, and job dissatisfaction, on the other? Does job satisfaction lead to positive emotional states and superior performance in sport enterprises? What does it mean to have a positive work attitude, and why is it important?

PART D: COMMUNICATION SYSTEMS AND SOCIAL PROCESSES

■ Chapter 12. Group behaviour: To what extent do sport enterprise staff work in groups to get things done? What are the strength and weaknesses of working groups? What developmental processes do work groups normally experience? How does group decision-making differ from individual decision-making? Under what conditions will group decision-making usually deliver the best outcomes?

■ Chapter 13. Team dynamics: What makes teams different from groups? How might teams in sport enterprises vary in their structure and purpose? What processes are needed to produce effective teams? What internal factors contribute to effective team performance? What contextual factors contribute to effective team performance?

■ Chapter 14. Interpersonal communication: What are the essential features and processes of interpersonal communication? What forms can communication take? Is there a one single best communication for all situations and circumstances? What factors lead to mixed messaging and distorted communication? What can be done to improve interpersonal communication systems in sport enterprises? What role is there for social media in a sport enterprise communication system?

■ Chapter 15. Leadership: What, exactly, is leadership all about? What makes for good leadership? Can leaders be made, or is more about innate qualities and appropriate personality traits? In what ways are task-centred leaders different from person-centred leaders? What differentiates a charismatic leader from a transformational leader? What can good leaders achieve that poor leaders cannot? What different leadership styles are displayed in sport settings and why have they been successful?

PART E: MANAGING PROBLEMATIC STRUCTURES, OPERATIONS AND BEHAVIOURS

■ Chapter 16. Safety and risk: How is the concept of risk best defined in today's sport environment, and how does it relate to the issue of safety? How important is a low-risk, safe climate to sport enterprises? How do you create a safe and risk-conscious sport environment and workplace?

■ Chapter 17. Stress and aggression: What is stress and what are its sources? What are the sources of workplace stress? What are the symptoms of workplace stress? What makes for anxiety and stress in work settings? How can aggression impact on stress? What forms can workplace aggression take? How might discrimination, bullying, harassment and homophobia engender aggression and how can it be managed? What might be done to reduce aggression in the workplace? What roles can education, training and counselling play in the elimination of workplace aggression?

■ Chapter 18. Conflict management and resolution: What causes conflict? What are the different models for managing conflict? Under what conditions should hard approaches be utilized, and under what conditions might soft approaches be the preferred option? How useful is dispute resolution in sorting out conflicts in sport enterprises? How might cases of misbehaviour lead to conflict? How might misbehaviour be best managed in sport enterprises?

PART F: POWER, CONTROL AND CHANGE

■ Chapter 19. Power and politics: What is power and how does it work? Where do people working in sport enterprises get their power from? Why do some people in sport enterprises have a lot of power and other very little? Does it matter, and if so, how can power be more equally distributed throughout a sport enterprise? How can the notion of 'empowerment' be used as a strategy to improve organizational performance? How are power and leadership related? Under what conditions will additional power produce more authoritative leadership?

■ Chapter 20. Bargaining and negotiation: What are the key theories and principles that underpin bargaining and negotiation processes? What specific sport enterprise operations most often involve bargaining and negotiation? How does a zero-sum-game view of bargaining and negotiation work? How does a win-win view of bargaining and negotiation work? What would a sport-enterprise-based bargaining and negotiation model that allows for a win-win outcome look like?

■ Chapter 21. Change and realignment: What are the key external factors that are forcing sport enterprises to re-examine their current structure, values, policies and day-to-day operations? What are the implications of these outside pressures for the interpersonal conduct of staff, volunteers, players and members? What change programmes could be implemented that can best deal with the issues of technological change, and cultural and social diversity within sport? Is there also a case for addressing dysfunctional stereotyping and discrimination?

Part A
Contextual, structural and operational features of sport enterprises

Part A

Chapter 1

Sport's special features

OVERVIEW

This chapter addresses the underlying structures, values and operational features of sport, and how they impact on organizational conduct, as well as on the behaviour – both individual and interpersonal – of managers, administrators, officials, players and members. Special attention will be given to the ways in which contemporary sport is both different from and similar to the world of commerce, and the implications it has for the management of staff in sport enterprises.

LEARNING OBJECTIVES

Having read this chapter, students will be able to:

1. Identify the diverse range of enterprises that constitute the sport sector;
2. Explain critically how sport has become increasingly corporate over recent times;
3. Understand why, despite this corporatization, sport has special features which define its organization, operation and ethos;
4. Understand the ways in which this corporatization has impacted on the conduct of sport enterprises, and the behavioural expectations and job requirements of managers, administrators, officials, players and members; and
5. Explain why volunteers are essential to the operation of sport enterprises around the world.

ENVIRONMENTAL PRESSURES ON SPORT ENTERPRISES

When examining the place of sport in contemporary society, the first point to note is that it is played out in a world markedly different from 50 years ago. This suggests that sport, too, has changed over this period. The second point to note is that sport does not operate in a social, cultural and economic vacuum, but is rather shaped by its context. This will be a major theme running throughout this book.

Many of these contextual forces were evident in the 1960s. It was, on one hand, a slower, less complicated time, and in many respects it was also a more conservative time, when traditions dictated social behaviour at both work and play. However, it was also a turbulent time, when the Western world experienced rapid industrialization, increasing urbanization, greater levels of household consumption and large-scale international migration. It was also a time of significant technological change. The jet airliner was in the prototype stage and international tourism expanded rapidly. But this was also a luxury that only the well-heeled middle classes could afford. Agriculture and manufacturing were the engines of growth for most economies, and the service sector was dominated by retail and Government employees. This had all changed by the 1980s, when economies were driven by consumption more than production, and the service sector grew rapidly. During the 1990s national economies became less regulated as Government enterprises were privatized, trade barriers were removed, the banking sector was deregulated and global trade expanded exponentially.

Guided capitalism and the welfare state gave in to a new form of economic management that was most often described as 'neo-liberalism'. Minimum wages were left to the market to determine, safety nets for the poor and disadvantaged were loosened, and the space was immediately occupied by the forces of liberalism and technological progress. Moreover, the desire for constant change not only accelerated product obsolescence, but also led individuals to use consumption as a means of defining their roles, social position, status relations and identity. At one level this was liberating since it allowed people to reinvent personal identity and reposition their social identity. But it was also problematic for some people, since it often undermined any sense of continuity and social connectedness.

This shift in economic and social structures produced a massive amount of introspective analysis that led many critics of capitalism to claim that modern Western nations had entered a new phase in their development. Modernity – the period from the 1940s to the 1960s – was based on a rational and linear view of the world, the assumption that real production centred on tangible products, the importance of clearly defined hierarchies and strict lines of command, the central place of nuclear families, fidelity and lifelong marriage, and an ideology that centred on Government regulation of markets. This all changed in the 1970s and beyond. This new world was dominated by constant change, an obsession with the consumption of leisure goods, a breakdown of all types of hierarchies, the privatization of Government services and the drive for more individual freedoms. Various labels were attached to what was seen to be a major break with the past. In the 1970s it was generally agreed that the world had entered a postmodern phase, but by the 1990s the term 'late-modern' was used to describe the changing world context. By the beginning of the new millennium – that is, any time after 2000 – the term 'hypermodern' was used to describe what came to be a significant break with the past. This was the world that sport had to deal with.

Thus, Western society entered an age of apparent excess where rampart consumerism was tempered by an expansion of individual rights and responsibilities. This was hypermodernity at work. There was a lot happening, but for some commentators not all of it was good. A breakdown of traditional hierarchies and authority relations meant that individual attitudes and behaviours were no longer constrained by the rigid social and moral demands of the family, the church and the State. People were faced with a smorgasbord of choices and options. One option was about how to best define one's sense of self, and how to go about constructing an identity that was no longer determined by virtue of family connections, religious affiliations, cultural traditions and occupational attachments. Another option centred on the problem of what to consume, and the immediate response was the adoption of hedonistic lifestyles, where individual pleasuring and social positioning were front and centre. As it turned out, the twin problems of identity and lifestyle choices were fused by the explosive use of consumption practices to build an identity around a lifestyle and leisure practices. This is where sport became an important determinant of personal and social identity.

But, as with most forms of economic and social change, not everybody benefitted from these newly won freedoms: whereas some people were able to prudently assess their lifestyle choices, and subsequently enhance their quality of life in response to technological advancement and economic growth, others were engulfed by a 'destructive irresponsibility'. In a world stripped of its traditions, responsibility for social and moral action now resided in the individual, and the pronouncements of authority figures that hitherto had moral gravity were dismissed as puritanical and prejudiced. Many individuals were overwhelmed by the moral and social space they now occupied, and their escalating desire for easy pleasures and self-aggrandizement crowded out any commitment to self-discipline, public interest and the idea of the greater good. And threading its way through this moral malaise, disconnect from the past and uncertainty about the future was an insidious uneasiness manifest as chronic and sometime disabling anxiety.

This was the price to be paid for securing a social and economic system that valued ambition, freedom and individual rights above all else. This focus on individualism and freedom was not only visible in people's social relationships – be it at work or at play – but was also evident in the economic and political push for the deregulation of markets, which went under the name of neo-liberalism. Neo-liberalism and the competitive hedonism that accompanied it sometimes undermined the protection afforded previously to disadvantaged communities by the welfare state, and very often destroyed the social institutions that had provided meaning and security. For many critics, hypermodernism created an enormous amount of social wreckage. On the other hand, it enshrined human rights as a fundamental ideal, and enabled resources to be allocated to a whole raft of agencies and groups whose prime role was the protection of people's rights.

In this new hypermodern inspired, neo-liberal society, the forces that had previously opposed a more liberalized modernity – communism, socialism and collectivism, for example – had been rendered ineffectual. The great alternative visions had collapsed under the weight of a rampaging individualism married to identity-defining consumerism. Society was now more fluid than ever before. It was now far complex as the Internet rendered the postal system obsolete and fixed-line telephones networks redundant. And, as explained in more detail later, the demarcation between sport and business became increasingly blurred. Although commercial businesses were taking on a range of social causes and spending time protecting the environment, sport enterprises were complementing their concern for social development and public value with things like strategic planning, organizational effectiveness, corporate partnering, staff development and employee productivity. They often seemed more concerned with profits than player participation, social inclusion and competitive success.

11

IMPLICATIONS FOR SPORT

Sport, like every other human endeavour and leisure practice, has found the forces of hypermodernism and neo-liberalism difficult to counter, and now, for the most part has given in to its demand for new, efficient and commercialized ways of doing things. Adaptability is the key to survival and sustainability, and thus flexible structures and systems have become central to sport's commercial viability and social relevance. As we approach 2020 we find that sport is not what it used to be. Sport is no longer able to run its affairs within a minimalist structure, nor rely on the goodwill of a few enthusiastic volunteers to deliver its services. It can no longer legitimize a job description by writing it down on the back of an envelope. Sporting clubs can no longer expect people to contribute to a sporting club's operations for the love of the game. And, neither can clubs assume that their officials will be up to the task of handling grievances and disputes, or allegations of internal misconduct just because they are committed to the club's sustainability. The fact of the matter is that the demands on sport officials are higher than ever before, and no matter what the level of operation, the key to good sport enterprise performance now, and in the foreseeable future, is a highly developed set of people-management skills.

The management of sport enterprises is made additionally difficult by their increasingly hybrid quality, which has already been noted briefly. Sport has a number of special features that make it different from most other fields of social and commercial endeavour. It is no longer just about playing games, but neither is it only about commercial gain. This hybrid quality is a double-edged sword. Some of its features make adaption to changing circumstances easy, whereas others do not. But taken together, they provide the context for understanding more clearly the way sport enterprises conduct their affairs, the ways in which staff, players, and members are likely to behave, and the problematic intra-organizational, interpersonal and individual issues they have to deal with in their day-to-day engagement with each other. An additional level of complexity arises when the demands of external stakeholders – especially Government, corporate sponsors, broadcasters and fans – are addressed. It is thus important to spend time examining sport's special features, and reflecting on what they mean for the management of people in sport enterprises. These special features are listed below.

DIVERSITY

Sport is an enigmatic institution and comes in many forms. For instance, the mainstay of sport in many countries is the community club that relies on the support of its members to sustain its activities. These clubs can be single-sport enterprises like tennis clubs and swimming clubs, but they can also be multifunctional and provide a range of sports under the same roof. They are managed frequently by volunteers who pay fees for the privilege of playing. There are also sporting associations whose primary role is to provide administrative support to clubs, organize competitions and generally develop the sport they represent, whether it is netball, table tennis or volleyball. Although these enterprises have many paid employees, they also rely on volunteer staff to run their programmes and manage their affairs. Then there are commercial leisure centres that provide sport services on a fee-for-service or user-pay principle. Gymnasiums and swimming centres often fall into this category, and can be either privately owned or owned by local councils. There is also a raft of professional sport clubs and leagues that play in large stadiums, attract thousands of spectators, and generate mass-media coverage. These sport enterprises are book-ended by first, Government and its agencies, and second, the media and sport merchandisers, who both promote sport and use its star players to attract customers.

The practice of sport can thus be viewed from two different perspectives. For some it is all about participation, playing the game for its own sake and using the game to develop character and leadership. In other words, sport can be a vehicle for making better people and improving communities. In these instances commercialism is often viewed as a problem by its tendency to overemphasize winning, encourage gambling and undermine the values of amateurism. On the other hand, some people believe that sport can only achieve its potential if it is well supported and funded. In other words, commercialized sport will not only increase standards of play by sustaining professional sport leagues, but also improve the productivity of its human capital; that is to say, its paid staff and volunteer officials. At the same time, the benefits of commercial sport are not always shared equally, since some sports are inherently more popular than others and attract more funding. As a result sports like canoeing, water polo and rowing will always be disadvantaged so long as they are played in the shadows of popular spectator sports like the various codes of football (American football, Australian football, Gaelic football, rugby league, rugby union and world football), tennis and cricket.

Essentially, sport practice comprises two distinctive but connected strands. The first strand is community sport, which comprises participant-based sport geared around the local club, the volunteer administrator, a simple organizational structure and the recreational player. Whereas a few talented young players will use the local club as the springboard for entry into the world of elite sport development, most club members will focus their energies on interclub competition and building their social networks. The second strand is professional sport, which is centred on the elite performer and geared around spectators who provide the catalyst for the sports' commercial development. It attracts media coverage which, in turn, provides a promotional impetus for further spectator interest. Broadcasting of events emerges, rights fees are negotiated, corporate sponsors see the benefits of linking their brands to a sport league or club, and all of a sudden professional sport leagues and mega-sport events begin to occupy large slabs of the sports landscape. When sport becomes commercial rather than recreational, officials, players and fans begin to take it very seriously.

CORPORATIZATION

A key feature of contemporary sport is its increasingly intricate links to the business sector. This process of corporatization is often problematic and has been labelled as the 'paradox of commercialism'. Although strategic advice is usually geared towards bolstering the commercial success of sport brands, there is an ongoing tension between sport as a business and sport as a game-centred, social institution. In this uneasy balance, sports are faced with the challenge of extracting commercial value from their brands without compromising the intrinsic integrity and spirit of the game. Fuelled by a celebrity ethos and the centrality of entertainment, it is easy to undermine the brand and diminish its status as a heroic form of human endeavour. As a consequence, sport's quintessential nature is at risk whenever it commercializes itself to secure a larger share of the market. However, it also means that unless sport commercializes itself, it will be unable to survive in the contemporary competitive landscape. However, despite the dire pronouncements linked to sport's commercialization, fears that members and fans will abandon professional sport have proved to be unfounded.

This corporate transformation has not, however, reduced the tension between the need to make a profit and the desire to achieve on-field success. But what it has done is to highlight the multiple demands that contemporary sport places on the enterprise and management of constituent enterprises. Stakeholders have a diverse set of needs and, in addition, they all believe that their needs have the highest priority. Management also understand that stakeholder aspirations will only be achieved if revenue streams are strong, staff are professionally trained and socially adept, and everyone is committed to the organizational cause. This requires not only strategic and technical skills, but also highly developed people-management skills.

BLURRING OF COMMERCIAL AND NOT-FOR-PROFIT BOUNDARIES

Forty years ago there were clearly different perceptions of the purpose of commercial enterprises and not-for-profit enterprises. Commercial business was in the business of building products, selling services and making profits. Not-for-profit enterprises, on the other hand, were more concerned with building communities, supporting the disadvantaged, providing mutual assistance and delivering public services like education. Apart from a few professional leagues, sport was very much part of the not-for-profit sector. It secured most of its funds from members, and used these funds to deliver a range of programmes centred on sport and active recreation.

Today the boundaries are blurred. Many commercial organizations are undertaking a raft of social development programmes aimed at building communities, assisting the disadvantaged and, more generally, supporting social causes that range from delivering literacy programmes to children in developing nations to raising funds to support breast-cancer research. And, as noted in the previous section, sport has also expanded its operating parameters. First, it now has a much deeper concern for building its revenue base and covering its costs. It has to be financially prudent. It also believes it has a responsibility to not only provide space for people to engage in healthy physical activity, but to assist people who have been disadvantaged or disabled in one form or another. Sport has entered the age of social causes, and consequently has invested in programmes that counter racism and homophobia, and educate young people about mental illness, anxiety and social isolation, and how to manage them better. In recent times sexual violence has become a focal point for the development of sport-centred promotional campaigns. Sports enterprises are now often multifunctional, where service to members is one among many of their civic responsibilities.

SPECIFICITY OF SPORT

The boundary-blurring issue provides a succinct lead-in to the idea that sport is qualitatively different from the world of 'normal' business. This idea has been given further impetus by the European Union's 2007 *White Paper on Sport*. When discussing the place of sport in contemporary society it gave special attention to its 'specificity'. It used this term to highlight significant features of sport that differentiate it from other fields of commerce and industry, while also acknowledging the thousands of intricate economic and social exchanges required for the delivery of sport experiences.

First, its activities are defined by a plethora of internal law, rules and customs. These laws, rules and customs not only determine what is, and is not, permissible in different games and contests, but also set the parameters for who is, or is not, permitted to play. Moreover, all sorts of rules and regulations are used to ensure fair and balanced competitions, and thus avoid situations where the inequities are so severe that the outcome of the contest is never in doubt. Thus, tacit approval is granted by the broader community – and Government especially – for the organizers of sport events to give the contest outcome a high degree of uncertainty that will attract both players and spectators. This can be done by giving the fastest runners a handicap (done in traditional forms of professional running), establishing a range of weight divisions (done in boxing, the martial arts and rowing) and segregating contests into male-only and female-only.

Second, sport is not only highly structured but is also organized around clearly defined hierarchies. It conforms to a pyramid mode, whereby the base of the pyramid includes community 'grass roots' sport, the middle level involves those sports that are seriously competitive and sometimes played for money, while the peak of the pyramid includes all the elite players, many of whom will have an international reputation, and many of whom will be paid handsome retainers. The peak of every sporting pyramid will also have a single governing body that sets the planning and operational parameters for all the associations and clubs under its governance.

Third, this sporting pyramid is tightly bound by a set of interdependencies that connect its different levels, although not always in positive ways. For example, the young athletes at the bottom of the pyramid need constant nurturing because they will inevitably become the talent pool from which the next bunch of elite performers will be selected. At the same time, retired elite players can be encouraged to re-enter their chosen sport at the grass roots level, since they can provide the experience and expertise to assist the establishment of the next talent pool of young players.

FISHBOWL EXPERIENCE OF PLAYERS

Players and athletes are at the heart of sport. This is especially evident in professional sport, where fans pay good money – sometimes a few hundred pounds – to attend games, watch events and exhilarate in the performances of their favourite players. The history of sport demonstrates that sporting heroes, particularly when they perform at the very highest level, will attract enormous crowds. Examples include Babe Ruth in American Major League Baseball, Stanley Matthews in English football (soccer), Donald Bradman in international cricket, Pelé in Brazilian and international soccer, and Michael Jordon in American basketball. There are many equivalent examples in contemporary sport, including Usain Bolt in athletics, Serena Williams in tennis, Tiger Woods in international golf, and Lionel Messi in world football. Even in local competitions there is an insatiable media interest not only in what players do on the field, but also in what they do off the field. In becoming the centre of media attention they have also become local celebrities, and every misdemeanour and ever-so-slightly socially deviant behaviour is allocated front-page headlines.

This development means that players live a fishbowl existence where their behaviour is scrutinized daily. Moreover, clubs, teams and leagues have become increasingly sensitive to any negative publicity that arises from player misbehaviour, and have put in place a raft of rules and codes of conduct that provide sanctions for players in contravention. Sport enterprises have hired lawyers, counsellors, agents and psychologists to assist players to manage their behaviour, and when players go outside of the narrowly proscribed limits, a team of experts and specialists is invariably there to guide them through the maze of media scrutiny and commentary that inevitably follows. The pressures on players to behave appropriately, and not to make fools of themselves or undermine the reputation of their clubs, are more onerous than in nearly any other occupation. Whereas music, film and television celebrities are almost expected to flaunt illicit drug use, sexual impropriety and financial extravagance, sports stars are expected to be exemplary citizens and solid role models for impressionable children. The media scrutiny becomes breathtakingly intense when sexual assaults or drug use are involved.

However, it is not just the media spotlight which has applied pressure to athletes to conform to behavioural guidelines. Professional sport organizations, in particular, have introduced conduct-related clauses in player contracts, which are also appearing in an increasing number of collective bargaining agreements. Nowhere are assumptions about sport's fishbowl more obvious than in the World Anti-Doping Agency's (WADA) rise to power, and the control it exerts over the lives of players and athletes. The prevailing policy approach to substance use in sport rests on the proposition that punitive sanctioning will deter drug use and remove 'drug cheats' from competition. The conduct of players has become a constant in the weekly reporting cycle of the media. It has also become an issue of other not-for-profit organizations with a particular social cause to push. Any conduct that deviates from the norm will inevitably fall under the watchful eye of anti-violence campaigners, equal opportunity proponents, anti-discrimination officials, gender equity activists, doping agency officers and drug investigators. The social-issues agenda has become so important to sport enterprises that many of them have appointed integrity offices to manage the media-commentary fallout. Again, sport managers will bear the brunt of these issues, and finely tuned interpersonal skills will be required to bring problematic player conduct to some sort of closure.

PLAYERS AS ASSETS

Another feature of contemporary sport is the massive increase in player salaries and recruiting costs, and how these impact the management process in professional sports in particular. Clubs are now confronted by the issue not only of how to deal with players who earn more than the clubs' chief executive officer and senior management team, but also how to deal with transfer fees. In these instances players are increasingly counted as assets, and indeed given a value in the same way that an item of machinery or office equipment is listed as an asset and allocated a value.

Treating players as assets can lead people to think that management have no empathy towards player problems, and see them as little more than machines that only need a bit of light maintenance to sustain their productivity. The additional implication is that whereas players can have enormous bargaining power, they can also be treated like cattle and traded at the whim of coaches and managers. As later chapters reveal, sport managers who believe that players work best when put under constant pressure, and praised only when it is absolutely necessary, will be in for a rude shock. Players like being praised, and carefully crafted rewards and incentives can boost player confidence and encourage them to play harder and think smarter. Praise can also balance the criticism that frequently comes from mainstream media, social media, television broadcasters and fans in general.

COMPETING VALUES

These discussions highlight the fact that sport enterprises are not just in the business of making money and winning games. They also have a responsibility to provide their communities with quality products that deliver positive experiences. Moreover, these experiences will involve not only short-term enjoyment, but also longer-term social connectedness and personal meaning.

Additionally, although effective structures and efficient operations are essential for delivering quality sport services, the key to a sustainable sport enterprise is its ability to handle the diverse needs of not only the people who consume its services, but also the people who supply them. This means that if sport is to manage its affairs effectively, it must balance the need for tight and systematic structures that guide effective action against the imperative of having staff, members, players and supporters who are engaged and motivated to contribute to the aspirations of the enterprise.

PUTTING IT ALL TOGETHER

Foster, Greyser and Walsh, in their 2006 publication *The Business of Sports*, tackled the sport–business nexus by compiling a list of things professional sport and business have in common, and areas where they differed. They concluded that whereas sport and business shared a common concern for value creation, branding, funding new sources of revenue product innovation and market expansion, sport was concerned more significantly with beating rivals, winning trophies, sharing revenue and channelling the passions of both players (the employees) and fans (the customers). Table 1.1 below lists these factors.

Table 1.1 The sport–business nexus

Areas of Commonality	Areas of Differentiation
Leadership and strategy matters	Winning on the field central
Value creation and value sharing	Diverse owner objectives
Search for revenue growth	Managing in the fishbowl
Value-chain encroachment and fluidity	Supporting the weakest
New product innovation	Handicapping the strongest
Astute and creative contracting	Revenue pools and allocation rules
Quality of the product matters	Athletes as business assets
Branding matters	Managing the badly behaving player
Fans and customers as a business pillar	Limited financial disclosures
Globalization	Sports as an entertainment cocktail

Source: Foster *et al.* (2006:2)

The other important point made by Foster *et al.* (2006) is that athletes are now business assets that are instrumental in attracting fans, sponsors and media exposure. And it therefore comes as no surprise that, unlike a commercial business, sports' service deliverers (the players) earn far more than their immediate supervisors (the club managers). This has important implications for the structuring of salaries in sport enterprises, and pay-relativities between different categories of employees.

IMPLICATIONS FOR EMPLOYEE COMPETENCIES

Sport is not simply just another form of business enterprise, but neither is it so special that it has no connection to business. Although the special features of sport already referred to suggest that it needs to be managed in ways that fit its idiosyncratic values and structure, it also works best under strong business models and sound management principles. One of the weaknesses of sport at the community level is its failure to grasp management theory and best-practice models, and use them to improve the performance of the sport system. At the same time, sport's unique structures and practices have important implications for the management of sport enterprises, especially when it comes to the relationships among professional staff, volunteers, players, members and fans.

And to repeat, sport enterprises do not usually aim to make profit their primary consideration. As most of them are legally set up as non-profit entities, they do not have shareholders and are not allowed to distribute profits or dividends to their owners or members. Their primary goals have more to do with service to members, or more generally, to the community. This has implications for the skills and capabilities – especially where leadership is concerned – that are valued by clubs and associations and agencies.

Sport enterprises also rely frequently on volunteers to make things happen, and plan and run events and activities. This means they must be skilled in motivating and training people to deliver things efficiently and enthusiastically. And these days, sport enterprises must be adept at securing resources and attracting members. Funds are often scarce and, as a result, membership is often the main revenue source, particularly for community clubs, associations and agencies.

In addition, the fact that sport has outcomes and expectations that are not so well rehearsed in the normal world of business means that it often has to meet a wide variety of often special needs. Diversity is a big deal in sport and is seen as a way of ensuring social inclusion. However, to be implemented successfully, it requires a broad array of management skills and competencies to ensure its effective operation. And when all the special features of sport are assembled, it is clear that highly developed interpersonal skills are a priority. Based on the discussion to date, the following competencies are required:

- Business acumen, such as a good knowledge of strategy and legal principles.
- Communication, such as good writing and oral skills, and a sharp marketing mind.
- Sensitivity to community relations, such as dealing with the public, and working with volunteers.
- Interpersonal skills, such as being able to handle conflict and being able to attentively listen to others.

- Staff-related problem solving skills, such as negotiating agreements, supervising, scheduling tasks and motivating others.
- Planning and evaluation skills, including building strategies and measuring performance, especially at the individual employee and volunteer staff level.

Although it might be said that these are really generic – that is, generalized – skills that any good sport enterprise manager needs, it is also important to note that they are heavily person-centred. As such, the effective application of these skills demands first, a deep working knowledge of people's traits, dispositions, and attitudes, and, second, a clear understanding of how the energies and capabilities of staff – be they administrative staff, coaches or players – can be harnessed to deliver the best possible outcomes for the communities they serve.

CASE STUDY

As the above discussion shows, sport is now a complex industry, where the commercial imperative of the business firm fuses with the social-value imperative of the not-for-profit enterprise. This complexity is compounded by the fact that sport is a person-centred experience where very close, and often intimate, relationships are formed between participants. This shifting web of relationships moves with every new management team, every newly trained collection of volunteer officials, every new group of members, every new coterie of corporate supporters, every new team of coaches, trainers and support staff and, of course, every new congregation of players. Players are also public figures, and need to behave impeccably when in the social spotlight. This is why there are so many issues to address when managing players in a professional sport league setting.

Consider the case of the Berlin Bears Football Club (BBFC). Johnny Joyride had been asked to examine the ways in which management could best accommodate the disparate needs of players. He was asked to not only consider in-house managers, but also those external to the club who took on the role of player agents. His initial point was to note that like all players employed by professional sports clubs, these BBFC players needed to be constantly protected from: (1) the risk of injury; (2) a possible loss of form; and (3) damage to their physical health. Johnny argued that the bodies of players and athletes were their greatest asset, since it was the means by which they earned themselves an income. If their body failed them, then their capacity to earn an income vanished. Johnny noted thoughtfully that this was not the case for administrators and officials, whose productivity was determined by their cognitive capabilities and their ability to think and act strategically. Johnny recommended that professional players be kept aware of the need to keep their bodies in good shape. Johnny also found that they could be thoughtless when it came to managing their personal affairs, be it their education on one hand, or their social life on the other. So, unlike most people who work for a living in traditional occupations like policing, teaching or practising law, the BBFC players understood the precarious nature of their career's demands, and the need for outside support and guidance.

Johnny also found that BBFC players were aware of their obligation to serve the interests of the club. They were also aware of the resources that the club had put at their disposal to assist their development, and maximize their contribution to the club's mission and vision. Johnny identified the mission to be essentially about both on-field success and off-field brand value. But, as Johnny also noted, players understood that their interests would not always be met by the demands of their employer, the BBFC. Hence their en masse decision to appoint personal managers, or 'agents' – as American sport officials like to call them. Johnny thought this initiative was a good one. While internal club managers were concerned with their contribution to the organization's future progress, external player-managers were there to maximize the players' personal benefits and stocks of capital.

Johnny concluded that the player-management role had become very important to BBFC players, and increasingly, players wanted their managers to take on a whole raft of roles and responsibilities to assist them to get though the highly competitive and fishbowl existence within which they operated. They wanted a lot more than just getting someone to negotiate a playing contact and an annual salary. As Johnny noted, it was now about putting together a full-service arrangement that provided support for the overall welfare and well-being of players that covered: (1) on-field performance; (2) training schedules and injury management; (3) their day-to-day football club activities; (4) their education; (5) their life outside of football; (6) sorting out personal crises when the need arose; and (7) designing a full-blown career-path, and even retirement and life plans that took them well beyond their football careers. According to Johnny, this sort of service required more than just a friendly face, a bit of smooth talking, a forceful personality and a network of industry mates. It needed a full range of professional support services, career advice and sensitively designed counselling, and general lifestyle support.

Johnny also reminded club management that the player-manager (PM) was not the coach, the club doctor, the conditioning supervisor, the team dietitian or the team manager. However, the PM was a confidante and mentor, and could guide the client along the path to successful sport performance. Johnny reckoned that in professional sport there was always the problem of deciding what should or should not be used to secure superior performance. Was training at altitude okay? What about caffeine tablets? How about a new lightweight pair of sport footwear? Where did food supplements fit in? Was something to calm the nerves okay? Was there anything wrong with using a seemingly innocuous anti-asthma spray? And how about some heavy-duty protein powders and amino acids? Johnny finished off by saying that while PM clients wished to become the best players and athletes they could ever be, there were limits on how they could do it. PMs needed to be able to tell them what those limits were.

Questions

1   Having considered the attitudes and commentaries of BBFC players, what makes the career of professional sports people so attractive on the one hand, and so stressful on the other?

2 Why couldn't the BBFC footballers be happy with the available internal club support, rather than seek out external personnel to act as their personal managers?

3 What does the BBFC case tell you about the range of skills that player-managers need to handle the many and varied needs of players?

4 If you were a manager, what rules would you put in place to secure appropriate player behaviour?

5 Is it better to have compliant players who not only do as they are told, but also do not answer back or challenge the manager's directions, or coach's instructions?

6 Is compliance enough to ensure high levels of performance by either players or, indeed, staff? What else might be needed?

7 What role can player-managers and player agents take in enhancing player performance, optimizing their contribution to the social life of the club and building its brand value?

Case exercise

The international governing body for basketball – FIBA – has successfully engineered an impressive growth in the game over recent years. It is also a flagship team sport at the Olympic Games. Having carefully scanned the FIBA website (www.fiba.com), explain how it has gone about the need to increase participation against the need to build the brand. And, having reflected on how FIBA achieved this balance, discuss the skills and competencies that were crucial in making it all happen.

SUMMARY

This chapter addressed the underlying structures, values and operational features of sport, and how they impact on the organizational conduct of sport, and the behaviour – both individual and interpersonal – of managers, administrators, officials, players and members. Special attention was given to the ways in which contemporary sport is both different from and similar to the world of commerce, and the implications of sport's special features for the effective management of the brand, organizational values and staff relations.

WEBSITES

See these sites for more information on the idea of brand-building and values management in sport.

FIBA.com. (2016). *International Basketball Federation*. Available at: www.fiba.com/nike.
Nike News. (2016). *Sustainable Innovation*. Available at: http://about.nike.com/sustainable-innovation.

REFERENCES AND BIBLIOGRAPHY

Belk, R. (1996). Hyperreality and globalization: Culture in the age of Ronald McDonald. *Journal of International Consumer Marketing*, 8(3–4), pp.23–37.

Bromley, P. and Meyer, J. (2014). 'They are all organizations': The cultural roots of blurring between nonprofit, business and government sectors. *Administration & Society*, 29(1), pp.1–28.

Commission of the European Communities (2007). *White Paper on sport*. White Paper. Brussels, Belgium: Commission of the European Communities. Available at: http://eur-lex.europa.eu/legal-content/EN/TXT/?uri=URISERV%3Al35010 (accessed 29 June 2016).

Foster, G., Greyser, S. and Walsh, B. (2006). *The business of sports: Texts and cases on strategy and management*. Mason, OH: Thomson/South-Western.

Gerrard, B. (2003). Efficiency in professional sports leagues. *European Sport Management Quarterly*, 3(4), pp.219–220.

Gerrard, B. (2005). A resource-utilization model of organizational efficiency in professional sports teams. *Journal of Sport Management*, 19(2), pp.143–169.

Lipovetsky, G., Charles, S. and Brown, A. (2005). *Hypermodern times*. Cambridge, UK: Polity.

Morris, D. (1981). *The soccer tribe*. London: Cape.

Rein, I., Kotler, P. and Shields, B. (2006). *The elusive fan: Reinventing sports in a crowded marketplace*. New York: McGraw-Hill.

Ritzer, G. (1998). *The McDonaldization thesis*. London: Sage.

Smith, A. and Westerbeek, H. (2004). *The sport business future*. Basingstoke, UK: Palgrave Macmillan.

Szymanski, S. and Kuypers, T. (2000). *Winners and losers: The business strategy of football*. London: Penguin.

Thibault, L. (2009). Globalization of sport: An inconvenient truth. *Journal of Sport Management*, 23, pp.1–20.

Trentmann, F. (2016). *Empire of things: How we became a world of consumers, from the fifteenth century to the twenty-first*. London: Allen Lane.

Chapter 2

Design and structure

OVERVIEW

This chapter examines the ways in which sport enterprises can be designed and structured. It begins with a discussion of the principles that underpin organizational structure, and then moves into a critical examination of the different models and design arrangements. It ends with a discussion of the ways in which structure can impact on individual behaviour and interpersonal relations in sport enterprises.

LEARNING OBJECTIVES

Having read the chapter, students will be able to:

1 Understand ways in which sport enterprises have been traditionally designed and structured;
2 Explain how sport's special features have shaped the design and structure of sport enterprises;
3 Critically review the features that can make contemporary sport enterprises more adaptable, flexible and decentralized; and
4 Explain the managerial, operational and behavioural benefits of adaptive, flexible and decentralized sport enterprises.

WHY ORGANIZE?

Sporting enterprises, like all other organizations, must have some sort of structure, otherwise they would collapse in on themselves and become an administrative 'black hole', where chaos replaces order and random decisions sideline systematically thought-through programmes. Organization and structure are essential if activities, programmes and events are to be carried out with some degree of efficiency and rationality. This does not mean, though, that every sport enterprise must be structured according to a standard blueprint. As the remainder of this chapter suggests, the ideal organizational structure is one that fits the specific operational needs of the people who work in it, and meets the aspirations of its members and clients.

While no two enterprises will be structured and organized in exactly the same way, there are a few fundamental principles that underpin the structure of all organizations.

The first point to make is that all sport enterprises have a mission or common purpose that acts as a focal point for the activities of members. This common purpose may not always be stated explicitly, and may not even be documented, but it is not, in practice, difficult to identify. For example, the mission or purpose of a suburban tennis club may be to provide the local community with the facilities by which they can engage in tennis games at the competitive and social level. In a wider context, the mission or purpose of a national governing body for track and field may be to coordinate the activities of associations and athletic clubs, and to promote and develop the sport of track and field to citizens around the nation.

The second point is that sport enterprises comprise many people playing and working together. This is a fundamental feature of organizational life, and highlights the fact that when people get together in groups they can achieve things that will be impossible if left to individuals working alone. Although getting people to unite in order to pursue a common cause is often fraught with difficulty, since it requires agreement and compromise on many initiatives, it is the only way of undertaking complex tasks with any degree of confidence. Running an event – be it the Olympic Games or a suburban fun run – requires the cooperation of many people sharing responsibilities and coordinating their efforts.

The third point, which arises directly out of the second, is that no one person is able to do every task that needs to be done. Consequently, specialized jobs, functions and tasks will be allocated to either individuals or small groups. This division of labour will occur no matter how small the sporting organization. It is unlikely that any person, no matter how intelligent or experienced they may be, or how small the sporting organization, could simultaneously be secretary, treasurer, coach, recruiting manager, junior development officer, fitness adviser, team manager, medical officer, property and supply officer, membership coordinator and promotions officer. The larger the sporting organization, and the wider its activity base, the greater the necessity to divide up tasks and functions and allocate them to different individuals and groups. We spend some time in Chapter 4 describing how one goes about designing jobs, creating job descriptions and providing job specifications.

The fourth point is that all sports enterprises have a hierarchy of authority. There will be people at the top of the hierarchy with significant levels of authority, and those at the bottom with far less authority. At the same time, it is expected that those with less authority will be receiving continual guidance or instructions from above on how and what should be done. For example, the management committee acting through the secretary will indicate to club members what procedures will be followed with respect to the season's competitive activities, their scheduling, and who is or isn't eligible to play in specific grades of competition. The hierarchy of authority also involves the creation of communication channels by which messages are sent, received, responded to, reflected upon, returned and reviewed. Chapter 14 has a lot more to say about communication networks.

The final point is that all sports enterprises have rules and procedures that govern the conduct of members. Whereas, on one hand, a massive stack of rules and regulations might suppress people's initiative, on the other hand, documented regulations provide for consistent, purposeful behaviour and equitable treatment of members and other participants. They can establish clear and unambiguous guidelines to assist and train new members and officials, and give players a good idea of how competitions will be organized and coaching will be administered. The only thing worse than a club or association with an authoritarian and dictatorial set of rules and processes is one with none. Chapter 11 will examine the ways in which organizational structures influence the emotional attachment to a job, and an employee's level of job satisfaction.

CORE THEMES

There are two key themes running though this chapter. The first is that there is no one best way to structure a sporting enterprise. Although it essential to have a clearly defined way of doing things, it is important to avoid rigid and didactic forms of organization, where things are put together so rigidly that there is no room for staff to take the initiative when special cases arise. It is important to create a structure that not only enables efficiency to flow, but also ensures adaptability and flexibility. The second theme is that all structures should start from the premise that an effective enterprise will always comprise two components or operational levels. The first component will be the 'steerers'. The primary concern of steerers is to set policy frameworks and provide a strategic direction. In a traditional sport setting, this role would have been known as the management committee or the executive. In larger enterprises it is the Board of Directors; a term that has been used in the business arena for many years. The second component will be the 'rowers', whose primary concern is to deliver the service or 'product' to the customer or client. They have their traditional equivalent in the committee members who have taken responsibility for creating a fixture, putting together an event, organizing a fund-raising activity or getting a sponsorship deal organized. Today, in light of the increased complexity of sport enterprises, staff will be grouped into functional areas like administration, finance, marketing, stakeholder relations, operations, and the like. This component aims to ensure that things actually happen at the right time and place, and that the event, tournament, show or activity provides appropriate levels of value, entertainment, excitement, pleasure and delight. The rower-steerer relationship is a neat way of illustrating how different structures can be used to achieve successful strategic outcomes. It also enables us to emphasize the critical importance of the mission, the strategic direction and the operating guideline. It also gives space to the discussion of the design of work groups and project teams, where clarity of purpose, mutual interdependency and shared decision-making are needed to ensure coordinated responses to a constantly changing and complex sporting environment. This issue will be given additional attention in Chapter 13.

WHERE TO BEGIN?

As already noted, no two sport enterprise structures will be exactly the same. This is because of differences in the nature of the sport being played and the scale of its operations, to name just two factors. At the same time, there are some guiding principles that underpin the structure of organization of all sporting enterprises. A useful starting point is to create a checklist of features that give a clear picture of how well structured a sports club or association is, and what needs to be done to provide it with the bare bones of a workable structure. Ten questions are posed below.

Structure checklist

1 Is the general purpose or mission of the enterprise well understood?
2 Can the core management team be identified?
3 Are the roles of this team known to everybody?
4 Are there clearly differentiated functional divisions within the club or association?
5 Can the essential tasks and responsibilities of each division be described?
6 Does every staff member have a clearly defined reporting relationship?
7 Does each staff member have a clearly defined set of responsibilities?
8 Do project teams have clear terms of reference?
9 Do project teams have a clearly designated reporting relationship?
10 Is there a precise set of operating guidelines for committees and work teams?

The above checklist of key structural features, will, when put into practice, create an organizational structure which can be represented visually in the form of an organizational chart.

Organizational charts

An organizational chart shows the tasks or responsibilities that need to be undertaken, the authority relationship between each person undertaking the tasks and the channels of communication that will be established.

This 'bare bones' structure can be easily given more administrative flesh by adding details about the functional responsibilities of each area, together with the number of people operating in each area. For example, the team manager in a football department of a semi-professional club may have a number of specific tasks in the form of a duty statement, and may be responsible for supervising the activities of a physician, psychologist/counsellor and three trainers. As far as committees are concerned, the management committee may have twelve members: the executive committee, four; the senior selection committee, three; and all other committees, four members. There may also be a statement that indicates the 'span of control' associated with each authority relationship. The coach's span of control may be five, being responsible for directing the activities of one assistant coach and four specialist coaches. The fitness coordinator, on the other hand, may have a span of control of two. There is no ideal span of control. Some people say three to seven is preferable. However, it all depends upon the jobs being done and how much responsibility has been given to each job.

Organizational charts, though, do not tell the whole story. They do not tell us much about the informal arrangements that exist between officials and members, or the ways in which the communication system really works. It often happens that some people, because of their expertise, experience, personality or political 'clout' and influence, become the focal point for communication and decision-making. All an organizational chart can do is to indicate that some attempt has been made to create an organizational structure, which will allow the

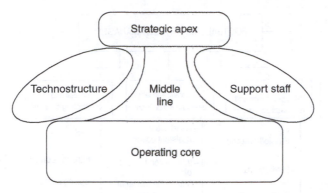

Figure 2.1 Mintzberg's model of organizational structure
Source: Mintzberg (1992).

club or association to work reasonably effectively. Charts also highlight the fact that structure is important, and that different structures will have different outcomes. A structure, which leads to effective coordination, good communication, the involvement of members, the delivery of quality service and successful performance is essential.

In terms of constructing an organizational chart and displaying visually what is going on, one of the best models for doing this was invented by Henry Mintzberg. It has five dimensions described in the following way:

- Operating core.
- Middle management/line.
- Strategic apex.
- Techno-structure.
- Support staff.

It can be displayed as shown in Figure 2.1 above.

This model provides a strong visual representation of just who is involved in running the show, what roles they play, who has the power and influence, and who does not. It can also show whether or not the organization is tightly organized and run, on one hand, where one person is clearly in charge and makes all the key decisions, or is decentralized on the other, where a lot of decisions are taken at the lower end or bottom of the hierarchy. It also, of course, illustrates how big or small each part of the organization happens to be.

PUTTING THEORY INTO PRACTICE

Theorizing about the structure of sport enterprises is one thing, but putting something together and setting it up as practical operating system is another thing. Figure 2.2 provides a pictorial representation of how the operational division of a professional football club might be organized.

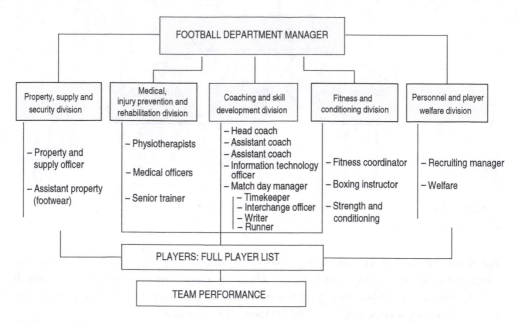

Figure 2.2 Organizational chart for football department of semi-professional sporting club
Source: adapted from Smith and Stewart (1999:239).

The chart highlights the principles that are used to design organizations, which are:

- Hierarchy of tasks and jobs;
- Vertical chain of command;
- Specialization of tasks and jobs based around specific functions; and
- Standard procedures for each task and job.

This chart is also structured on the basis of function; that is, the football department is organized around a collection of five different, but interrelated functional areas, which are:

- Property, supply and security;
- Medical and rehabilitation;
- Coaching and player development;
- Fitness; and
- Player recruitment and welfare.

IS THERE 'ONE BEST' SPORTS ORGANIZATIONAL STRUCTURE?

It is clear that any sport enterprise, no matter what its size, must have some structure in order to achieve its mission and vision. Additionally, it must address all of the above structural principles if it is to function properly. But, as we noted early on in this chapter, there is no single structure that can best fit every sporting organizational circumstance. Size, in particular, is a major influence on structure.

Take, for example a small suburban sporting club. Most small-scale sporting enterprises make use of an Executive Committee comprising the President, Secretary, Treasurer and another senior official. The role of the executive committee and its powers are usually established by the Management Board. A third tier of committees will also usually exist. Commonly called subcommittees, these units will be given specific functions, which will involve either or both administrative tasks and advisory roles. Subcommittees have traditionally been divided into Finance, Social, Coaching, Selection, Junior Development and Facilities. Large sporting enterprises, on the other hand, will have a Board of Directors and a number of sharply defined functional divisions with clearly defined chains of command.

IS THERE AN ALTERNATIVE WAY OF STRUCTURING SPORTING ENTERPRISES?

There is a growing body of literature which demonstrates that traditional structures and ways of organizing sporting and recreational activities are no longer able to achieve optimal results, particularly where there is a growing commercial dimension which may involve extensive event management, marketing, fund-raising and sponsorship programmes. They are frequently unable to adapt to rapidly changing circumstances like changing customer tastes and new communication and computer technologies. Tom Peters, the prominent American management consultant, believes that business has now entered the age of 'unstructure'. Peters argues that the traditional concept of an organization is no longer useful to managers, and that it is now simplistic to think of an organization 'as a single entity standing on its own'. Peters cites the production and sale of ice-hockey equipment as an example of how the final result is achieved through a network of loosely connected, flexible but interdependent arrangements. The equipment is designed in Scandinavia, engineered in the USA to meet the demands of a massive North American market, manufactured in Korea and distributed through a multinational market network with initial distribution from Japan. In this and many other cases, according to Peters, there is no one single best organization design. And it is no longer essential to have engineering, manufacturing and sales under the one corporate roof. Instead, temporary manufacturing teams, work groups, design groups and sales forces are brought together quickly and efficiently to create the final product and the end experience.

Gifford and Elizabeth Pinchot (1993), writing in *The End of Bureaucracy and the Rise of the Intelligent Organization*, developed a similar theme. They concluded that bureaucratic structures – which emphasize hierarchy, authority, rationality and subordination – no longer work and should be replaced by an underlying operational philosophy, which privileges 'freedom and community'. In other words, the rigid hierarchy referred to earlier will be replaced by a network of semi-autonomous work groups (or, as they are alternatively called by the Pinchots, 'liberated teams'), which provide the customer service in ways they think are best, and make things happen on their own initiative, but always with clear guidelines.

The concept of the flexible organization is also developed David Osborne and Ted Gaebler (1992), in *Reinventing Government*, where they make the distinction between the core policy and decision-making processes, and the operational or service delivery area. They make two important points, both of which were noted in the early part of this chapter. First, they claim that the policy and strategy formulation – that is, the steering function – is integral to the organizational purpose, and must be directly resourced and internally controlled. Second, the delivery of products to customers can be organized in a number of ways, and can be delivered either by permanent internal staff or by sessionals, casuals and subcontractors. And, as noted earlier, the policymakers and strategists are called 'steerers', while the service deliverers are called 'rowers'.

Pinchot and Pinchot (1993) talk about the same thing when they distinguish between insourcing and outsourcing as ways of obtaining supplies and delivering services. They give the example of Nike outsourcing supply. Nike effectively subcontracts 100 per cent of its athletic shoe manufacture to production partners, and concentrates its energies on research, design marketing and sales. A good rule of thumb for determining what is insourced or outsourced is to ask two questions. The first is: What are our strongest skill sets and core competencies? In other words, what are we very good at, and what are we particularly better at than our competitors? In these instances we should not outsource, but rather retain. The second question is: Are there some things that we do only fairly well, or not very well at all? In these instances, it makes good sense to find someone who can work with us, who can do it well, and who will provide a quality service to customers.

It is already the case that many sporting enterprises have become flexible providers of services. For example, sporting associations frequently contract a special event organizer to manage an event or tournament, or to design a schedule of fixtures. They are therefore well positioned to use the steerer and rower model, and the insourcing and outsourcing approach when they structure their organization. There is, as a consequence, other ways of designing an organization and constructing an organizational chart. For example, instead of a pyramidal configuration, a 'concentric' configuration can be put in place. The concentric model will involve a central circle surrounded by outer circles joined up in such a way to look like a bicycle wheel. The hub will comprise the Management Core and Executive Committees, the spokes will designate the communication channels, while the rim(s) will designate the functional divisions, subcommittees or project groups.

The concentric model, while in practice not radically different from the pyramidal model, aims to create a different set or organizational relationships. It constitutes an attempt to spread the decision-making among the lower tier of committees and work groups, and to encourage each of these groups to communicate with each other, as well as with the centre or peak of the pyramid. In some respects it is a 'federal' system of organization; that is, each of the functional areas acts in an autonomous way, with most of the interaction being between the units rather than between the unit and the senior administrator.

CENTRALIZATION VERSUS DELEGATION

The above discussion brings into focus the tension between centralized models of organizational design on one hand, and delegated decision-making models of organizational design on the other. Since most sporting enterprises rely heavily on volunteers and unpaid labour it is important that they are given sufficient levels of responsibility to challenge and stimulate them. At the same time they should not be given jobs that will overburden them, or cause debilitating anxiety and stress. The delegation of decision-making is often not as simple as it sounds. A number of issues should be considered before it can be successfully implemented.

In the first place there are a number of preconditions for delegation on the part of the controlling officials. Delegation will be possible where senior officials are:

■ Receptive to ideas of subordinates;
■ Willing to let go of tasks;
■ Willing to let others make mistakes; and
■ Willing to trust subordinates.

On the other hand, subordinates may show resistance to delegation. This may result from the following concerns:

■ Fear of criticism over possible mistakes;
■ Easier to seek advice from a more senior official;
■ Lack of confidence;
■ Inadequate resources to do job; and
■ Insufficient incentive to take on additional responsibilities.

If these concerns can be allayed, and the controlling officials have confidence in subordinates, then delegation is workable.

Delegation is not just a way of involving more people; it is a way of tapping into skills and abilities and getting the most from those who want to contribute. Effective delegation will also make for greater clarity of what needs to be done, since the delegation process requires a clear statement of the jobs and responsibilities involved. It is also likely to make for faster decisions since those actually involved in the activity or programme no longer need to seek approval for the actions. Delegation therefore allows the rowers to act quickly and responsively when dealing with the client or customer, and to be better able to enhance stakeholder satisfaction. It also has the potential to deliver a significant increase in staff morale and job satisfaction. These issues are discussed in more detail in Chapter 11.

ON REFLECTION

Most sporting enterprises are relatively small, but this doesn't stop them from often being fairly rigid and tightly administered. That is to say, most governing bodies and sporting clubs are controlled centrally, with power in the hands of a few influential people at either the 'Board' level or at senior management level. It is also the case that even though they do not have a large staffing establishment, they can be very hierarchical. That is to say, decisions are made at the top, communication is usually from top to bottom, and power is not relinquished without a fight. As we will see in the following chapters, overly tight structures may stifle individual initiative and incur lower levels of job satisfaction. It has been shown that organizational hierarchies that are excessively rigid can:

■ Create communication barriers;
■ Filter information as it is passed upward;
■ Stifle fast and flexible action;

- Lead to top management losing touch with grass-roots practices;
- Discourage individual accountability;
- Slow the adaptation to changing circumstances; and
- Create a plethora of restrictive policies and rules.

The other issue worth reflecting on is the argument that there is no best structure to achieve optimal operational performance. This position is defended on the principle that different structural arrangements are possible, no matter what the context or sport being managed. At one end of the structural continuum is a mechanistic, pyramidal structure (traditional, formal and centralized) and at the other end is an organic, concentric model (flexible, informal and decentralized). Neither one is necessarily better than the other, but one may be more appropriate. The trick is to work out which will work best for your sport enterprise. However, we would suggest that in these turbulent times, a flexible structure that allows staff to act creatively and with energy, and enables them to get close to customers, members, clients and players, will in most cases produce the best results.

CASE STUDY

Despite the many different ways of designing organizations, and despite research that suggests productivity improves when authority is delegated and semi-autonomous work groups are introduced, there are critics who believe that enterprises – including those in the sports sector – have become less rather than more flexible. By reinvigorating the critique of modern industrial society by the German sociologist Max Weber, they proclaim that organizations are becoming increasingly standardized, and returning to the mode of operation that featured in bureaucracies of the 1950s and 1960s. But, instead of using the word 'bureaucracy' to describe the return to rigid conformity, they have used the term 'McDonaldization' (MCD).

Lance Lukewarm has just been appointed the CEO of the Scandinavian Handball Association (SHA). He has been asked by the Board of Directors to undertake a review of the organizational structure. He has a number of options from which to choose. He has consulted with other governing bodies, and in each case has been advised to adopt a flexible structure that would allow the association to adapt more quickly to changes in the broader economic and social environment. He came across an article that looked at the so-called MCD of sporting enterprises. It captured his imagination, and he decided to give it a lot of thought, mainly because he was aware of the international successes achieved by the McDonald's fast-food business. He thought it might be applicable to SHA. An abridged version of the article is reproduced below.

In 2004 George Ritzer, an American sociologist, wrote a book titled *The McDonaldization of Society*. It examined 'the processes by which the principles of the fast-food restaurant are coming to dominate more and more sectors of American society as well as the rest of the world' (Ritzer 2004:1). Using Weber's theory of rationalization, Ritzer argued that MCD affected not only the restaurant business, but also education, work, health care, travel, leisure, politics, the family and sport. He reckoned that MCD was 'an inexorable process, sweeping through seemingly impervious institutions and regions of the world' (Ritzer 2004:10). And, in line with Weber's notion of formal rationalization, Ritzer believed that the MCD process was underpinned by the operating principles of efficiency, calculability and predictability. According to Ritzer, MCD was, in the end, all about securing control not just over the labour process, but also the people undertaking the process. So, let us have a look at these four operating principles in more detail.

Efficiency

According to Ritzer, efficiency means choosing the optimum means to a given end. Ritzer noted that the fast-food restaurant 'has spearheaded the search for optimum efficiency and has been joined in that quest by other elements of our MCD society' (Ritzer 2004:40). He said there were innumerable ways to search for ever-greater efficiency, but in MCD systems that search has taken the form primarily of streamlining a variety of processes, simplifying goods and services and using the customer to perform unpaid work that paid employees used to do (Ritzer 2004:61). For example, customers are expected to stand in line and order their own food rather than a waiter [or waitress] doing it.

Ritzer did not dispute the fact that greater efficiency brings many advantages. However, he also noted that methods used to increase efficiency were typically organized and operated by organizations to further their own interests, and these were not always the same as the customers' interests. Ritzer also argued that the drive to become more efficient was addictive; that is, the more we encounter efficiency, the more of it we crave, even when it leads to exploitation, highly repetitive work and mass tedium.

Calculability

Ritzer also cited calculability as part of the MCD creed. According to Ritzer it involves an emphasis on things that can be calculated, counted and quantified. It thus results in an emphasis on quantity rather than quality. This leads to a sense that quality is equal to large quantities of things. Also, there is an emphasis on the efforts to create the illusion of quantity, and the tendency to reduce production and service processes to numbers. Ritzer conceded that calculability brings with it many advantages, such as the ability to obtain large numbers of things at a relatively low cost. But he also suggested that in a society that emphasizes quantity, the pursuit of quality is forgotten, and as a result goods and services tend to be increasingly mediocre and ultimately unsatisfying.

Predictability

Ritzer identified predictability as the third dimension of the MCD process. He reckoned it involves an emphasis on discipline, systemization and routine. This means that things are the same from one time or place to another. Predictability is achieved in various ways, including 'the replication of settings, the use of scripts to control what employees say, the routinization of employee behaviour, the offering of uniform products and processes and the minimization of danger and unpleasantness' (Ritzer 2004:102). Ritzer also noted that in today's complex society consumers neither want nor expect surprises. As far as their fast-food experiences are concerned, they want to know that the Big Mac they ordered today will be identical to the one they had yesterday, and the one they will eat tomorrow. Ritzer understood the need for predictability, since it allows us to do things knowing what the outcome is likely to be. It reduces risk and uncertainty and, for the most part, this is a good thing. However, Ritzer also asserted that a predictable world can easily become a boring world, where the excitement of the unexpected sinks into a swamp of banal normality.

Increasing control of humans through non-human technologies

In short, Ritzer asserted that control through the MCD process is achieved primarily through the replacement of people with machine-based technologies. One of the most important objectives here is to increase the control over uncertainties created by people – particularly employees and customers. In controlling employees and customers, these non-human technologies would also lead to a greater control over work-related processes and finished products. However, increased control through technology not only includes machines and tools, but also materials, skills, knowledge, rules, regulations procedures, and techniques. In support of this claim, Ritzer cited soft-drink dispensers which have sensors that automatically shut off the dispensers when the cup is full. Ritzer also noted the use of French-fry machines that buzzed when the fries were done, and additionally, lifted the baskets automatically out of the hot oil. All of these initiatives, according to Ritzer, eliminated the errors resulting from human fallibility and misjudgement.

At the same time, Ritzer understood that MCD could sometimes deliver benefits to both staff and customers. They included the following.

- A wider range of goods and services are supplied.
- The availability of goods becomes more geographically dispersed.
- Customers secure almost instantaneous service and thus save time.
- Products have uniform quality; at least some people get better goods and services than before the MCD process.
- Customers have access to more low-priced alternatives to high-priced customized products.
- Longer opening hours provide a significant increase in customer convenience.
- In a rapidly changing and seemingly hostile world, MCD provides a comparatively stable, familiar and safe space.
- Because of the MCD emphasis on quantification, consumers can compare one product with another more easily.
- MCD provides employment opportunities for young people entering the workforce.
- MCD provides a range of work-related training experiences.

Lance was impressed with the arguments Ritzer was putting forward. He understood how the application MCD principles might assist SHA to improve its operations and use its resources more efficiently. However, he was concerned that the MCD process might not only stifle the creativity and imagination of staff, but also make the sport bland and unexciting. He felt that he could not progress with any change management plan until he had consulted with other experts in organizational design. He had many questions to ask, some of which are listed below.

Questions

1   What is the essence of the MCD process?
2   What are its three driving principles?
3   What are the core strengths of MCD?
4   What are its main weaknesses, especially when applied to the operation of sport enterprises?
5   Which of MCD's key features are most visible in sport enterprises?
6   To what extent might these features actually improve the overall performance of a sport enterprise like SHA?
7   How might the implementation of MCD processes affect the work arrangements of staff at SHA?
8   How might the implementation of MCD processes affect staff morale, satisfaction and productivity?

Case exercise

Take a look at the International Cycling Union website (www.uci.ch). Having explored its roles and operational demands, prepare a visual representation of its structure. Does its structure strike you as tightly bureaucratic or decentralized and flexible? Do you think its structure fits its operating environment?

SUMMARY

The conservative traditions of sporting enterprises are exemplified in their structures and supporting operations. Most local sporting clubs and, indeed, many of the larger sporting associations have organized themselves around the conventional roles of President, Secretary and Treasurer, which are subsequently supported by multiple committees that implement the 'executive' decisions. However, these structures are essentially second best, and the constantly changing and highly competitive environment that now surrounds sporting enterprises would seem to demand a more sharply defined set of organizational arrangements with a raft of policies and operating guidelines. However, there is always the risk of becoming too well-defined, too formal and too bureaucratic. It is also important to have a more flexible organizational structure, where staff are given the space to take the initiative when operationalizing strategies. So far, the evidence indicates that a more decentralized and fluid internal operation, where leadership, power, information and decision-making are diffused, will deliver higher levels of staff morale, satisfaction and productivity.

WEBSITES

International Cycling Union (Union Cycliste Internationale). (2016). Available from: www.uci.ch/. See this site for details on the International Cycling Union roles and its operational demands.

International Olympic Committee (IOC). (2016). *The International Olympic Committee: The Organization.* Available from: www.olympic.org/about-ioc-institution. 2016. This is another site worth visiting for details on the organization and structure of the IOC.

REFERENCES AND BIBLIOGRAPHY

Cunneen, P. (2008). *Organizational structure: An essential lever in managing change.* Dublin: Black Hill.

Mintzberg, H. (1992). *Structure in fives: Designing effective organizations.* Upper Saddle River, NJ: Prentice Hall.

Mintzberg, H. (1994). *The rise and fall of strategic planning.* New York: Free Press.

Osborne, D. and Gaebler, T. (1992). *Reinventing government.* Reading, MA: Addison-Wesley.

Peters, T. and Waterman, R. (1982). *In search of excellence.* New York: Harper & Row.

Pinchot, G. (1985). *Intrapreneuring.* New York: Harper & Row.

Pinchot, G. and Pinchot, E. (1993). *The end of bureaucracy and the rise of the intelligent organization.* San Francisco: Berrett-Koehler.

Ritzer, G. (2004). *The McDonaldization of society.* Thousand Oaks, CA: Pine Forge Press.

Smith, A. and Stewart, B. (1999). *Sports management.* St Leonards, NSW, Australia: Allen & Unwin.

Weber, M. (1922). *Wirtschaft und Gesellschaft.* Part III, Chapter 6, pp.650–678, VIII. Bureaucracy. Tubingen: J.C.B. Mohr.

Chapter 3

Culture and climate

OVERVIEW

This chapter examines the overlapping concepts of organizational culture and operating climate, and the ways in which they shape the behaviour of sport enterprise staff and members. Different cultures and climates are discussed, and their origins and impacts are explained.

LEARNING OBJECTIVES

Having read and discussed this chapter, students will be able to:

1   Identify the dimensions of organizational culture;
2   Explain how culture shapes the organizational ethos and operating climate of sport enterprises;
3   Understand the ways in which the ethos and climate shape interpersonal and individual behaviour within sport enterprises;
4   Distinguish between desirable and productive cultures on one hand, and dysfunctional cultures on the other; and
5   Map an organization culture, and identify strategies for introducing new and improved cultures.

ESSENTIALS OF ORGANIZATIONAL CULTURE

Whereas the management of organizational culture is well understood within the commercial and Government sector, it is frequently just taken for granted within the sport enterprise domain. Although a lot is said about player cultures in professional sporting clubs, there is little analysis of club cultures in the broader organizational sense. Neither is there much discussion about the theory of culture, nor about how it can be managed. This is unfortunate, since 'corporate culture' is a powerful determinate of individual and group behaviour, and has the ability to reshape and create strong and appropriate operating climates. It is also a powerful tool for improving the morale, satisfaction and productivity of staff, be they administrators, coaches or players. But what is organizational culture really about? People talk about it a lot, but it is rarely explained in any deep or meaningful way. Nor is there much discussion in sporting circles about the different types of cultures that can be put in place, and their strengths and weaknesses.

To put it succinctly, organization culture comprises a pattern of values, beliefs and expectations that are common to members of an organization, and which set the behavioural standards and norms for employees. It establishes the climate and sets the tone, if you like. Culture may be encased in the organization's mission statement and distributed to employees through an array of policy statements. It may also be promulgated more subtly through unwritten assumptions about what constitutes appropriate and inappropriate conduct, and an understanding of how things get done. Additionally, organizational culture has a number of recurring features: first, its core assumptions are frequently taken for granted; second, it is intrinsically inflexible and difficult to change in the absence of a major trauma or crisis; and third, the more that organizational members share a common culture, the more influential it becomes.

Another important feature of organizational culture – especially in sport – is its capacity to expose both insiders and outsiders to what might be called 'culture-revealing' situations. This means all those practices and ways of behaving that reinforce the core values and beliefs of the organization. They are often highly visible, since they include all the artefacts, which, in a sport club situation, will include things like trophies, honour boards, publically displayed slogans and memorabilia that confirm the club's achievements and highlights its traditions and longevity. They also involve the observable behaviour of staff, officials, members and players. These behaviours may, on one hand, be aggressive, individualistic and discriminatory, and on the other, be accommodating, communal and supportive. The third culture-revealing situations are work practices. They may feature multiskilling, ongoing professional development and employee autonomy on one hand, and narrowly defined tasks, training by trial and error and strict supervision on the other. There are also other culture-revealing situations and these are addressed in later parts of this chapter.

Unfortunately, many sport cultures have not been positive, or put clubs and associations in a good light. Additionally, they not have been conducive to the building of morale and productivity either. For example, clubs and associations sometimes refuse to embrace new information technologies, are sceptical of the value of sport science, fail to train their casual and volunteer staff properly, encourage hypermasculine leadership to the point of condoning bullying, and discourage the full involvement of women. These are not the sort of practices that will assist sporting enterprises to prosper or achieve their sporting potential. In today's highly competitive leisure marketplace, visionary thinking, innovation, continual improvement, risk-taking, inclusiveness, adaptability and flexibility are essential for growth and development.

However, as noted previously, it is not easy to change the culture of a sporting enterprise, since sport is by nature a conservative institution, and as Chapter 1 suggests, values its traditions and history highly. Sometimes a sport enterprise's current values and practices are based upon the way things were done more than 100 years ago. For instance, the reason that 'test match cricketers' wear all-white, 'neck-to-ankle' uniforms is because that is the way it has always been. Yet, change is essential if sporting enterprises are to meet the challenges and opportunities of today's dynamic society. Lawn bowls clubs are a case in point. Where image is now nearly everything, lawn bowls cannot fully shake off the perception that it is dominated by traditionalist administrators, who value a weighty set of dress codes and strict game rules more than the delivery of an engaging and comfortable pastime.

Another recurring theme throughout studies of organizational culture is the notion that, ideally, culture should be appropriate to the environment or context in which the organization functions, and that effective strategy is dependent upon the degree to which the culture supports the organization in its relations with stakeholders. Therefore, an organization should foster the development of cultural traits which are consistent with – or fit – the challenges and expectations of its internal and external environments. Thus, the appropriateness of culture is clearly linked with organizational success.

In addition to appropriateness, the strength of a culture has also been associated with corporate performance. Strength refers to the intensity or pervasiveness of the culture, and measures the degree to which organizational members embrace the prevailing assumptions and values integral to the culture. It has been argued that strong cultures lead to appealing outcomes such as unity, commitment and coordination, thus contributing to enhanced performance throughout an organization. However, strong organizational culture can sometimes be problematic when it does not align with its operating environment. This occurs when a business or sport enterprise operating in a constantly changing industry is resistant to change. Thus, strong cultures must also be 'appropriate' for performance to be affected positively. Therefore, the trick to culture management is the development of a strong yet appropriate culture that aligns with the organization's objectives and change strategies. Thus an appropriate culture for an elite sporting club that places a premium on winning is a strong work ethic and competitive ethos.

CONCEPTUALIZING AND CATEGORIZING CULTURE

As already noted, culture can be described as the 'personality' of an organization. It represents a shared value and belief system that tempers all organizational activity. However, this deceptively simple but succinct description camouflages a number of complex ingredients that make up culture. It also fails to reveal the different ways culture can be perceived, understood and typologized. Many attempts have made to conceptualize and categorize organizational culture, and some of the illuminating ones are discussed below.

A Jungian approach to culture

The eminent Swiss psychologist, Carl Jung, provided a useful construct for the analysis of cultural meaning through a three-tiered pyramid model. This construct was subsequently adopted by Edgar Schein (2010), an American organizational theorist, and it formed the basis of his acclaimed book titled *Organizational Culture and Leadership*. According to Jung and Schein, organizational culture can be represented as a three-tiered pyramid. At the apex are the rational elements of culture, in the middle are the so-called non-rational elements, while the base contains all the underlying assumptions and archetypes.

The starting point for the discussion of the Jung–Schein model is thus the rational level, which includes those readily apparent and observable qualities of a sporting enterprise. They include the physical environment, including the structure and layout of offices, the public statements of officials, the way individuals communicate, the form of language used, what clothes are worn and the memorabilia that fills the rooms and offices. One of the most important observable qualities involves the place of sporting heroes. They are culturally rich and are highly visible indicators of the culture that is being pursued. Heroes give an insight into the culture of an organization, since they are selected by both the rank and file, and the bosses and powerbrokers. In addition, they indicate those qualities for which individuals are respected and admired by a wider audience. The hero is a powerful figure in a sporting organization, and may simultaneously be an employee and a former player. The hero may also be charismatic, entrepreneurial or just plain administrative, which often characterizes business enterprises. By understanding the orientation of heroic figures, both past and present, it is possible to map cultural change. Heroes can be both reactionary and progressive. Heroes that reinforce the dominant culture will solidify the values and attitudes that the culture emphasizes. On the other hand, a hero that transcends and transforms the dominant culture will be a catalyst for change in the behaviours and values of a club. Often a hero – especially a sporting hero – is the most powerful medium for successful change management.

Tradition is another window into the material culture of an organization. Like heroes, traditions are readily observable via document analysis and the investigation of memorabilia, but it is important to note that the underlying values and assumptions that give meaning to heroes and tradition reside in the deeper levels of the Jung–Schein model. Tradition may, on the one hand, be preserved by the present cultural identity, whereas, on the other hand, the sporting enterprise may have developed a contemporary cultural personality based on some historical incident. Thus, it is important to acknowledge the role of tradition and history in creating the personality of sporting organizations, because it may be a cultural linchpin and a stepping stone to cultural renewal.

The second and middle level of the Jung–Schein model is the personal unconscious in which resides the deeper feelings, moods and emotions that shape behaviour. This equates to the non-rational level of culture that incorporates the beliefs, habits, values, behaviours and attitudes prevalent in a sporting enterprise. An accurate assessment of this level of culture is difficult and fraught with danger, since what employees think and how they behave may be at odds with their actual conduct. This is especially relevant to the problems of bullying and sexism, where the real feelings and emotions may most times be hidden from the public gaze.

Finally, the deepest level of the psyche is the collective unconscious. The collective unconscious is an innate, primal and difficult-to-access part of the mind. This correlates to the archetypal level of culture in organizations. This is revealed in the history, tradition, legends, myths and stories of a sporting club, which are, in turn, a reflection of deeply held views about the meaning of sport and its social and communal significance. An investigation of this level, for example, can expose core assumptions about manliness, the role of women, leadership, competition and aggression. These deeper forces are the ones that must be addressed when undertaking a programme of culture change.

Harrison's take on organizational culture

Roger Harrison (1972) pioneered the analysis of organizational culture and, in order to unravel the complexities of cultural practices, constructed 'ideal' categories and cultural types that defined the type of organizations to which individuals perceived they belonged. Effectively, Harrison's survey sought to identify values and styles of behaviour found within the organization. He also sought to identify the individual's own set of values and beliefs. What Harrison found was that within each organization, there was likely to be a combination of four major 'organization ideologies' or cultures. He termed them power, role, task and person cultures. Harrison found that while one of these cultures may predominate, elements of all four may exist, and frequently, their differentiation and integration are left to be handled by middle-managers, rather than by senior executives. Harrison belongs to the school of 'contingency theory', which advocates that there is no one best way to manage an organization. Many of these contingency theorists concentrate on the task and role cultures, frequently renaming them 'organic' and 'mechanistic', respectively. Although Harrison classified the four cultures, it was left to Charles Handy (1993; 2000) to develop them into workable models.

Handy's adaptation

Charles Handy took, as his starting point, Harrison's four types of culture – power, role, task and person – and used them to develop a detailed analysis of organizational structure and behaviour. According to Handy, each type of culture produces specific organizational outcomes.

Power culture

The power culture originates from a central source, much like a spider's web, and provides excitement and exhilaration for some, and discomfort and intimidation for others. Within a power culture, the organizational structure is centred around a select few, relying on strong leadership, and a figurehead to manipulate and orchestrate all activity. In many cases, the power figurehead is surrounded by technical specialists who provide advice and guidance, further enhancing the leader's omnipotent image. Power-centred organizations depend heavily upon the quality of individuals in the central roles; decision-making being undertaken by these select few, whose power base is resource-orientated rather than expertise-focused. Subsequently, this centralized decision-making process is rapid, facilitating a competitive, risk-taking environment, capable of undertaking considerable change quickly, concentrating on results, irrespective of means. In organizations typified by this culture, there are few written rules and procedures, with control being exercised centrally. Inevitably, therefore, power organizations' heroes will traditionally involve larger-than-life inspirational, entrepreneurial leaders who lead 'from the front'. The strengths of such an organization include its speed of reaction to environmental change, its ability to adapt to focus shifts and its willingness to capitalize on high-risk opportunities. Its weaknesses are that it has difficulty accommodating growth in size and relies too heavily upon the abilities of a select few individuals. A power culture is frequently found in small entrepreneurial organizations, occasionally in trade unions, and may also be found in some sporting enterprises. One might imagine that a sport enterprise led by Sepp Blatter, former FIFA president, would display elements of a power culture. Such a culture puts faith in the individual, judges by results and is tolerant of rule-breaking as long as things get done. Unfortunately, the loss of a power leader might cause strong reverberations, which may undermine the stability of an organization. It is possible, for example, that the loss Frank Lowry as the Chairman of the Football Federation of Australia may allow the chronic tensions that once characterized Australian soccer to resurface.

Role culture

The role culture is, in contrast, highly bureaucratic. It is typified by functional specialization, control, rules and procedures, and hierarchy. The main function of senior management is coordination and direction rather than adventurous decision-making. In this case, decisions are based upon lengthy formal procedures, culminating in predictable low-risk strategies. Concomitantly, managers of role-centred organizations are reluctant to undertake change to accommodate environmental variables. The major orientation of the role culture is the job to be filled rather than the individual who is to fill it. The allocation of work and responsibility determines the efficiency of their culture instead of the individual ability. As a consequence, there are few heroes in organizations in which role culture predominates, with strengths being its stable, secure and predictable outlook, and weaknesses being its inflexibility and protracted change processes.

The role organization needs a stable environment in which to function. The public service, automobile and oil industries, life insurance and banking are examples of usual role culture. Again, it may be applicable to sporting enterprises, an example of which might be the English Marylebone Cricket Club, or the All England Tennis club.

Task culture

Task cultures are job- or project-orientated, and organizations with this culture usually develops a decentralized organizational structure. As this emphasis is on task achievement, decision-making tends to be undertaken by specialists and experts rather than those in power positions. Subsequently, decisions are implemented rapidly and opportunistic risks are regularly engaged in. The predominant style of task culture is to work in team settings, which encourages a flexible attitude towards projects. Formal roles have little meaning in task groups and procedures are adaptable and pliant. Task cultures are cohesive, innovative and competitive, with the ability to conform where appropriate. The group dynamics are complex and can be difficult to control. Heroes in these types of organizations are rare and the focus is on groups of individuals and team accomplishments. Task-culture organizations which possess adequate time and resources are usually most successful. Hence, small organizations set up for specific tasks or periods, such as in wartime, are effective. However, when speed is of the essence, and resources become difficult to acquire, management begin to feel the need to control methods as well as results. As a result, task culture can readily change to role or power culture. Task cultures are frequently seen in sporting enterprises, because influence is widely dispersed, so effectiveness must rely on overall team strength. Outcomes and results will depend upon team members subsuming individuality, particularly status and power, to the common good. There are signs that as sport enterprises become more complex, the need for high-performance work groups becomes greater. Indeed, we argue that task cultures, where project teams provide the management energy, are the future for successful sport administration.

Person-orientated culture

A person-orientated culture exists to serve the individuals in the organization. As a result, the organizational structures, rules, procedures and roles are formulated according to the requirements of the individual members. Decision-making can only occur with the mutual consent of all members, and can, therefore, be tentative. Similarly, high-risk activities are barely engaged in because consensus is rarely achieved among individual members, leading the organization to resist change and encourage resolute stability. While person-orientated cultures aim to be cooperative, they also allow individual members to be elevated to hero status by their peers, and admired for their individual accomplishments. The strength of a person-orientated culture is its solidarity, which can unite its members against management, creating control difficulties for employers. Advertising agencies, hippie communes, fundamentalist religious groups, welfare agencies and even families often have this 'person' orientation. If this type of culture exists in sporting enterprises, then it resides with the amateur clubs and with those individuals who gather together to play their sport in their own way. They lack the formality to undertake serious training and, indeed, such sporting clubs rarely have a paid coach or any work-like structure. On the other hand, sociability and conviviality are often highly valued. After-game drinks, 'dinner dances' and weekend car rallies epitomize the person-centred sporting enterprise. This form of culture clearly has its place. However, sport enterprises that pretend to reflect changing community leisure needs, but which are dominated by person-centred cultures, are not likely to progress beyond their own self-contained smugness.

Deal and Kennedy's modifications

Deal and Kennedy also developed a four-sector model of organizational of culture. These sectors or segments, as they were sometimes called, were labelled as: first, driving; second, outgoing; third, specialist; and fourth, control. The driving culture correlates almost exactly to the power culture described by Handy. Its organizational structure is highly centralized with decision-making undertaken responsively by a select few. Its heroes have a tough, individualistic attitude and can tolerate all-or-nothing risks. In addition, they are flexible to changes and focus primarily on the ends rather than the means. Organizations attributed with a driving culture have the ability to accomplish tasks expeditiously, although their lack of procedures and rules contributes to their failure to learn from past errors. Furthermore, the driving culture espouses the virtues of individual performance and reward, and consequently suffers from a lack of teamwork.

The outgoing culture approximates Handy's task culture. Although organizations with this culture are unprepared to assume high-risk responsibilities, they are resolute and instantaneous decision-makers. The organizational structure of a company with an outgoing culture is largely decentralized, and orientated around group leadership and teamwork. This allows for responsive and adaptive change under certain circumstances. Heroes in an outgoing culture are personified by a friendly attitude, and prevail upon teamwork to solve problems. They are able to produce a high volume of work rapidly, but possess a short-term perspective and are more committed to action rather than problem-solving.

The term 'specialist' is used by Deal and Kennedy to describe their third culture category, which is synonymous with Handy's 'role' culture. A specialist culture is hierarchical, with decision-making constrained by bureaucratic processes. In contrast to role cultures, organizations exhibiting specialist characteristics are attracted to high-risk activities. Heroes within specialist cultures demonstrate obstinate endurance and a tolerance for long-term ambiguity. They recalculate their decisions repeatedly, and display loyalty and respect for authority. Specialist cultures in organizations have the potential for high-quality inventions and significant scientific breakthroughs. Unfortunately, they are slow converting plans into action.

The control culture is not unlike the specialist culture, but has little in common with Handy's person culture. The control culture is process-orientated, opting for controlled, low-risk endeavours in preference to more speculative undertakings. Such organizations are cautious and protective of their members. They tend to be orderly and punctual, attending to the last detail via established procedures, bringing order and system to the workplace. Initiative is discouraged, since bureaucratic red tape prevails.

GOFFEE AND JONES' BINARY MODEL

Another model of culture type was offered by Goffee and Jones (1998), who focus on two organization determinants: sociability, a measure of friendliness among members of an organization; and solidarity, a measure of an organization's ability to pursue common objectives. These two behavioural dimensions are combined to produce a typology comprising networked, mercenary, fragmented and communal organizational models.

Networked organizations are high in sociability but low in solidarity, which means that they focus on personal relationships rather than organizational objectives. They possess formal hierarchies, but also informal methods of getting around them. In this model, the opposite type is the mercenary organization, which is typified by a lack of interest in interpersonal relationships and a focus on business performance. At the other extreme, the fragmented organization is low on both scales, and reinforces an 'every person for themselves' attitude. Finally, the communal organization is high on both scales, reinforcing the importance of both organizational goals and kinship.

To sum up, the above approaches to organizational culture have their strengths and weaknesses, but they all promote the notion of 'ideal' cultures. Although this approach fails to account for the needs of different members and different environmental demands, they highlight the enormous variety of cultures that can exist. They also demonstrate that, in these turbulent times, cultures that stifle inventiveness and discourage quick decisions will fail to grasp opportunities when they present themselves. For sport organizations, it becomes clear that creating conditions that allow the display of heroic qualities is essential for successful performance.

MAPPING ORGANIZATIONAL CULTURE

A major problem associated with assessing organizational culture is the difficulty that arises in teasing out its submerged elements. This is the important insight offered by the Jung–Schein model. A quantitative approach which uses questionnaires and scaled responses to generate data from sporting club officials, players and members is unlikely to elicit these hidden aspects of culture. Only a detailed examination of an organization, using 'deep' interviews, close but discrete observation of behaviour, and the systematic analysis of statements and documents would be able to draw out these core, but often-submerged characteristics. Assumptions, values and beliefs can be so thoroughly embedded that they are difficult to bring to the surface to investigate. Whereas exposing the depth of organizational culture is a formidable task, the rewards are rich since it can deliver a clear and precise understanding of what really drives a sporting enterprise's practices.

In constructing a cultural map, it is important to first identify the features of an organization that will contain cultural indictors. The second step is to identify specific indicators for each feature. The final step is to attach a cultural meaning to each indicator. Table 3.1 illustrates how the process works.

Table 3.1 Template for culture mapping

Enterprise feature	Culture indicator	Cultural meaning
Mission statement		
Core values		
Policy statements		
Organization structure		
Physical environment		
Communication and language		
Leadership		
Responsiveness to change		
Role models and heroes		
Artefacts and memorabilia		
Stories, myths and legends		
Rites, rituals and ceremonies		

CASE STUDY

Barry Bigwave had spent most of his life surfing. He was introduced to surfboard riding in his early teens and quickly immersed himself in both the practice and the culture of the sport. He soon understood that surfing was both highly individualistic but also communitarian. It was individualistic in the sense that catching and riding a wave was a very personal experience, but it was also communal in that once surfers were back on the beach and in the clubhouse a lot of time was spent sharing their experiences, both good and bad. Barry was also aware of the ways in which surfers viewed the surf in a spiritual way. For instance, they were never interested in controlling or taming the wave; their total concern was accommodating themselves to the shape of the wave and immersing themselves in the power of the wave. It was also, for the most part, a very masculine culture: while a small coterie of females also surfed, most of the space was taken up by males. There was a subsequent hint of sexism. It was rarely conceded that females could ever surf at the level of the men and although the women's surfing techniques were aesthetically appealing, their manoeuvres were limited and predictable. However, as the years passed, Barry became increasingly sensitive to the female push for equal treatment and recognition. Many of the older male surfers initially resisted, but they understood that a surfing culture that pushed females to the margins was counterproductive. In addition, Barry enjoyed the freedom and autonomy that came with being a surfer. Rules were sparse, but there were sufficient protocols in place to ensure an orderly experience.

However, at the age of 50, Barry was struck down with a serious back injury and his surfing career came to an abrupt end. His physician made it clear that vigorous aquatic activities could disable him for life. He was thus forced to find another leisure activity in which he could immerse himself. This was not an easy task to achieve since his local community was short on sports facilities. He was left with the option of either becoming a couch potato or taking up lawn bowls. Two of his close but older friends had joined the bowls club and persuaded him to join. His initial experience was thoroughly enjoyable. The membership manager was extremely helpful and the club president made a point of introducing him to a number of members, all of whom were welcoming. However, once he began to immerse himself in the lawn bowls culture he quickly understood that it was radically different from the surfing culture. First, lawn bowls was highly communal and provided little space for individual expression. The needs of the team dominated any individual need for something as simple as self-expression. Barry was also struck by the long list of rules and regulations that set the parameters for the behaviour of club members. Although the club had a licence to sell alcohol, the licence placed rigid restrictions on its sale. But what was even more problematic for Barry was the strict dress code. The idea of a formal dress code was completely foreign to surfing. When he questioned the severity of the dress code, he was told in no uncertain terms that 'this is the way we do things around here'. He got the message.

Barry also had to confront a tournament and event schedule that was strict and unbending. This was again foreign to him, since surfboard riding was an organic experience, where surfing time was dictated by the natural environment and the ebb and flow of tides. Barry understood that lawn bowls was not only structurally different from surfboard riding, but also had a very different set of traditions. He became increasingly aware that the culture of lawn bowls was embedded in both the organization of the game and the values of the participants. Initially, he thought this was heavily problematic, but having reflected on his surfing experiences, conceded that surfing also had an embedded culture that shaped the structure of the sport and the conduct of its participants. At the same time, he wasn't able to work out why the cultures were so distinct and different. After all, he thought, they were both sporting activities that engaged with the environment and involved some degree of competition. He also realized that having experienced both cultures it was difficult to see how either of them would change, or indeed, whether they should have to change. But he also had the nagging feeling that neither culture was perfect, and that in each case some of the cultural practices marginalized potential members and stopped participants from doing things differently, and possibly even more pleasurably.

Questions

1   Describe the culture of the surfboard club.
2   Describe the culture of the lawn bowls club.
3   How can the differences in organizational culture be explained?
4   Reflecting on the organizational cultures, what are their strengths and weaknesses?
5   Is it reasonable to conclude that a strong culture is a good culture, or is this too simplistic?
6   If you were a consultant to these clubs, how might you go about improving their cultures?

Case exercise

Take a look at the international governing body for triathlon (www.triathlon.org). Start with the mission and vision statements, and then go to its organizational chart. Examine the chart and get a feel for which roles and responsibilities it prioritizes. Use the theories and models discussed in this chapter to help you work out which cultural type seems to best fit triathlon at the international level.

SUMMARY

Although culture and climate are slippery concepts, their impact upon organizational behaviour and performance is significant, and can profoundly influence the way an organization thinks strategically, as well as the way it plans formally. Just as nations have cultures that dictate how their citizens will act towards each other and outsiders, organizations have cultures that govern how their members behave and how they go about their daily tasks.

Culture conveys assumptions, norms and values, which in turn impact upon activities and goals, and in so doing, orchestrate how employees undertake their work, and determines what they view as significant within the workplace. Thus, employees' work-related behaviours, beliefs and understandings are determined largely by the organization's culture. Culture has been related to performance and excellence in the marketplace, as well as employee commitment, cooperation, efficiency, job performance and decision-making. Organizational culture has proven to be a significant tool in unravelling the conundrum of troublesome organizational behaviour.

And, to repeat, it is not easy to change the culture of sporting enterprises overnight, since they are by nature conservative institutions which value their traditions and history highly. Whereas organizational culture is troublesome to reveal and difficult to manage, it remains the cornerstone of any successful change strategy. Despite the conceptual messiness that surrounds culture, a detailed cultural map is the most effective tool for coming to grips with the culture of a sporting club or organization. Some cultures are clearly engines of energy and innovation, but others can be negative, distorted and, in a word, 'dysfunctional'. Although it was once believed that a strong culture was a good culture, this is no longer the case. For culture to be useful and productive, it must be appropriate to its operating environment, as well as strong.

WEBSITES

International Triathlon Union. (2016). *The Official Triathlon Resource*. Available from: www.triathlon.org/. See this site for the structure of the International Triathlon Union, which can be explored by examining the mission, vision statements and organizational chart.

The Sport Journal. (2009). *An Ethnographic Study of the Skateboarding Culture*. Available from: http://thesportjournal.org/article/an-ethnographic-study-of-the-skateboarding-culture/. See this site for a study on the culture of skateboarding.

REFERENCES AND BIBLIOGRAPHY

Deal, T. and Kennedy, A. (1985). *Corporate cultures: The rites and rituals of organizational life*. Reading, MA: Addison-Wesley.

Goffee, R. and Jones, G. (1998). *The character of a corporation*. New York: Harper Business.

Handy, C. (1993). *Understanding organizations*. London, UK: Penguin.

Handy, C. (2000). *21 ideas for managers*. San Francisco, CA: Jossey-Bass.

Harrison, R. (1972). Understanding your organization's character. *Harvard Business Review*, 50(May/June), pp.119–128.

Schein, E. (2010). *Organizational culture and leadership* (4th edn). San Francisco: Jossey-Bass.

Trice, H. and Beyer, J. (1993). *The cultures of work organizations*. Englewood Cliffs, NJ: Prentice Hall.

Part B

Job-task processes in sport enterprises

Chapter 4

Job analysis and selection

OVERVIEW

This chapter begins with an understanding of the different functions of job analysis. The chapter continues by describing the various processes and tools required to clearly define a job using qualitative, quantitative and mixed methods. Personnel-selection theories, such as person-job fit and person-organization fit, set the framework for the chapter. Special attention is given to the process of applicant selection by examining how to attract, identify and choose the most appropriate candidate for the job.

LEARNING OBJECTIVES

Having read this chapter, students will be able to:

1   Comprehend the functions of job analysis in sport enterprises;
2   Learn the qualitative, quantitative, and mixed methods for analysing job requirements;
3   Understand the theoretical underpinnings of personnel selection; and
4   Be able to develop and apply selection criteria to find and decide on an appropriate job candidate for a sporting enterprise.

INTRODUCTION TO JOB ANALYSIS AND SELECTION

In sport enterprises, like any other organization, job analysis is the process of gathering, analysing and structuring information about a job's components, characteristics and job requirements (Sanchez and Levine 2000). In today's competitive sport business environment, the recruitment of qualified employees is one the keys to sustained competitiveness. As well as job analysis playing an important role in recruitment and selection, it also underpins job evaluation, job designing, deciding compensation and benefits packages, performance appraisal, analysing training and development needs, assessing the worth of a job and increasing personnel and organizational productivity.

Job analysis helps to determine what kind of person is required to perform a particular job. It points out the educational qualifications, level of experience and the technical, physical, emotional and personal skills required to carry out a job in an appropriate way. The objective is to fit the right person at the right place in the sport enterprise. The importance of job analysis at application level can be explained by referring to the real-life case study of Internet company Yahoo! Specifically, Carol Bartz was named Yahoo! CEO in January 2009, despite lacking experience of leading an Internet-based company, only to be removed two years later owing to systematic failures. This situation could have been avoided by conducting an appropriate job analysis for the Yahoo! CEO position, as such analysis would have identified previous experience of leading an Internet company as a compulsory requirement for candidates (Dudovskiy 2013). In sport we witness these types of problems. For example, the appointment of the Australian National Rugby League (NRL) CEO Dave Smith was marred with controversy. A banker with great business acumen, and trumpeted by Australian Rugby League Commission chairman John Grant as a person who 'knows business and knows how to lead', he was unable to solve many of the problems confronting the game. When his three-year reign came to an end crowds were still down, junior participation was reduced and yet when the strategic plan had been done at the beginning of his tenure, all these key elements were supposed to have been on the rise. His critics argued that Smith did not understand the game and therefore his banking background would limit his ability to solve the game's problems by uniting the stakeholders. Smith insisted the fans were the NRL's most important shareholders, but he hardly endeared himself to them by failing to know that Cameron Smith was the captain of the Kangaroos. This need to have a detailed understanding or experience in the administration of the game could have been identified through a detailed job analysis. Figure 4.1 captures the key components that shape the purpose of job analysis.

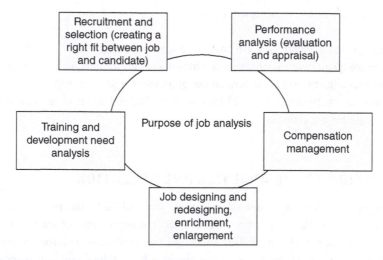

Figure 4.1 Purpose of job analysis

Source: Purpose of Job Analysis (2016).

FUNCTIONS OF JOB ANALYSIS

Examining the function of job analysis in more detail we are able to capture the key components within it. First, it entails staff planning. This includes recruitment, retention, training and mentoring strategies for all staff (Whitmell 2005). If a sport enterprise is seeking to employ a new staff member it should not only consider the recruitment phase, but also how it intends to train the new employee and mentor the person so they fulfil their potential. Finally, it needs to consider strategies for staff retention. Retention of the best staff is essential to long-term competitiveness and reduces recruitment costs by not having to go to the market again.

Classifying jobs is component of job analysis. Job classification is a scheme of classifying a job according to the current responsibilities and duties associated with the job. It is different from job design in that the person assigned to the job is not taken into consideration. Jobs are classified with the purpose of studying jobs in a holistic perspective. It takes into account the following:

1 Classifying workers: often based on the number of hours worked and job duties performed, and typically determine eligibility for benefits.
2 Generating job descriptions: proposed initially as a draft, job descriptions and specifications are reviewed with the participation of management, and this is followed by finalizing job descriptions and formulating relevant recommendations. They are descriptive in nature and provide both organizational information (like location in structure and authority) and functional information (what the work is).
3 Performance appraisal: systematic evaluation of the performance of employees, to understand the abilities of a person for further growth and development. Performance appraisal is generally done in systematic ways which are as follows:
    i   Sport managers measure the pay of employees and compare it with targets and plans.
    ii The sport manager analyses the factors behind work performances of employees.
    iii The management of the sport enterprise are in a position to guide the employees to improve individual and organizational performance.
4 Identifying training needs: training assists employees to enhance their capabilities and acquire new skills and knowledge, and helps employees come up with unique and innovative ideas, meet targets within the desired time frame and therefore improve the efficiency of the sport enterprise. It is important to recognize that loss of time, money and energy goes in designing training programmes for employees. Sport managers need to understand where all their team members are lacking and need improvement. They need to be very clear how training programmes can benefit the employees. Sport managers need to sit with human resource professionals and design specific training programmes keeping in mind the needs and requirements of employees and the organization. Training programmes conducted just for the sake of it yield no results. Types of training include: induction training; refresher training; on-the-job training (coaching, job rotation); and off-the-job training (seminars/conferences, simulation exercise, vestibule training).

53

5   Job restructuring: includes revising, analysing, altering, reforming and reshuffling the job-related content and dimensions, to increase the variety of assignments and functions to motivate employees and make them feel like an important asset of the sport organization. The main objective of conducting job redesign is to place the right person in the right job and get the maximum output while increasing their level of satisfaction. This issue is discussed in more detail in Chapter 11.

JOB ANALYSIS METHODS

Although there are several methods of collecting job-analysis information, choosing one or a combination of more than one method depends upon the needs and requirements of the sport organization and the objectives of the job-analysis process. Typically, all the methods focus on collecting the basic job-related information, but when used in combination these may bring out hidden or overlooked information and prove to be great tools for creating a perfect job-candidate fit. Selecting an appropriate job-analysis method depends on the structure of the sport enterprise, hierarchical levels, nature of job and responsibilities and duties involved in it (see Chapter 2 for more discussion of this area). Before executing any method, all advantages and disadvantages should be analysed, because the data collected through this process serves a great deal and helps sport organizations cope with current market trends, organizational changes, high attrition rates and many other day-to-day problems. We shall look at a number of job-analysis methods that are commonly used by sport enterprises to investigate the demands of a specific job.

Qualitative methods

Qualitative job-analysis methods rely typically on an interview and/or direct observation. These methods range from informal to highly structured, and can be subjective as they depend on the objectivity and analytical ability of the analyst, as well as the information provided by job incumbents and other informants. To enhance reliability and validity, it is common practice to secure acceptance from both the job incumbents and managers before the resulting job descriptions are considered final.

Interviews

The advantages of the interview are that the incumbent can describe their work and it can yield data about cognitive and psychomotor processes that are difficult to observe. This method helps the interviewer know exactly what a sport enterprise employee thinks about their own job and the responsibilities involved in it. It involves an analysis of a job by an employee. In order to generate honest and true feedback or collect genuine data, questions asked during the interview should be decided carefully. To avoid errors, it is always good to interview more than one individual to get a pool of responses. Then this can be generalized and used for the whole group. The disadvantages of the interview are that it requires an experienced interviewer and well-designed questions. It can also be difficult to combine data from disparate interviews, and data gathered is subjective and should be verified. Interviews may also elicit extraneous data.

In undertaking a job analysis you can interview each employee individually: these people are generally the most knowledgeable people about the duties and responsibilities of their job. Alternatively, a group interview with several employees, three to five people who are familiar with the job, works well. If only interviewing a sport manager(s), if the interviewee provides the answer 'that's the way we've always done it', it is important to check the rationale for the process or procedure with a more senior manager within the sport enterprise. Typical questions to ask before undertaking a job analysis include: What does each person do in their role? What level of detail is necessary for a good job analysis? Ask for clarification on terminology and be cautious of duplication or overlap in the terminology.

Observation

In observation a job analyst observes an employee and records all their performed and non-performed tasks, fulfilled and unfulfilled responsibilities and duties, methods, ways and skills used by them to perform various duties and their mental or emotional ability to handle challenges and risks. The advantages of observation are that it provides first-hand information, is simple to use, verifies data from other sources and is useful for manual and psychomotor tasks. The disadvantages are that it is time-consuming, may bias worker performance, usually comprises a small sample size, requires a skilled observer, validity and reliability may be problematic, and it is not useful for jobs consisting mostly of mental tasks.

Although it may seem one of the easiest methods to analyse a specific job the truth is that it is the most difficult one. This is because every person has their own way of observing things. Different people think differently and interpret the findings in different ways. Therefore, the process may involve personal biases or likes and dislikes and may not produce genuine results. This error can be avoided by the proper training of the job analyst or whoever will be conducting the job-analysis process. This particular method includes three techniques: direct observation; work methods analysis; and critical incident technique. The first method includes the direct observation and recording of an employee's behaviour in different situations. The second involves the study of time and motion, and is used especially for assembly line or factory workers; for example, in a Nike clothing and shoe factory. The third is about identifying the work behaviours that result in positive or negative performance.

Quantitative methods

Qualitative approaches, like interviews and observation, are not always suitable. For example, if your aim is to compare jobs for the purpose of remuneration, you may need to say that, in effect, Job A is twice as challenging as Job B, and so is worth twice the salary. To do this, it can help to be able to assign quantitative values to each job. Examples of quantitative approach of job design are discussed in the following.

Position Analysis Questionnaire (PAQ)

The Position Analysis Questionnaire (PAQ) is a questionnaire used to collect quantifiable data concerning the duties and responsibilities of various jobs. Data is collected on 194 items across five basic activities. The advantage of the PAQ is that it provides a quantitative score or profile of any job in terms of how that job rates on five basic activities. These activities are:

55

1 Having decision-making/communication/social responsibilities;
2 Performing skilled activities;
3 Being physically active;
4 Operating vehicles/equipment; and
5 Processing information.

The job analyst decides if each item plays a role and if so to what extent. For example, if processing skills received a rating of 4, this would indicate that processing skills (the ability to synthesize information) play a considerable role in this job, as may be the case in a performance-analyst position for a professional baseball team.

Functional job analysis (FJA)

This method tries to examine the fundamental components of 'data, people and things'. The rationale behind functional job analysis (FJA) is that jobs must be defined in terms of the interaction among the task, the individuals responsible for accomplishing the task and the environment in which the task is to be performed. FJA also determines the extent to which specific instructions are necessary to perform the task, the extent to which reasoning and judgement are required to perform the task, the mathematical ability required to perform the task and the verbal and language facilities required to perform the task.

Critical Incident Technique (CIT)

In contrast to FJA, where experts make judgements about the content of job, the Critical Incident Technique (CIT) utilizes actual episodes of on-the-job behaviour. This job-analysis method grew out of experiences with selecting candidates for flight training during World War II. Standards for acceptance or rejection were lax, and vague reasons such as 'lack of inherent flying ability' were used to disqualify individuals who might have been good crew members. In an attempt to avoid relying on the impressions of examiners to assess the suitability of candidates, the Air Force Aviation Psychology Program developed a series of standards for performance, using examples of behaviour that had occurred in military situations. In other words, CIT asks employees for specific examples of on-the-job behaviour that demonstrate both high and low levels of performance. The advantage of CIT is that the analysis is based on concrete behaviour, whereas the disadvantage is that developing the scales to access employees requires some expertise.

Other methods for job analysis

Mixed methods are a combination job-analysis method; for example, a multimethod design questionnaire could be developed to be distributed among the workers. The workers answer the questions to the best of their knowledge and belief. The Job Element Method (JEM) of job analysis focuses on the human attributes necessary for superior performance on the job. Earnest Primoff originally developed JEM, which aims to identify the superior workers on a job according to their performance. A list of characteristics of superior workers that is essential to superior performance is then developed.

APPLICANT SELECTION METHODS

Applicant selection methods vary, based on a sport enterprise's staff and resources. Sport enterprises should consider the 'reliability' and 'validity' of the methods they use as part of the selection process. This means that the selection methods should be consistent and measure what they are intended to measure. *Reliability* refers to how dependably or consistently a test measures a characteristic. If a person takes the test again, will they get a similar test score, or a much different score? A test that yields similar scores for a person who repeats the test is said to measure a characteristic reliability. Validity is the most important issue in selecting a test. *Validity* refers to *what* characteristic the test measures and how well the test measures that characteristic. Validity tells you if the characteristic being measured by a test is related to job qualifications and requirements.

It is important that when selecting applicants there are key selection criteria for potential employees. For example, which qualifications, attributes, skills, knowledge and organizational or person fit is required for the position. To establish this, a properly constructed position description should be developed that includes the following.

1   Identifying the right candidate in the recruitment and selection process.
2   Linking positions with workplace design.
3   Creating role clarity.
4   Defining reporting lines and delegations.
5   Linking the performance development framework.
6   Identifying areas of professional development.
7   Defining the knowledge, skill and attribute requirements of the job.
8   Being person-centred rather than task-centred.

Common mistakes in this process include: having too many selection criteria; a need to prioritize; too many key elements in one criterion; the position purpose is not being clearly defined; a tendency to create a list of tasks rather than the main responsibilities of the position; and ignoring the immediate and longer-term requirements of the sport enterprise.

INTERVIEW SELECTION PROCESS

The job interview process can be lengthy. Being interviewed once and receiving a job offer is typically a thing of the past. Today, many sport enterprises have an extensive interviewing process starting with screening interviews, followed by in-person interviews, second interviews and even third interviews. Interviews can take place via telephone, video conferencing, Skype or in person. It is also important to ask the right questions. As a guideline you should ask all candidates the same core questions, help to focus the candidate, make the candidate feel welcome and as relaxed as possible, use experience-based questions, ask open-ended questions, and look for the competencies the sport enterprise needs.

It is also important to complete reference checks. When contacting and evaluating references it is important to consider when to contact the individual providing the reference (often called a referee), what to expect from the reference, and decide what questions you need to ask. When it comes to the personnel selection, decision-making process be aware of *false positives*: this is a candidate who looks great on paper or in the interview but does not perform when they are in the job. Identify *true negatives*: if you believe the candidate is not acceptable and they are not a good fit for the position, this correctly identifies weak candidates. *False negatives*, however, can have a detrimental impact on the sport enterprise. This is when you believe the candidate is not acceptable but they would have been a good fit for the position. You assessed the candidate incorrectly. If this occurs you need to revisit your job-analysis process to identify the errors within it. *True positives* are the best outcome from the interview process. The goal of the job analysis and selection process is to select true positive candidates. True positives are when you believe the candidate is acceptable and they are a good fit for the position, meaning you correctly assessed the candidate as good.

CASE STUDY

Under Armour is a US-based sportswear enterprise. According to Euromonitor International's latest research, it has become the world's second-biggest sportswear brand (Ho 2016). By the end of 2015, Under Armour had made extraordinary growth in size and scope, highlighted by a 30 per cent average top-line growth and 23 consecutive quarters of 20+ per cent net revenue growth. The incredible success of the brand, both within and outside North America, is attributed to many reasons. One of the reasons for Under Armour's success that other sport enterprises can learn from is how discreet and effective Under Armour has been in the recruitment and selection of its employees, especially for higher managerial posts.

According to Under Armour's annual report in 2015, the international revenue outside of North America increased to 11.5 per cent from 8.7 per cent in 2014. Global expansion presented a valuable opportunity for the company to grow its revenue and income base and create a global brand. Under Armour seized the opportunity by developing its strategy of expanding its overseas market in Europe (including the United Kingdom and Germany) and Asia (Japan, Hong Kong, Shanghai and Guangzhou, China). However before 2014, the revenue generated from Under Armour's overseas market was not increasing as expected. From 2009 to 2013, the net revenue produced through international sales had stagnated at around 6 per cent of total revenue. It was also becoming difficult to take Chinese market share off Adidas and Nike. It was therefore decided that market expansion in China required a change of strategy and new managerial personnel to boost sales and take market share away from its two major competitors.

Under Armour recruited the former managing director of Adidas Ltd's India operations, Erick Haskell, to lead the organization's China operations. Haskell had senior-level managerial experience in the sporting goods sector in China and Asia, as well as an understanding of the Asian market. Haskell had the managerial skills, knowledge and experience that Under Armour required to build a market presence in China. The selection and recruitment of Haskell based on his managerial experience and achievements were justified by the remarkable sales revenue growth in China of over 100 per cent in 2015. In the same year, Under Armour opened its largest international brand-house store of 15,000 square feet on Weihai Lu Road in downtown Shanghai, which was followed by planning for an additional 100 more stores to be opened in China.

Adapted from: *Under Armour looks at new markets to grow sales*. Retrieved from: http://finance.yahoo.com/news/under-armour-looks-markets-grow-210113574.html

Questions

1 Why is job analysis and selection an important recruiting process for Under Armour?
2 What is the relationship between job analysis and selection in this case?
3 What makes Eric Haskell an appropriate candidate to lead the Under Armour's China office?
4 Should the revenue growth in China be attributed to the appointment of Eric Haskell? Provide reasons for your answer.
5 Discuss if Under Armour should have expanded so aggressively into China after a small period of sales revenue growth.
6 Why is job analysis so important to the long-term competitiveness of sport enterprises?
7 Identify the key functions of job analysis.
8 There are numerous job-analysis methods: discuss three of these.
9 How can interviews and observation methods complement each other when selecting the best candidate for the position?
10 Identify five questions that would be appropriate and five questions that would *not* be appropriate to ask a potential employee during a job interview.

Case exercise

Review the Speedo recruitment site (www.insidespeedo.com/careers) and the link to its 'People's Page' (www.insidespeedo.com/people). When you have done this identify how Speedo aims to attract the best people to its organization. What does this tell you about their approach to recruitment and the development of staff? Does it make you want to work at Speedo (provide reasons to support your answer)? Based on the content of this chapter, can you think of anything else that Speedo could put on this webpage?

SUMMARY

This chapter provided an understanding of the different functions of job analysis. The chapter described the various processes and tools required to define a job clearly, using qualitative, quantitative and mixed methods. Personnel-selection theories, such as person-job fit and person-organization fit, set the framework for the chapter, discussing the process of applicant selection by examining how to attract, identify and choose the most appropriate candidate for the job.

WEBSITE

GlobalSportsJobs.com website: Available from: www.globalsportsjobs.com. See this site for an overview of the global expansion of positions available in the sport sector. It also provides key insights into industry trends.

REFERENCES AND BIBLIOGRAPHY

Cornelius, E.T., Schmidt, F.L. and Carron T.J. (1984). Job classification approaches and the implementation of validity generalization results. *Personal Psychology*, 37, pp.247–260.

Dudovskiy, J. (2013). Job analysis as an important HRM function. Retrieved from http://research-methodology.net/job-analysis-as-an-important-hrm-function.

Embrey, D. (2000). Task analysis techniques. *Human Reliability Associates Ltd.*, pp.1–14.

Fleming, M.J. and Wilson, J.B. (eds) (2001). *Effective HR measurement techniques*. Alexandria, VA: Society for Human Resource Management.

Ho, A. (2016) *Can Under Armour replicate its North American success in Asia Pacific?* Retrieved from: http://blog.euromonitor.com/author/adalineho.

Jenkins, S. (2013). David Clutterbuck, Mentoring and coaching. *Sports Science & Coaching*, pp.139–254.

Kram, K.E. and Ragins, B.R. (2007). The roots and meaning of mentoring. In B.R. Ragins and K.E. Kram, *The handbook of mentoring at work: Theory, research, and practice* (pp.3–15). Thousand Oaks, CA: Sage.

Levine E.L. (1983). *Everything you always wanted to know about job analysis*. Tampa, FL: Mariner.

Purpose of Job Analysis. (2016). Retrieved from www.managementstudyguide.com/purpose-of-job-analysis.htm.

Sanchez, J.I. and Levine, E.L. (2000). Accuracy or consequential validity: Which is the better standard for job analysis data? *Journal of Organizational Behavior*, 21, pp.809–818.

Taylor, T., Doherty, A. and McGraw, P. (2008). *Managing people in sport organizations: A strategic human resource management perspective*. Abingdon, UK and New York: Routledge.

The New Daily (2015). NRL CEO Dave Smith gives up the worst job in sport. Retrieved from http://thenewdaily.com.au/sport/2015/10/20/dave-smith-gives-worst-job-sport/.

Whitmell, V. (ed.) (2005). *Staff planning in a time of demographic change*. Lanham, USA and Oxford, UK: The Scarecross Press.

Chapter 5

Orientation and induction

OVERVIEW

This chapter discusses processes to introduce people into the work environment from both individual and organizational perspectives. Adjustment antecedents are introduced, followed by a description of both proximal and distal outcomes of adjustment. The concepts of socialization, including fit, psychological contracts, familiarity and formalization, are described in both theoretical and practical terms. The chapter concludes with a discussion of orientation strategies and practices.

LEARNING OBJECTIVES

Having read this chapter, students will be able to:

1   Understand the antecedents and outcomes of adjusting to new organizational settings;
2   Understand the process of socialization in accepting new people into a sport enterprise and work environment;
3   Learn orientation strategies and techniques to assist in socialization, integration and productivity into a sporting enterprise; and
4   Understand the unique circumstances of sport enterprises, including working with volunteers.

INTRODUCTION TO ORIENTATION AND INDUCTION

In the final stage of recruitment and selection process there is a need to have an appropriate introduction to the new work environment for employees and volunteers. This period of early entry is a critical phase in organizational life, and is the part of the orientation process in which a new sport enterprise employee is introduced to their fellow workers, and given information such as working hours, place of work, performance standards, benefits and facilities, and the names of the immediate and other senior employees. Orientation is critical for aligning or realigning new employee expectations about the sport enterprise, and their role within the organization. A well-designed orientation process is important for the sport enterprise as it lets the organization control what information new employees receive and how they receive it (Taylor *et al.* 2015). Sport volunteer orientation must also be considered. Like employees, new sports volunteers are likely to have preconceived ideas and expectations about the sport enterprise that may not be consistent with the organizational reality, or may not be complete. Therefore, the various strategies and practices for orienting and socializing employees are also applicable to sport volunteers (Taylor *et al.* 2015).

Sport event organizations are often referred to as 'pulsating organizations'. These are organizations that expand and contract in size. In these cases, induction refers to a programme covering facets of the major sport event organization, and information to assist sport managers with their roles and responsibilities. Major sport event organizations such as an organizing committee for an Olympic Games or Commonwealth Games have adapted their induction methods from generic organizations (Hanlon and Cuskelly 2002). Pulsating organizations are quite different from 'generic' organizations. The latter organizations have a relatively stable workforce and hence, established relationships between personnel. The induction of new personnel is also commonly performed on an individual basis. In contrast, induction is more likely to be performed on a group basis at pulsating major sport event organizations, owing to the influx of personnel over a limited period of time (Hanlon and Cuskelly 2002).

ADJUSTING TO NEW SPORT ENTERPRISE

In today's global sport market it is highly likely that individuals will change jobs and take new career paths at some stage of their working life, so sport enterprises need to know how to assist in integrating new employees to increase the likelihood that they will remain with the sport enterprise for a significant period of time (Taylor *et al.* 2015). Establishing a process to assist new employees to adjust to the organization – often called 'organizational socialization' – may take weeks or months to achieve. During this early time new employees determine what their new sport enterprise is like and whether they fit in. At the heart of this early organizational adjustment is the concept of new employee adjustment, which includes knowledge, confidence and motivation for performing a work role, and commitment to the organization and its goals (Kammeyer-Mueller and Wanberg 2003).

In their book *Managing People in Sport Organizations: A Strategic Human Resource Management Perspective*, Taylor *et al.* (2015) provide a perspective on organizational adjustment process for new employees (or newcomers). Drawing on the work of Kammeyer-Mueller and Wanberg (2003), they examine how these antecedents of adjustment relate to variables that are more 'proximal' to the process of organizational adjustment and more global, or are 'distal' indicators of a new employee's organizational adjustment (see Figure 5.1) on the next page. In summarizing the component parts of the model they begin by reviewing the *Antecedents of Adjustments*. This includes pre-entry knowledge and refers to the knowledge about the sport enterprise and the new employee's role within it; it can affect a new employee's ability to select jobs that match their skills and abilities, and facilitates the acquisition of information regarding the new environment.

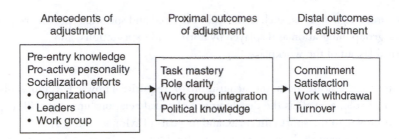

Figure 5.1 Model of newcomers' organizational adjustment

Source: adapted from Kammeyer–Mueller and Wanberg (2003).

Proactive personality is a new employee disposition towards proactive behaviour. It determines the individual's propensity to seek out information. Being proactive increases their acquisition of knowledge of the work environment and their willingness to modify their work role to match their preferences. The final element of this part of the model highlights the socialization influence – influences through formal organizational training and orientation, materials produced by the sport enterprise, its leaders, and co-workers and the work group – and provides important social information (Taylor *et al.* 2015).

Through their organizational efforts new staff and volunteers may have acquired some degree of familiarity or pre-entry knowledge about the sport enterprise and their particular role, as part of the recruitment and selection process. A candidate who is enthusiastic and well-researched is likely to have familiarized themselves with the sport enterprise prior to being interviewed. For example, a potential board member may enquire about the time commitments and the role. A Director of Coaching within a State hockey association may wish to meet their staff and understand how their budget is controlled and distributed. Leaders within the sport enterprise also contribute to the socialization efforts through shaping the organizational culture, structure and goals of the organization (Taylor *et al.* 2015).

The middle component of the model refers to the *proximal outcomes* of adjustment (short-term). Taylor *et al.* (2015) identify four short-term outcomes that are considered to be direct representations of the quality of an employee's adjustment. These outcomes are:

1   Task mastery – skill and confidence;
2   Role clarity – direction and purpose;
3   Work group integration – perceived approval and inclusion; and
4   Political knowledge – understanding of the informal power relationships.

To develop task mastery, role clarity, work group integration and political knowledge, the new employee needs to become familiar with:

■   Understanding formal work-related aspects; e.g. mission and goals, rules and regulations, organizational structure and chain of command, reporting relationships, the evaluation and reward system, health and safety standards, disciplinary and grievance procedures;
■   Formal personnel-related policies and procedures; e.g. pay, employee benefits;

- Roles and assigned tasks, such as the skills required and specific reporting requirements;
- Work group integration as displayed by norms and expectations; and
- Physical layout of the workplace.

These outcomes indicate both the acquisition of requisite knowledge and skills for the organizational role, as well as the development of social relationships that will help to bind the new employee to the sport enterprise and its goals (Taylor *et al.* 2015).

The final component of the model relates to *distal outcomes*. Distal outcomes of adjustment (longer-term) include organizational commitment, job satisfaction, work withdrawal and turnover. Organizational commitment stems from recognition of both the short-term objectives and longer-term impact of this process (Taylor *et al.* 2015). Work withdrawal is a combination of behaviours that reflect an attempt to disengage psychologically from work tasks. As well as indicating poor adjustment, work withdrawal also reflects poor performance and should be of concern to the sport enterprise. Turnover hazard is the complete withdrawal of an individual from a work setting. Institutionalized socialization, a more structured process of socialization, has been shown to promote new employee loyalty, commitment and consequently, reduced turnover (Taylor *et al.* 2015).

SPORT ENTERPRISE SOCIALIZATION AND SOCIAL EXCHANGE

Socialization shapes our behaviour to the norms of an organization, culture or society. Organizational values and beliefs have been shaped through this process of socialization. We are socialized whenever we become involved in a new situation through learning mutual expectations, taking roles, developing expectations, feedback and developing new self-concepts (Taylor *et al.* 2015).

The employment relationship is a social exchange or transaction, where member effort and loyalty are given in return for fair rewards. Beyond the formal agreement that forms the basis of that relationship is an individual's psychological contract with their sport enterprise. The psychological contract comprises an individual's beliefs about what they can expect to receive from the organization in return for their work, effort, performance and commitment. Perhaps most importantly, the psychological contract is based on the individual's belief that it is a mutual agreement between themselves and the sport enterprise; that is, both parties understand their respective obligations. What employees expect to receive in return for their effort, loyalty and commitment may vary between individuals and sporting enterprises. However, in general, expectations include fair compensation, guaranteed work of a minimum specified duration, a safe work environment, socio-emotional security, training and development as required, and a sense of community (Taylor *et al.* 2006).

Volunteers will not have any expectations of financial compensation. However, their psychological contract may comprise expectations that their needs and motives for volunteering will be met; for example, that there will be an opportunity to make a difference and to connect with others through sport volunteering (Cuskelly *et al.* 2006). In a study of the psychological contracts of community rugby volunteers in Australia, Taylor *et al.* (2006) found that the participants were in fact most focused on the intrinsic characteristics of their volunteer role; specifically, their expectation for rewarding work, social environment and networking opportunities, and recognition and appreciation for their contributions. Their next greatest focus was working conditions; specifically, expectations about the number of volunteers to do the work and support from the club.

The psychological contract is an individual's way of compartmentalizing their expectations of the sport enterprise, and the organization's expectations in return. When an individual's expectations are not met by the sport enterprise, or do not meet the expectations of the sport enterprise, the contract is violated (Johns and Saks 2001). For example, a sport manager of merchandise for a professional sports franchise finds out that they do not actually have as much decision-making discretion as they thought they were going to have, with regard to selecting new products. The fallout may be that they become frustrated, dissatisfied or disillusioned which then impacts on their work behaviour (Taylor *et al.* 2015).

STAGES OF SPORT ENTERPRISE SOCIALIZATION

A new employee goes through a process of transitioning to become an insider. Feldman (1976) identifies three fundamental stages in the work socialization process. These are: (1) anticipatory socialization; (2) encounter socialization; and (3) role management. This framework acknowledges that an employee's understanding about a sport enterprise begins before they even enter the workplace, and continues as they adapt to their role. To understand this further we shall looks at each of the three stages in greater detail.

Stage 1. Getting in: Anticipatory socialization

As a result of anticipatory socialization, most newcomers have some preconceived ideas or expectations about what it means to work in a particular segment of the sport industry, in a particular role, or in the new sport enterprise itself. Therefore, employees may enter the work setting with preconceived ideas about:

- The new job
- The sport enterprise
- The sport
- The sport industry.

The pre-entry ideas, expectations, and knowledge may be formed by a variety of sources (e.g. friends, family, fans, media, formal education, previous volunteering or work experience). Often sport business graduates may want to work for their favourite sport team. However, there may be gaps between what the individual thinks it will be like to work for a team or sport enterprise and what it is actually like (Taylor *et al.* 2015).

Stage 2. Breaking in: Encounter socialization

Differences or disparities will become evident during the second stage. Orientation is important to help new employees develop accurate perceptions of the sport enterprise. Encounter socialization takes place at or immediately following entry to the sport enterprise

65

as a member, rather than as an outsider trying to gain entry. This is when the individual begins to gain deeper insight into the reality of the sport enterprise, and their identity in the sport enterprise begins to take shape (Beyer and Hannah 2002). The new employee is formally introduced to their role and initiated into the work group. According to Johns and Saks (2001), if this outcome is reached the new employee will have identified critical organizational norms and start to identify with experienced organizational members. Moreover, Johns and Saks suggest that the socialization challenge is to sufficiently orientate new employees into the sport enterprise 'without frustrating them or stifling their uniqueness' (Johns and Saks 2001:247).

Stage 3. Settling in: Role management

This is a process of adaptation socialization that involves fine-tuning expectations about the sport enterprise and understanding reciprocal obligations. This stage may not be as clearly defined in terms of start and end points as the first two stages. In most cases it is defined by the new employee rather than by the sport enterprise, as the individual comes to terms with the final stage of organizational adjustment. Nonetheless, it is important to recognize that orientation to the sport enterprise does not end for new employees after the formal entry stage of encounter socialization. They will continue to adapt and alter their behaviour to align with the culture of the sport enterprise (Taylor *et al.* 2015).

ORIENTATION STRATEGIES AND PRACTICES

Taylor *et al.* (2015) use the framework developed by Van Maanen and Schein (1979) to describe the different and contrasting types of orientation strategies that may be utilized in a sport enterprise, for both paid employees and volunteers. The six strategies are:

1   *Collective v. individual.* With the collective approach, a sport enterprise may provide orientation to several new employees as a group. An advantage of this approach is that the sport enterprise is the ability to orientate several new employees together rather than individually. Taylor *et al.* (2015) note that the collective approach is the preferred approach when there are several employees commencing at the same time, all requiring the same information. This might be the case with new corporate sales staff for a football stadium. It would also be favoured for more routine and more technical jobs, where employees need to know the rules and procedures in order to do their job effectively; for example, stadium security staff. The individual approach is a contrast to the collective approach, which is a tailored orientation for each new employee. When standard information about the sport enterprise and the position is seen as less valuable than on-the-job training as a means of organizational socialization this approach is better suited. This approach works less routine jobs; for example, a head of performance analytics or sponsorship director position (Taylor *et al.* 2015).

2   *Formal v. informal.* Planning an approach to orientation requires formal strategies. In these cases strategically selected information is shared and how that information is communicated is carefully designed. The contrasting approach is the use of informal

strategies. Essentially, orientation is unplanned and spontaneous. It occurs on an ad-hoc or 'as needed' basis, leaning towards on-the-job learning rather than sessions of a formalized nature. As expected, consistent messages tend to be associated with formal strategies, whereas informal strategies can result in greater variation of the message between individuals, within or across groups (Taylor *et al.* 2015).

3   *Sequential v. random.* Relying on a step-by-step formula that has been determined to provide appropriate stages in learning about the sport organization is described as sequential orientation strategies (Taylor *et al.* 2015). For example, a newly hired and qualified football stadium security staff member may be expected to be orientated about the stadium and specific safety and risk management measures for fans through a sequence of formal learning. This process may then involve observing or partnering an experienced security staff member. The individual may then progress to taking individual responsibility for a security function and being evaluated by a senior security staff member. The sequential approach reduces uncertainty and anxiety for new employees as the orientation process is well planned. A random approach contrasts the sequential approach in that the process is less staged. It tends to be arbitrary where the new employee works it out as they go (Taylor *et al.* 2015).

4   *Fixed v. variable.* Orientation approaches that occur within a set timeframe (e.g. over a day(s), week(s), or month(s)) are known as fixed approaches. The timelines for a fixed approach are dependent on the employee. A new employee may require a longer fixed period, whereas an employee who has been with the sport enterprise for a longer period and is being orientated into a new role may require less time. A variable time frame, where there is no specific end to the orientation, is known as a variable approach. A variable approach may continue until there is confidence that the new employee is able to perform their tasks, has a clear understanding of their role within the sport enterprise, has been integrated into their work group and has an understanding of the political dynamics within the sport enterprise (Taylor *et al.* 2015).

5   *Serial v. disjunctive.* This refers to whether regular members are directly in the orientation of new employees. When current employees are involved directly in the socialization of a new employee this is considered a serial approach (Taylor *et al.* 2015). For example, this may involve formalized mentoring and orientation sessions run by existing employees. This may be the case when new corporate box sales staff are recruited and orientated to the sport enterprise by experienced sales staff. The orientation may involve formal information sessions on how to sell corporate packages, on-the-job shadowing by the new corporate sales staff member and finally, monitoring and evaluation by the senior sales employee. When orientation does not involve regular members formally in new employees' socialization this is known as disjunctive orientation. Like the random approach, new employees tend to be left to figure it out on their own. The major benefit of the former approach is that integrating new employees with regular employee facilitates social learning and opportunities for informal socialization that can take place in this form of shared environment. Informal socialization involves learning about the sport enterprise and its employees beyond organized or mandated information sharing (Taylor *et al.* 2015).

6   *Investiture v. divestiture.* Focusing on what positive and unique attributes the employee has to contribute to the sport enterprise is a form of induction known as investiture. This approach recognizes it is important for individuals to understand how they fit in and build a positive personal workplace identity. Experienced organizational employees need to positive social support (Kossek *et al.* 2011). Contrasting this approach is induction, known as divestiture. This approach breaks down any misconceptions the new employee may have about the sport enterprise, and inducts them into the ways of doing within the sport enterprise. Taylor *et al.* suggest that 'divestiture often involves debasement or humiliation through one or more "tests" that are intended to show the newcomer that they do not, in fact, really know what goes on in the organization' (2015:94), and is essentially 'negative social feedback [about preconceptions] until newcomers adapt' (Taylor *et al.* 2015:240). Moreover, Taylor *et al.* suggest this approach is common in sports teams and is based on removing bad habits and socializing new employees into the right way of doing things in the sport enterprise.

ORIENTATION PRACTICES

The job preview is an orientation practice that is used to give candidates a greater sense of the job and the organization (Johns and Saks 2001). Rather than focusing on the positive aspects alone, in order to present the sport enterprise in a positive light to a potential new employee, it is advantageous to display the sport enterprise in an honest and genuine way throughout the recruitment and selection process. Presenting work expectations in this way to the potential employee (including both positive and negative aspects of the sport enterprise and the position) allows the individual to assess if the position is attractive and aligned with their own needs and values. If the individual accepts the position with a greater understanding of the sport enterprise, their expectations of the sport enterprise and work experience have greater likelihood of matching. This increases the possibility of short- and longer-term organizational adjustment (Taylor *et al.* 2015).

As with paid employees, sport volunteers need a well-designed orientation process reduces stress on new volunteers, makes them feel welcome and may reduce the likelihood of turnover (Hanlon and Cuskelly 2002; Taylor *et al.* 2015). Sport volunteers need to be provided with the organization's constitution, introduced to and provided with the names and contact information of key volunteers and any staff, familiarized with the responsibilities and accountabilities of their new role and how their role relates to others in the sport enterprise, and familiarized with any facilities, equipment or resources that are used regularly by the sport enterprise. It should not be assumed that new volunteers know what they are supposed to be doing, how, when and with whom, just because they have offered their free time to help a sport enterprise. Rather, it is important to orientate volunteers effectively, so that they develop a strong, realistic, psychological contract with the sport enterprise (Taylor *et al.* 2006).

CASE STUDY

The National Basketball Association (NBA) in USA has the longest tradition in professional sports of providing an orientation and induction programme for the successful transition of its players to a professional career. The NBA and National Basketball Players Association (NBPA) created the NBA Rookie Transition programme in 1986. This orientation and induction is important for players as it makes newcomers to the league feel welcomed and empowered, especially those who have travelled from a different country, or who speak different languages. As Chris Bosh wrote about his rookie year of 2003/2004:

> Becoming a complete NBA player, however, doesn't happen overnight. You don't just push a button and suddenly think, act and even view yourself as a professional athlete. I told the guys that, sure, their lives were about to suddenly change in many obvious ways. But their lives would also change gradually in more profound ways. They would mature, learn about responsibility and become their own men during the course of their rookie seasons.

Each September, every rookie takes part in this mandatory six-day seminar and workshop programme that provides first-hand knowledge of what to expect as a player in the NBA, and how to balance these pressures and demands. Sessions generally run from 9 a.m. to 9 p.m. and are conducted by league and player association personnel, current and former players and experts in each of the fields covered. The programme is designed to teach players techniques to cope with unique stresses inherent in their lives, and how to utilize the various resources available to them throughout their NBA career. The 'rookie' programme uses presentations, role-playing, skits and interactive workshops, as well as group breakout sessions. At the end of each day, players participate in an interactive activity designed to highlight the day's lessons. The diverse offering of sessions includes:

- Professional and life skills;
- Player development;
- Personal development and education;
- Media and community relations;
- Legal education; and
- Special sessions, i.e. cultural adaptations and acclimating to the NBA-style of play.

It is also rewarding for the NBA itself when the programmes are implemented successfully. With this comprehensive induction programme, the Player Development Departments from the NBA and NBPA are able to make sure that new NBA players understand the challenges and pressures they are about to confront, how to deal with them, and that support mechanisms and programmes are in place to them when embarking throughout their NBA careers.

Source: adapted from: www.nba.com/news/rtp_030919.html

Questions

1   Why is the transition programme important to an NBA rookie?
2   What outcomes should an induction programme in professional sport try to achieve?
3   How could you evaluate if the orientation and induction was successful or not?
4   As a human resource manager of a professional sport enterprise, how would you design a comprehensive and effective induction programme for a women's professional sporting team? Would it be different from a men's programme? Justify your reasoning
5   As a professional athlete, how would you make the most of the orientation and induction programme provided by your employer?
6   Explain the three components of the Newcomers Organizational Adjustment model and apply the principles to a sport organization.
7   What is meant by the psychological contract?
8   Explain the three basic stages of the work socialization process.
9   Outline why sport volunteers need 'a well-designed orientation process'.

Case exercise

Review the Sport England webpage on training sport volunteers (www.sportengland.org/our-work/volunteers-and-coaches/volunteering-explained/support/how-do-i-train-new-volunteers/). Identify the key principles of its volunteer induction programme. Compare these principles with the NBA Rookie Transition Programme and explain why the two programmes are different. Do you feel some elements from the Sport England programme should be embedded into the NBA transition programme? Justify for your reasons for this.

SUMMARY

This chapter discussed processes to introduce people into the work environment from both personal and organizational perspectives. Adjustment antecedents were introduced, followed by a description of both proximal and distal outcomes of adjustment. The concepts of socialization, organizational fit, psychological contracts, familiarity and formalization, were described in both theoretical and practical terms.

WEBSITE

Organizational behaviour: Terms and definitions. Available from: http://cw.routledge.com/textbooks/champoux/ch06-guide6.asp. See this site for definitions of key terms associated with orientation and induction.

REFERENCES AND BIBLIOGRAPHY

Beyer, J.M. and Hannah, D.R. (2002). Building on the past: Enacting established personal identities in a new work setting. *Organization Science*, 13(6), pp.636–652.

Cuskelly, G., Evans, G. and Hoye, R. (2004). Problems and issues in the recruitment and retention of sports officials: A report prepared for the Australian Sports Commission. Queensland, Australia: Griffith Business School, Griffith University.

Cuskelly, G., Hoye, R. and Auld, C. (2006). *Working with volunteers in sport: Theory and practice.* London: Routledge.

Doherty, A. (1998). Managing our human resources: A review of organisational behaviour in sport, *Sport Management Review*, 1(1), pp.1–24.

Feldman, D.C. (1976). A contingency theory of socialization. *Administrative Science Quarterly*, 21(3), pp.433–452.

Hanlon, C. and Cuskelly, G. (2002). Pulsating major sport event organizations: A framework for inducting managerial personnel. *Event Management*, 7, pp.231–243.

Johns, G. and Saks, A.M. (2001). *Organizational behaviour: Understanding and managing life at work.* Toronto: Addison Wesley Longman.

Kammeyer-Mueller, J.D. and Wanberg, C.R. (2003). Unwrapping the organizational entry process: Disentangling multiple antecedents and their pathways to adjustment. *Journal of Applied Psychology*, 88(5), pp.779–794.

Kossek. E.E., Pichler, S., Bodner, T. and Hammer, L.B. (2011). Workplace social support and work–family conflict: A meta-analysis clarifying the influence of general and work–family-specific supervisor and organizational support. *Personal Psychology*. 64(2), pp.289–313.

National Basketball Association. Orientation Week. Adapted from: www.nba.com/news/rtp_030919.html.

Taylor, T., Darcy, S., Hoye, R. and Cuskelly, G. (2006). Using psychological contract theory to explore issues in effective volunteer management. *European Sport Management Quarterly*, 6(2), pp.123–147.

Taylor, T., Doherty, A. and McGraw, P. (2015). *Managing people in sport organizations: A strategic human resource management perspective* (2nd edn) New York: Routledge.

Tosi, H., Rizzo, J. and Mero, N.P. (2000). *Managing organizational behavior.* Oxford, UK: Wiley-Blackwell.

Van Maanen, J. and Schein, E.H. (1979). Toward a theory of organizational socialization. *Research in Organizational Behavior*, 1, pp.209–264.

Chapter 6

Reward systems

OVERVIEW

This chapter explores the different rewards that organizations provide to employees, including extrinsic and intrinsic rewards. The chapter also discusses ways to improve reward effectiveness. A thorough discussion of the unique aspects of rewarding volunteers is included owing to the high volunteer base of sport organizations.

LEARNING OBJECTIVES

Having read the chapter, students will be able to:

1   Learn to differentiate between extrinsic and intrinsic rewards;
2   Understand what reward practices are preferred in different circumstances;
3   Learn how to improve reward effectiveness in sport enterprises; and
4   Comprehend how to reward volunteers and the differences between employee and volunteer motivation.

INTRODUCTION TO REWARD SYSTEMS

An employee reward system should motivate employees to perform at their highest level. Job security and opportunities for advancement encourage employees to take pride in their work. As you devise an employee reward system for your business, keep in mind there is no right or wrong system. Ask for input from your staff and let them help you create a system that works for you (Brown 2016).

Every company needs a strategic reward system for employees that address these four areas: compensation, benefits, recognition and appreciation. The problem with reward systems in many businesses today is twofold: they are missing one or more of these elements (usually recognition and/or appreciation); and the elements that are addressed aren't properly aligned with the company's other corporate strategies (Entrepreneur 2016).

A winning system should recognize and reward two types of employee activity: performance and behaviour. Performance is the easiest to address because of the direct link between the initial goals you set for your employees and the final outcomes that result. For example, an incentive plan or recognition of the top sales people for attaining periodic goals could be implemented.

Rewarding specific behaviours that made a difference to the sport enterprises is more challenging than rewarding performance, but this obstacle can be overcome by asking, 'What am I compensating my employees for?' and 'What are the behaviours I want to reward?' For example, are employees being compensated for coming in as early as possible and staying late, or for coming up with new ideas on how to complete their work more efficiently and effectively? In other words, is someone being compensated for innovation or for the amount of time they're sitting at a desk? There's obviously a big difference between the two (Entrepreneur 2016).

When we talk of rewards we can also think of them as being extrinsic or intrinsic rewards. We shall now look at these two types of rewards.

EXTRINSIC REWARDS

Extrinsic rewards are administered by external agents, such as a supervisor. They are usually reflected in factors such as salary increases, bonuses or promotions (Chelladurai 2006). Extrinsic rewards are not necessarily related to performance. For instance, the sport enterprise may base a promotion on seniority rather than performance. Extrinsic rewards played a dominant role in earlier eras, when work was generally more routine and bureaucratic, and when complying with rules and procedures was paramount. This work offered workers few intrinsic rewards, so that extrinsic rewards were often the only motivational tools available to organizations. When we consider extrinsic rewards it is helpful for us to understand what the extrinsic needs of the employees are and identify some examples of extrinsic rewards and how they operate.

1   Extrinsic needs
    i   Physiological/survival (e.g. food, shelter, clothing). Once these basic needs are met an employee can evaluate whether or not there is sufficient security in the job to meet their subsequent need for a stable environment.
    ii Security: part of safety needs (e.g. security, stability, health). If an employee decides that there is not sufficient security in their job to meet their need for stability, then they are likely to try and secure an adequate paying job at another organization.
    iii Social: interaction through group work and customer service. Sport organizations rely heavily on volunteers' attraction to helping out in sport because of a desire to help others, the social benefits of interacting with others and the personal rewards of contributing one's skills and making a difference (Cuskelly *et al.* 2006).
2   Money in the workplace
    i   The meaning of money differs. The strength of an individual's need for money can determine the strength of their desire to exert effort in a given direction for a period of time.

3   Financial reward practices

i   Membership-based and seniority: Membership-based rewards are allocated solely for being part of a group within an organization. These rewards commonly include annual cost-of-living increases to a base salary or support for an equity policy. For example, if a local government park and recreation department was looking to encourage staff to have master's degrees or obtain certification, they might offer pay incentives for having either or both. Membership-based rewards are also often tied to length of time with an organization. For instance, after a certain length of service with a sport organization, employees may receive a certain percentage increase to their pay or be eligible for additional benefits. In a unionized environment, many of these rewards are spelled out in a labour agreement.(Hurd *et al.* 2008).

The basis of the pay structure may be based on seniority. However, just as short-term employees can be discouraged when seniority is the only factor considered for advancement or pay increases, not rewarding employee seniority at all can discourage those faithful employees who have put in years of service. With a seniority-based reward system, the pay structure reflects longevity in the organization. The assumption is that employees should be rewarded for staying with the organization because they have acquired skills and knowledge over time that are valuable to the sport enterprise. For the staff member, there may be motivation to join and stay with an organization with this type of financial security. With this type of system, an employee knows there will be incremental pay increases over time and this kind of security can be very attractive to staff. It is also a relatively easy system for a sport organization to administer, and labour costs can be forecast. However, there may be no further motivation to work hard because longevity rather than behaviour or performance is linked to compensation.

ii   Job-based status: Job-based status rewards compensate employees for their individual job performance. They aim to maintain internal equity and motivate employees to compete for promotion. Specific examples of these rewards can include a higher salary, profit sharing, and bonuses. These rewards are distributed through job-evaluation methods. Job evaluations analyse the performance of an individual in the workplace. Typically, evaluations distribute more credit to jobs that demand a higher level of effort and responsibility. Job status rewards contribute to employee motivation in the workplace. However job-based rewards are inconsistent with market responsiveness, encourage employees to compete with each other and can lead to organizational politics.

iii   Competency-based: Organizations that use competency-based pay structures reward employees based on the skills, knowledge and experience they apply in the workplace rather than on their job title or position. This approach is designed to motivate employees to become aspirational, build on their existing skills and apply these in their job. Competency-based rewards are becoming increasingly popular because they improve workforce flexibility and are consistent with the emerging idea of employability. Competency-based rewards, however, tend to be measured subjectively, and can result in higher costs as employees spend more time learning new skills.

iv Performance-based (individual, team, organizational rewards): Linking valued rewards with effort and performance can be expected to motivate employees to exert effort and perform at a higher level. However, providing rewards that are not commensurate with one's perceived effort can be expected to detract from work motivation. With a performance-based reward system, the pay structure provides compensation in return for acceptable results or behaviour. Rewards may be provided on a continuous scale, where the better one performs the better the rewards, or on a graduated scale, where there are set levels an individual must reach in terms of performance before the next level of rewards is provided. Providing rewards for individual results is synonymous with a commission system, where compensation is directly linked to the quantity of the employee's output, such as number of units sold. Compensation by results is not uncommon for employees such as sporting goods sales staff or personal trainers at a fitness club. In addition, a winning season may be the basis for determining whether a collegiate coach can expect a raise in pay, or a financial bonus, or to keep their job.

4   Promotions and advancement

i   The advancement of an employee from one job position to another job position that has a higher salary range, a higher-level job title, and often more and higher-level job responsibilities, is called a promotion. Sometimes a promotion results in an employee taking on responsibility for managing or overseeing the work of other employees. Decision-making authority tends to rise with a promotion as well. Promotion and advancement are tools that can be used to reward achievement, retain staff in a competitive market or give an ambitious employee the reassurance that they are progressing within the organization. Unlike in a lateral move, the promotion can result in more status within the organization. But, along with the authority and status conveyed with the new position title come additional responsibility, accountability and expanded expectations for contributions. Indeed, one standard joke in organizations that promote employees is 'Be careful what you wish for'. However, promotion and advancement does not necessarily mean an increase in financial pay. The employee may be compensated in other ways and later in their career receive a higher salary as a consequence of the experience they gained. Overall, the keys to developing a reward programme are:

- Identification of company or group goals that the reward programme will support;
- Identification of the desired employee performance or behaviours that will reinforce the sport organization's goals;
- Determination of key measurements of the performance or behaviour, based on the individual or group's previous achievements;
- Determination of appropriate rewards; and
- Communication of programme to employees.

INTRINSIC REWARDS

In a general sense intrinsic rewards are the psychological rewards that employees get from doing meaningful work and performing it well. Just as with extrinsic rewards it is important for us to understand what the intrinsic needs of the employees are and identify some examples of intrinsic rewards and how they operate.

1   Intrinsic needs
    i   Esteem: Esteem needs are higher order needs that relate to a person's desire to have others recognize him or her and to have status among them. According to Maslow (1954), esteem needs include a desire for strength, achievement, adequacy, confidence (self-esteem), recognition and respect (esteem) from others.
    ii   Self-esteem and self-worth: Self-esteem and self-worth are closely aligned with a productive employee. It is safe enough to observe that self-esteem makes the path to achievement easier and more likely. Sport organizations need their employees to have a level of independence, self-reliance, self-trust and the capacity to exercise initiative; in brief, employees must have ample self-esteem. There are several ways you can satisfy this deep subconscious need for self-esteem and personal importance. You can do this by showing 'Appreciation', providing 'Approval' and giving employees the 'Attention' they need.
    iii Self-actualization: Self-actualization is 'to become everything that one is capable of becoming' (Maslow 1954:382). The content of some values focuses on personal competence, knowledge, accomplishments and wisdom. People's desire to understand their context and the events therein, and to be clear and consistent in their own perceptions and beliefs, reflects this function (Chelladurai 2006).
    iv   Sense of meaningfulness: This reward involves the meaningfulness or importance of the purpose you are trying to fulfil. You feel that you have an opportunity to accomplish something of real value; something that matters in the larger scheme of things. You feel that you are on a path that is worth your time and energy, giving you a strong sense of purpose or direction.
       Building blocks:
- A non-cynical climate: freedom to care deeply;
- Clearly identified passions: insight into what we care about;
- An exciting vision: a vivid picture of what can be accomplished;
- Relevant task purposes: connection between our work and the vision; and
- Whole tasks: responsibility for an identifiable product or service.
    v   Sense of choice: You feel free to choose how to accomplish your work, to use your best judgement to select those work activities that make the most sense to you and to perform them in ways that seem appropriate. You feel ownership of your work, believe in the approach you are taking, and feel responsible for making it work.
       Building blocks:
- Delegated authority: the right to make decisions;
- Trust: confidence in an individual's self-management;
- Security: no fear of punishment for honest mistakes;

- A clear purpose: understanding what you are trying to accomplish; and
- Information: access to relevant facts and sources.

vi Sense of competence: You feel that you are handling your work activities well, that your performance of these activities meets or exceeds your personal standards, and that you are doing good, high-quality work. You feel a sense of satisfaction, pride or even artistry in how well you handle these activities.

Building blocks:

- Knowledge: an adequate store of insights from education and experience;
- Positive feedback: information on what is working;
- Skill recognition: due credit for your successes;
- Challenge: demanding tasks that fit your abilities; and
- High, non-comparative standards: demanding standards that don't force rankings.

vii Sense of progress: You are encouraged that your efforts are really accomplishing something. You feel that your work is on track and moving in the right direction. You see convincing signs that things are working out, giving you confidence in the choices you have made and confidence in the future.

Building blocks:

- A collaborative climate: co-workers helping each other succeed;
- Milestones: reference points to mark stages of accomplishment;
- Celebrations: occasions to share enjoyment of milestones;
- Access to customers: interactions with those who use what you've produced; and
- Measurement of improvement: a way to see if performance gets better.

2 Intrinsic reward process

i Create goals for achievement: Encouraging employees to set goals and to reach them provides intrinsic rewards and motivation. A company should require all employees to set goals with regard to personal growth at work, education and the completion of projects. Provide employees with training on how to set measurable goals and encourage them to set a variety of short- and long-term goals. Give employees input into company goals, as well, to make them feel like they are working towards a bigger cause. As employees meet goals and set new goals, they will receive intrinsic rewards and increase their motivation. Goals should be challenging, but not impossible to reach. They should spark ingenuity and creativeness, and stretch workers to go beyond their previous results. However, if goals are viewed as unrealistic, the process can leave employees disheartened. The discouraging effects of unachievable goals can leave employees unwilling to even make the attempt to reach them.

ii Develop objectives and action plans for employee recognition: all employees like to be recognized and appreciated. An employee recognition programme can be the key to motivating employees and infusing a healthy dose of creativity into an otherwise 'stale' corporate culture. The number of recognition strategy/services firms, employee recognition programme vendors and corporate rewards/corporate loyalty sponsors has increased dramatically in the past 20 years. Bob Nelson,

President of Nelson Motivation Inc. and best-selling author of *1001 Ways to Reward Employees*, estimates that the US incentive industry is a $27 billion-dollar enterprise. Employee recognition programmes, when developed and administered appropriately, can improve communication between employees and management, as well as increase employee loyalty by giving employees more of a stake in their company's success (Whitney and Bombard 2012).

iii   Enable fairness, clarity and consistency: Establish clear and concise goals for employees to follow. Ideally, goals point employees in the direction you want them to go. If those goals are not properly laid out, understandable and comprehensible, employees can be left with feelings of frustration and failure, which defeats the purpose of the performance and reward strategy.

iv   Provide day-to-day guidelines for both managers and employees: A successful employee recognition programme is one that allows employees to participate easily. Employees are more likely to participate in an employee recognition programme if they are made aware of the programme's existence at the outset. To promote awareness of an employee recognition programme among its employees, an employer should advertise its programme details in conspicuous workplace locations, such as in the cafeteria and on company bulletin boards. Employers may also wish to include an explanation of the programme's rules and procedures in the orientation packets distributed to new employees and in the employee handbook.

IMPROVING REWARD EFFECTIVENESS

Linking reward to performance is now a key part of an increasing number of successful, large organizations as they are achieving better results, and greater employee engagement, by linking reward directly to performance. Creating a performance-based reward culture can unlock employee potential, retain and motivate your high performers, and ultimately deliver healthier financial results (Qikker 2014).

Ensuring the rewards are relevant is also important. For instance, rewarding bonuses to the top sport enterprise executives that are based on the organization's overall performance, whereas middle-management employees may earn bonuses on the basis of the sales figure or targets attained by their organizational function.

Use team rewards for interdependent jobs: team-based incentives were found to be more effective at increasing performance than individual incentives. If team-based rewards are not already included in the company strategy, they should be. Additionally, the resources devoted to team-based rewards should be substantial. This could have a significant impact on cooperation, employee cohesiveness and the company's bottom line.

Team-based awards are monetary compensation that rewards individuals for teamwork and/or rewards teams for collective results. Team-based incentive programmes can be extremely effective in increasing individual and team performance. They can also be very effective in shaping employee performance to be more in line with company values and goals. Team-based reward systems have been found to increase employee performance by as much as 48 per cent.

Regardless of the reward system you employ, sport enterprises need to ensure the rewards are valued. Including employees in the reward programme development process is critical to ensuring that they value the rewards and see them as worth the effort. Sport managers should value employee input and select rewards accordingly. Employees who see the rewards as worth the effort will be more motivated to work hard to obtain them.

REWARDING SPORT VOLUNTEERS

The sport sector is dependent on volunteers for the everyday functioning and success of their organizations. Increasingly, it is also recognized that the organizational commitment of volunteers is essential for the successful management and delivery of community-based sport. Committed individuals are believed to be more likely to remain in their organizations and to participate wholeheartedly in organizational activities, thereby contributing to organizational goals and success (Engelberg *et al.* 2011). People volunteer for different reasons and examples of why people choose to volunteer include:

- Normative incentives (motivated by the opportunity to help a cause; e.g. sport programme). Older adults (60 years or older) are more likely to be motivated by normative incentives and social benefits.
- Affective incentives (motivated by the opportunity to work with others, develop friendships, and identify with a group).
- Utilitarian incentives (motivated by the opportunity to use their skills or sport background, to develop new skills and work experience, to network in the community and help their child to participate in sport). Younger adults (younger than 35 years) are more likely to be motivated by utilitarian incentives relating to their own personal development. Those in the middle (35–60 year olds and most likely to have children participating) are likely to be motivated by utilitarian incentives, followed by social benefits (Engelberg *et al.* 2011).

Regardless of the reason people have for volunteering, sport organizations need committed volunteers, and as such we need to be aware of the different reward systems we can use. To begin, recognition of volunteers is vital. Recognition can be provided through intrinsic and non-financial rewards For example, in London, every June, as part of national celebrations of Volunteers' Week, Volunteer Centre Hackney hosts Hackney's Volunteer Achievement Awards. All groups in Hackney that use volunteers can nominate people for the awards and an independent panel chooses the winners. They also give appreciation certificates out to volunteers from lots of different groups as part of the celebration.

It is necessary to have excellent communication practices to tell volunteers – and show them – the difference they have made. Make sure service users know their helpers are volunteers, so they can say thank you. This is often more meaningful than anything staff say or do. An automatic thank you will be seen as insincere, but genuine recognition for a task well done will always be appreciated. Other ways of rewarding volunteers include:

- Parties: Invite volunteers to your staff Christmas party or hold a party in Volunteers' Week and get staff to act as hosts and waiters for the day.
- Thank you gifts: This should be unexpected and appropriate. Any merchandise should be simple and not too expensive. Your volunteers, especially if they are involved in fund-raising, won't want to see hard-earned money spent on them.
- Training: This helps people provide a better service and shows that you think that what they do is important enough to invest in.
- Public recognition: Make sure you have a volunteer section on your website or in your newsletter, and that this is not just a call for more help but a space to shout about the great things your volunteers achieve.
- Birthday cards, signed by all the staff.
- References: You should be willing to provide a reference for a volunteer when they apply for a job (even if, in some cases, this means you might lose your volunteer, be happy about their achievement).
- A final thought: Unappreciated volunteers are unhappy volunteers, and unhappy volunteers leave. Reward and recognition is not just about making volunteers feel good, it is about making your volunteer programme a success, keeping your volunteers and offering a better service to clients and the community (Volunteer Centre Hackney 2010).

CASE STUDY

Volunteers and the act of volunteering are considered to be at the heart of the world's sporting landscape and the sport participants' experience. In Australia, in 2015, sport and recreation volunteers represented 37 per cent of all volunteering activity. Volunteers have been an indispensable part of sport events. It could be relatively easy to recruit, select and induct volunteers for an activity. However, to manage and retain the volunteers in your team requires greater effort and commitment. Realizing that the more volunteers you can keep means the less time and energy you have to spend on recruiting new ones, sport organizations worldwide come up with various programmes to reward the volunteers who have participated in, and contributed their time and energy to, the sport community.

There are three types of volunteer recognition in Australian Football League (AFL). The first type is called 'State Volunteer of the Year'. There is a nomination process, in which each club, league or association can put forward someone who has contributed voluntarily to the completion of a major or significant project throughout the year, or someone who has contributed in a number of roles over a longer period of time. The prize for the winner is two AFL Grand Final tickets, a return flight and accommodation, and the opportunity to participate in the Grand Final Parade. The 'AFL Volunteer Merit Awards' are for AFL volunteers who have contributed significantly to Australian Football in a number of roles for a period of at least ten years. Finally, the 'AFL Volunteer Certificate Recognition Program' rewards volunteers by presenting them with AFL-branded volunteer recognition certificates.

Although the idea of rewarding volunteers can be seen as desirable and necessary to encourage engagement, on one hand, and against the ethos of volunteerism on the other, the act of volunteering should always be valued and acknowledged, either through material awarding, a personal education and development scheme, or just a simple thank you. The AFL is an example of a major sporting organization that has done this and reaped the benefits of having a committed and sound volunteer base.

Source: adapted from: www.volunteeringaustralia.org/wp-content/uploads/
VA-Key-statistics-about-Australian-volunteering-16-April-20151.pdf and
www.aflcommunityclub.com.au/index.php?id=60

Questions

1   Why is a volunteer reward system necessary in for a sport organization?
2   Do you consider the AFL reward system effective? Provide reasons for your answer. How could it be improved?
3   Identify strategies that could be used to retain sport volunteers.
4   Outline the purpose of a reward system.
5   Distinguish between extrinsic and intrinsic rewards; provide examples to support your answer.
6   How may a reward system such as the AFL's demotivate other AFL volunteers?
7   Explain why it is important that sport volunteers receive adequate recognition?
8   Discuss how the effectiveness of rewards can be improved.

Case exercise

Review the Nike webpage (http://jobs.nike.com/article/benefits) and identify the different types of rewards it offers to its employees. Are these mainly extrinsic or intrinsic? Provide examples of this to support your answer. Do you think all the rewards listed would be available to all employees, or are dependent on the position they have at Nike? Provide reasons to support your answer.

SUMMARY

This chapter explored the different rewards that organizations provide to employees, including extrinsic and intrinsic rewards. The chapter also discussed ways to improve reward effectiveness. A thorough discussion on the unique aspects of rewarding volunteers was included, owing to the high volunteer base of sport organizations.

WEBSITE

JoinInUK (2015). *Show your support for local sport: Join in today! Sport Club Volunteer Support.* See www.youtube.com/watch?v=hj1fx1Hn_tk&feature=youtu.be to understand ways you can support your local sports club.

REFERENCES AND BIBLIOGRAPHY

AFL and Volunteers. Rewarding Volunteers. Adapted from: www.volunteeringaustralia.org/wp-content/uploads/VA-Key-statistics-about-Australian-volunteering-16-April-20151.pdf and www.aflcommunityclub.com.au/index.php?id=60.

Brown. D. (2016). What are successful employee rewards systems? Retrieved from http://work.chron.com/successful-employee-reward-systems-12291.html.

Chelladurai, P. (2006). *Human resource management in sport and recreation* (2nd edn). Champaign, IL: Human Kinetics.

Cuskelly, G., Hoye, R. and Auld, C. (2006). *Working with Volunteers in sport: Theory and practice.* London: Routledge.

Engelberg, T., Skinner, J. and Zakus, D. (2011). Exploring the relationship between commitment, experience, and self-assessed performance in youth sport organizations. *Sport Management Review*, 14(2), pp.117–125.

Engelberg, T., Skinner, J. and Zakus, D. (2014). What does commitment mean to volunteers in youth sport organisations? *Sport and Society: Cultures, Commerce, Media, Politics*, 17(1), pp.52–67.

Entrepreneur (2016). Retrieved from www.entrepreneur.com/article/75340.

Hurd, A.R., Barcelona, R.J. and Meldrum, J.T. (2008). *Leisure services management.* Champaign, IL: Human Kinetics.

Maslow, A.H. (1954). *Motivation and personality.* New York: Harper & Row.

Qikker. (2014). *The missing link: Improving your organisation, by linking reward to performance.* Manchester, UK: Qikker Solutions Ltd.

Volunteer Centre Hackney (2010). Retrieved from: http://vchackney.org.

Whitney, M.M. and Bombard, J.M. (2012). *Strategies for developing a successful employee recognition program.* Boston, MA: Morgan, Brown, and Joy, LLP.

Chapter 7

Training and development

OVERVIEW

This chapter discusses the training and development of people in the workplace. It begins by explaining the rationale behind training, then progresses to a discussion of cost-effective training. The chapter then describes the four phases of the Instructional Systems Design system: needs assessment; design and development; delivery using mechanisms of mentoring, coaching, leadership development and career planning; and evaluation.

LEARNING OBJECTIVES

Having read the chapter, students will be able to:

1   Understand the purpose of training and development;
2   Learn the reasons why a training programme is needed;
3   Be able to design and develop a training programme;
4   Understand what it takes to deliver a training programme effectively; and
5   Be able to evaluate the effectiveness of the training programme.

INTRODUCTION TO TRAINING AND DEVELOPMENT

Within sport, a tremendous amount of effort is committed to the on-the-field performance of athletes and coaches, neglecting the off-the-field performance and development of sport managers. The management of sport is assuming an ever more important role in the wake of the technological advancement that has resulted in ever-increasing competition, a rise in customer's expectation of quality and service and a subsequent need to lower costs. It has also become more important globally, in order to prepare workers for new jobs. In the current write-up, we will focus more on the emerging need for training and development in the sport sector, and its implications for individuals and employers.

Purpose of training

Whether it is induction, on-the-job training, coaching, mentoring, cascade training or in-house courses, the purpose of internal training is to create a motivated, skilled and effective workforce through which organizational goals are achieved. Internal training has certain advantages over learning through external provision and formal qualifications, including job relevance and cost. Employees, however, might find it is less transferable to other employment if it is too specific. The following are the two biggest factors that contribute to the increased need for training and development in organizations:

Change: The word 'change' encapsulates almost everything. It is one of the biggest factors that contribute to the need of training and development. There is, in fact, a direct relationship between the two. Change leads to the need for training and development, and training and development leads to individual and organizational change, and the cycle goes on and on. More specifically, it is technology that is driving the need; changing the way sport businesses function, compete and deliver.

Development: This is the other main reason for training and development becoming all the more important. Money is not the sole motivator at work and this is especially true for the twenty-first century. People who work with organizations seek more than just employment from their work; they look at the holistic development of self. Spirituality and self-awareness, for example, are gaining momentum the world over. People seek happiness in jobs that may not be possible, unless an individual is aware of the self.

A comprehensive training and development programme might include the following.

- Training for new staff who've never done this particular work before.
- Training for new staff who may be experienced in the work of the position, but not in the particular method or style which your organization uses.
- Staff development: Ongoing training for all staff.
- Professional development. Although this term is often used interchangeably with staff development, we've chosen to define it as leading either to specific new knowledge, or to the next level of expertise. Professional development might encompass several possibilities:
  - □ Graduate university courses.
  - □ Attendance at conferences.
  - □ Study circles: Groups of professionals who meet regularly to discuss readings and/ or members' writing and research on topics of mutual interest. A study circle may have a facilitator to help guide reading and discussions, or members may take turns acting as facilitator.
  - □ Field-generated courses or workshops: Courses or workshops that grow out of the needs of practitioners, who find people to teach them.
  - □ Institutes: Courses run by non-academic institutions, often involving observation and hands-on practice instead of, or in addition to, lectures, discussion and reading.

Common reasons for engaging in specific programmes of training and development include the need for training about a specific topic or skill, are part of an overall professional development programme, occur when a performance appraisal indicates the performance improvement is required, are a planned succession management strategy, and foster a common and shared development mindset.

COST-EFFECTIVENESS OF TRAINING

Kirkpatrick (1959) developed a four-level model for determining the effectiveness of a training programme. The model was then updated in 1975, and again in 1994, when he published his best-known work *Evaluating Training Programs*. The model portrayed the assumptions that the four levels are arranged in ascending order, causally linked and positively correlated (Alliger and Janak 1989). However, the specifics of each level were not explored in depth and the model acted more as a classification system rather than an explanatory representation. Scholars claimed that the model neglected to present a systematic view of the relationships between these constructs (Alliger and Janak 1989; Holton 1996). The four levels are:

- *Level 1. Reaction*: to the training. Reaction implies how favourably the participants have responded to the training. This evaluation is primarily quantitative in nature and is a feedback to the training and the trainer. The most common collection tool is the questionnaire that analyses the content, methodology, facilities and the course content.
- *Level 2. Learning*: There is a need to measure the learning that takes place as a result of training. At the level of learning the evaluation is done on the basis of change in the ASK (Attitudes, skills and knowledge) of the trainees. The evaluation involves observation and analysis of the voice, behaviour, text. Other tools used, apart from observation, are interviews, surveys, pre- and post-tests etc.
- *Level 3. Behaviour*: Understanding how much changes result from training. Behaviour evaluation analyses the transfer of learning from the training session to the workplace. Here the primary tool for evaluation is predominantly observation. Apart from observation, a combination of questionnaires and 360 feedback are also used.
- *Level 4. Results*: Identifying the final results that occur due to training. The results stage makes evaluations towards the bottom line of the organization. Here the definition of the results depends upon the goal of the training programme. The evaluation is done by using a control group, allowing certain time for the results to be achieved.

Although Kirkpatrick's Four-Level Training Evaluation Model is popular and widely used, there are a number of considerations that need to be taken into account when using the model. One issue is that it can be time-consuming and expensive to use levels 3 or 4 of the model, so it's not practical for all organizations and situations. This is especially the case for organizations that don't have a dedicated training or human resource department, or for one-off training sessions or programmes. In a similar way, it can be expensive and resource-intensive to wire up an organization to collect data with the sole purpose of evaluating training at levels 3 and 4 (whether or not this is practical depends on the systems already in place within the sport organization).

The model also assumes that each level's importance is greater than the last level, and that all levels are linked. For instance, it implies that Reaction is less important, ultimately, than

Results, and that reactions must be positive for learning to take place. In practice, this may not be the case. Most importantly, sport organizations are changing in many ways, and behaviours and results change depending on these, as well as on training. For example, measurable improvements in areas like retention and productivity could result from the arrival of a new CEO or from a new technology, rather than from training. Kirkpatrick's model is great for trying to evaluate training in a 'scientific' way. However, so many variables can alter in fast-changing sport organizations that analysis at level 4 can be limited in usefulness.

METHODS FOR DETERMINING COST-EFFECTIVENESS

Sport enterprises, like any other organizations, seek a return on investment (ROI). Organizations spend huge amounts of money on employee development, and it is therefore very important to ascertain the benefits of training. Different studies have been conducted to evaluate the effectiveness of training programmes. In one of the studies it was found that sales and technical training gave better ROI compared to managerial training programmes.

To reach this conclusion a basic formula for calculating the ROI for training is used: *ROI (in per cent) = Programme benefits/Costs × 100*. It is important to determine the Cost-benefit ratio of training. Cost-benefit analysis (CBA) is used in both planning and evaluation. When used in evaluation, CBA is used to estimate the actual organizational results. After training or another type of intervention has been implemented, cost-benefit analysis can be used to determine whether there was any real benefit in comparison to the actual costs.

Some skills and values that are taught in training do not contribute directly to the 'bottom line' in a measurable way, yet they are presumed to make a valuable contribution to performance. The results of teaching such skills, which are often found in 'soft' skills training or in development programmes, are called 'intangible benefits', and are difficult to measure. Intangibles can include a range of behaviours, qualities or conditions that have value but can be difficult to quantify. Although showing operational results usually means reporting outcomes in 'hard' numbers, intangibles often have influential effects on the organization's performance despite the difficulty in quantifying them. A procedure for valuing intangible benefits, called 'shadow pricing', is to identify the intangibles; for example, more harmonious working conditions. You then need to determine what is required to implement the solution; for example, co-worker cooperation and teamwork as a result of a diversity training course. Finally, determine the implications. A diversity training course might result in less workplace discrimination, increased job satisfaction and a work environment that is more conducive to high productivity (Keller 2004).

Another way of looking at ROI is to calculate how many months it will take before the benefits of the training match the costs and the training pays for itself. This is called the 'payback period'. Expressed as an equation we could do it this way: *payback period = costs/monthly benefits*. The payback period is a powerful measure. If the figure is relatively low – perhaps only a few months – then management will be that much more encouraged to make the training investment. As a measure, it also has the advantage of not requiring an arbitrary benefit period to be specified.

INSTRUCTIONAL SYSTEMS DESIGN (ISD) MODEL: 4 PHASES

Instructional Systems Design (ISD) is the practice of creating instructional experiences which make the acquisition of knowledge and skill more efficient, effective and appealing. The process consists broadly of determining the state and needs of the learner, defining the end goal of instruction and creating some 'intervention' to assist in the transition. There are numerous ISD models and most are based on the same principles, a number of five phases, but we will focus on a four-phase model (Dick and Carey 1996).

Phase 1 has a focus on needs assessment. The rationale for this phase is that organizational investment is associated with employee loyalty and facilitating a sense of obligation to give back to the organization. Needs-based training leads to increased job satisfaction and morale among employees and volunteers. As a consequence, there is reduced turnover of employees and volunteers, and increased employee and volunteer motivation. This leads to improved efficiencies and procedures and an enhanced capacity to adopt new technologies and methods.

Phase 2 is about the design and development of the training. The concept of organizational learning – the development of skills, knowledge, and associations between past actions, the effectiveness of those actions and future actions (Fiol and Lyles 1985) – influences this phase. The design phase is the planning stage of ISD. Its purpose is to transform relevant content into concise, behavioural objectives, creating the instructional 'blueprint' that will direct the development of all training materials, tests and methods. Training requirements and outcomes identified during analysis are written as goals and objectives. The goals developed for training and development should state what will be accomplished as a result of the training, and should be specified in light of the needs identified. These will arise out of gaps and deficiencies identified in the preceding needs analysis. Training goals and objectives indicate the sport organization's expectation of the employee or sport volunteer in relation to their understanding of relevant concepts (e.g. privacy requirements), ability to perform a skill (e.g. public speaking) or demonstration of a change in behaviour (e.g. improved decision-making). Common training programmes for the employees and volunteers in sport organizations include: communication, negotiation, customer service, developing codes of conduct, issues of conflict of interest and corporate social responsibility, good corporate governance, diversity issues, volunteer management, and coaching and officiating. The latter training is usually located within a State or national accreditation framework (Taylor *et al.* 2015).

Phase 3 is the delivery phase. This involves implementing the strategies and conducting the activities, sharing feedback about the programme and training methods, administering tests, modifying the design of the trainings and its materials based on feedback from participants. Training may also be delivered through mentoring. Aubrey and Cohen (1995) identify a number of mentoring techniques. *Accompanying* is a technique that involves taking part in the learning process side by side with the learner/mentee. *Sowing* is the technique used when it is clear to the mentor that what they want to teach may not be understood by or be acceptable to the mentee at first, but will make sense and have value to the mentee only when the situation requires it. *Catalysing* is a technique used when the mentor chooses to plunge the mentee right into change, provoking a different way of thinking, a change in identity or a re-ordering of values. *Showing* involves developing a mentee by demonstrating an activity or a skill, and *Harvesting* is the technique used to create awareness of what was learned by experience and drawing conclusion therefrom. Each technique is useful and dependent on the development needs of the employee.

Coaching is another approach to delivering training. Coaching as a training mechanism aims to provide direction, improve performance, develop capabilities and remove obstacles that may be inhibiting the development of the employee. To many, organizational coaching and mentoring are considered very similar. However, there are differences between them. Coaching targets high performance and improvement at work, and usually focuses on specific skills and goals, although it may also have an impact on an individual's personal attributes, such as social interaction or confidence. The process typically lasts for a relatively short, defined period of time, or forms the basis of an ongoing management style. Mentoring involves the use of the same models and skills of questioning, listening, clarifying and reframing associated with coaching. Traditionally, however, mentoring in the workplace has tended to describe a relationship in which a more experienced colleague uses their greater knowledge and understanding of the work or workplace to support the development of a more junior or inexperienced member of staff.

One key distinction is that mentoring relationships tend to be longer term than coaching arrangements. In a succession planning scenario, for example, a regional coach development director might be mentored by a group-level counterpart over a lengthy period to develop a sound understanding of dealing with coaches, presenting to sporting organizations and challenging embedded coaching practices, all in a supportive environment. The sport organization should consider mentoring when the organization is seeking to develop its employees in specific competencies, using performance-management tools and involving the immediate manager when: the organization has a number of talented employees who are not meeting expectations; the organization is introducing a new system or programme; the organization has a small group of individuals (between five and eight) in need of increased competency in specific areas; and a senior manager needs assistance in acquiring a new skill as an additional responsibility.

Drawing a distinction between mentoring and coaching is a contested debate. The general consensus is that mentoring is relationship-orientated. It seeks to provide a safe environment where the mentee shares whatever issues are affecting their professional and personal success. Although specific learning goals or competencies may be used as a basis for creating the relationship, its focus goes beyond these areas to include things, such as work–life balance, self-confidence, self-perception, and how the personal influences the professional. Coaching, however, is considered task-orientated. The focus is on concrete issues, such as managing more effectively, speaking more articulately and learning how to think strategically. This requires a content expert (coach), who is capable of teaching the coachee how to develop these skills. Taylor, Doherty and McGraw (2015), however, identify key differences across a number of domains, which are highlighted in Table 7.1 opposite.

Management and leadership development, along with team-building programmes and initiatives, are important developmental areas. Included are on-the-job training, external short courses, special projects, residential courses and executive development courses. These development programmes are delivered either through internal processes or externally by training companies, Government bodies or universities. External programmes can be designed specifically for the sport organization and its personnel, or the employee/volunteer

Table 7.1 *Differences between mentoring and coaching*

	Mentor	Coach
Focus	Individual	Enhance performance
Role	Facilitator with no agenda	Specific agenda
Relationship	Self-selecting	Assigned
Source of influence	Perceived value	Position
Personal returns	Affirmation/learning	Teamwork/performance
Arena	Life	Task-related

Source: Taylor *et al.* (2015: 122).

may be integrated into 'open' programmes that comprise participants from a range of organizations, such as the Canadian Association for the Advancement of Women and Sport programme. Assessing the requirements of training and development for leaders and managers involves the complex task of identifying the competencies relevant to any given job, and there are many instruments which aim to measure managerial and leadership behaviours and skills. As with all forms of training and development, programmes which develop management, leadership and team capabilities should be entered into with due consideration about how this development will enhance the sport enterprise's ability to meet its strategic objectives (Taylor *et al.* 2015: 126).

Career planning and development are also important developmentally to employees. Career development is a combination of career planning, which is the individual's responsibility, and career management, which relates to the organization's training and development requirements and initiatives. Career planning is the process that the individual undertakes to assess their strengths and development opportunities relative to the job they are currently performing, and the future career that they aspire to. Career management refers to the support an organization affords an individual, through the delivery of training and development and performance feedback, to assist in the implementation of the individual's career plan.

Phase 4 is the evaluation phase. The evaluation of training and development activities should occur before, during and after implementation. The evaluation process has been described as having four different levels, commonly referred to as the Kirkpatrick levels. In relation to effectiveness, the goals and objectives of the training and development programme determine the most appropriate criteria for assessment. Evaluations should be valid, accurate and reliable, practical and relevant. Evaluation can also be formative and summative. Formative evaluation monitors the training as it proceeds through the ISD process. Monitoring involves reviewing the analysis and design documents periodically, to confirm that objectives are being developed and delivered as originally intended. Summative evaluation is the process of reviewing a course or training after it is taught. It includes measurement of training outcomes in terms of trainees' opinions about the training, test results, on-the-job performance, and the benefit or return on investment of the training to the trainees' organization.

Dynamic feedback loops are very important parts of the ISD evaluation process. If the training under development does not proceed satisfactorily through a particular ISD phase, checking it against specifications from an earlier phase may identify the problem. If a problem is identified, the training product must be corrected in the deficiency phase. For example, if the delivery phase training does not teach actual job skills performed at the trainees' job sites, the initial job analysis may be in need of revision. Back in the analysis phase, the training package must be corrected and redeveloped from that point forward.

CASE STUDY

The English Football Association (FA) has responsibility for retaining and growing the football workforce in the UK. It aims to provide the highest quality of football education programmes through the FA Learning project, and caters for the learning demands of people from all backgrounds who are interested in being part of the football community.

The 'Coaching Pathway' is one of the many learning pathways offered by FA Learning, and provides training courses to football coaches from grassroots to elite level. There are three strands of coaching courses: the main strand covers the entry Level One coaching certificate and leads up to the Union of European Football Associations (UEFA) Pro Licence (held by top club and national side managers). The second strand features specialist courses, including goalkeeping, Futsal and disability football. The third strand covers age-appropriate courses, including the FA Youth Award.

The Level One Certificate in Coaching Football, which is available throughout the country, is normally the first step new coaches would take. The minimum course duration is 24–32 hours, which provides an introduction to the organization and delivery of safe and enjoyable coaching sessions for players. Building on the initial skills learned from the Level One course, new coaches can then decide if they want to progress to the Level Two Certificate in Coaching Football, which aims to provide a deeper understanding of coaching for those on a pathway to professional coaching. Both of the above courses are available at local level (County FA), while the Level Three Certificate in Coaching Football (UEFA B Licence) runs at a national level. The UEFA A Licence is the highest practical coaching award available. It follows the UEFA B Licence and can lead onto the FA Academy Managers or the UEFA Pro Licence award.

The FA Coaching pathway programme offers other coaching courses that are dedicated to coaching for younger players or teams, and for particular groups such as goalkeepers, disabled footballers and coaching Futsal. Online courses across different disciplines are also available for those who prefer learning at their own pace. Once registered, candidates have six months to finish the course and receive a certificate upon completion.

The FA is a prime example of a sporting organization that makes training and development one of its top organizational priorities. It has established a career-progression pathway for those interested in coaching from community level through to the professional game.

Source: adapted from: www.thefa.com/my-football/football-volunteers/coaching volunteering/get%20into%20coaching/coachingpathway

Questions

1   What are the benefits for coaches who take the training programme?
2   Why is it important for FA to develop education programmes for coaches?
3   How would you evaluate the effectiveness of the FA Learning programme for coaches?
4   What makes the FA the authoritative sport organization for coaching training and development in the UK?
5   Design a training and development programme similar to the FA Coach Pathway programme for football referees.
6   Describe what a comprehensive training and development programme might include.
7   Explain Kirkpatrick's four-level model for determining the effectiveness of a training programme.
8   Explain the term 'return on investment' when applied to training and development.
9   Distinguish between formative and summative evaluation. What are the benefits of each?

Case exercise

Go to the Queensland Academy of Sport Career development website (www.qasport.qld.gov. au/services/athlete-career-and-education/index.html).

Browse through the site and identify the training and development opportunities offered to its athletes. In doing this, describe what the training and development is focused on, and if you feel it adequately prepares athletes for their sporting careers and a career when they have finished competing.

SUMMARY

This chapter discussed training and developing people in sport enterprise workplaces. It began by explaining the rationale behind training, then progressed to a discussion of cost-effective training. The chapter then described the four phases of the Instructional Systems Design system: needs assessment; design and development; delivery using mechanisms of mentoring, coaching, leadership development and career planning; and evaluation.

WEBSITE

Sport Nottinghamshire. (n.d.). *Jobs in sport.* Available from: www.sportnottinghamshire.co.uk. See this site for insight into the type of courses and training events available for individuals in the sport sector.

REFERENCES AND BIBLIOGRAPHY

Alliger, G.M. and Janak, E.A. (1989). Kirkpatrick's levels of training criteria: Thirty years later. *Personnel Psychology*, 42, pp.331–342.

Aubrey, R. and Cohen, P.M. (1995). *Working wisdom: Timeless skills and vanguard strategies for learning organizations.* San Francisco, CA: Jossey-Bass

Dick, W. and Carey, L. (1996). *The systematic design of instruction* (4th edn). New York: HarperCollins.

England Football Association. Coaching Pathway. Adapted from: www.thefa.com/my-football/football-volunteers/coachingvolunteering/get%20into%20coaching/coachingpathway.

Fiol, C.M. and Lyles, M.A. (1985). Organisation learning. *Academy of Management Review*, 10(4), pp.803–813.

Holton, E.F., III (1996). The flawed four level evaluation model. *Human Resource Development Quarterly*, 7(1), pp.5–21.

Keller, J.M. (2004). *How to estimate the cost-benefit of training: Calculating return on investment.* Tallahassee, FL: John Keller Associates.

Kellett, P. (1999). Organisational leadership: Lessons from Professional coaches. *Sport Management Review*, 2(2), pp.150–171.

Kirkpatrick, D.L. (1959). Techniques for evaluating training programs. *Journal of ASTD*, 11, pp.1–13.

Millar, P. and Stevens, J. (2012). Management training and national sport organization managers: Examining the impact of training on individual and organizational performances. *Sport Management Review*, 15, pp.288–303.

Taylor, T., Doherty, A. and McGraw, P. (2015). *Managing people in sport organizations: A strategic human resource management perspective* (2nd edn). New York: Routledge.

Part C

Employee traits, dispositions and behaviours

Chapter 8

Personality

OVERVIEW

This chapter examines the ways in which the personality of staff, volunteers, players and members can impact on their conduct and job performance. Different personality theories will be used to demonstrate the broad range of traits that exist, and the ways in which different traits influence individual conduct. Special attention will be given to the strengths and weaknesses of different traits, and how to best match traits to job requirements.

LEARNING OBJECTIVES

After critically reviewing this chapter, readers will be able to:

1 Define the notion of personality;
2 Identify key personality traits across the population;
3 Discuss the strengths and weaknesses of different traits; and
4 Explain how sport managers can best match specific traits to identifiable job requirements.

BASIS OF PERSONALITY

Everyone has a personality. It is embedded in our psyches. Moreover, each individual has their own unique personality, which is expressed through their emotions, beliefs, attitudes and conduct. Additionally, all people bring their personality to the workplace. Particular types of personality are valued in sport and, stereotypically, officials and players can make their mark by projecting personalities that are larger than life on one hand, or eccentric and quirky on the other.

The workplace exposes everyone's personality. This is because working in an organizational setting demands frequent interaction with other employees, and the exchanges that follow are in part shaped by each individual's personality. Sometimes dealing with workplace personalities can present a bigger challenge than the work itself. Interpersonal disputes and tensions are often explained by problems resulting from a 'personality clash'.

So, what exactly is personality? It is often associated with terms like 'temperament', 'disposition' and 'character', and thus says something about the ways in which individuals present themselves to others in different social situations. Personality thus has a lot to do with the visible aspect of someone's character. Additionally, personality is more than exhibiting a specific trait; rather, it is about the embodiment of a collection of qualities. Overall then, personality can be broadly described as the organized pattern of behavioural characteristics of individuals, being the sum total of their physical, mental, emotional and social dispositions.

Understanding one's own personality, and the personality of others, can assist people to make sense of why their co-workers behave the way they do. This can allow us not only to accommodate the eccentricities and foibles of others – we become more tolerant – but also alerts us to the possibilities of using these differences to approach tasks, problems and projects in diverse and creative ways. It is also important to understand that people do not choose their personality: part of it is laid down at birth, while other parts of it are shaped by a multitude of childhood and adolescent experiences, some of which will be highly rewarding, and some of which will be difficult and occasionally traumatic.

UNDERSTANDING PERSONALITY: MYERS BRIGGS TYPE INDICATOR MODEL

How might we get a better grip on personality and understand the different ways in which people respond to different experiences more clearly? There are many models of personality, but one of the most popular and most engaging is the Myers Briggs Type Indicator model (MBTI). Created specifically for evaluating personality in relation to jobs and occupations, the MBTI evaluates personalities in four fields: energizing; attending; deciding; and living. Each of these four fields has two possible rating categories: extraversion or introversion; sensing or intuition; thinking or feeling; and judging or perceiving. Each of these four personality fields are discussed below.

Field 1. Energizing: Extraversion v. introversion

Extraversion and Introversion provide the foundation of all personality models. First used by the Swiss psychologist Carl Jung in the early part of the twentieth century, it explains different ways in which people direct their psychic energy. Whereas extraversion is frequently associated with wanting to dominate and push dissenters to the side, and introversion is linked to shyness or reclusiveness, they are often used to provide exaggerated descriptions of the traits. In reality, they are more nuanced and diverse than that, as the following explanations indicate.

Extraversion (E)
Extroverts like receiving their energy from active involvement in events and having a lot of different activities. They become excited when being around people; enjoy energizing with others; like moving into action and making things happen; are gregarious; and generally feel

at home in their social world. Finally, extroverts understand problems more acutely when they can talk out loud about it and bounce ideas off others.

The following statements apply to extroverts:

- I am outgoing, and I see myself as a people-person.
- I feel comfortable in groups and like working in them.
- I have a wide range of friends and know lots of people.
- I sometimes jump too quickly into an activity and don't allow enough time to think it over.
- Before I start a project, I sometimes forget to stop and clarify what I want to do and why.

Introversion (I)

Introverts secure their psychic energy from an array of different places. They get it from dealing with the ideas, pictures, memories and reactions that are inside their heads. They are more tuned into their inner world; generally prefer doing things alone or with one or two people they feel comfortable with; and take time to reflect to make sure they have a clear idea of what they will experience after they have decided to act. Ideas are almost solid things for introverts. And, at the extreme, they may even like the idea of something better than the real thing.

The following statements generally apply to introverts:

- I am seen as 'reflective' or 'reserved'.
- I feel comfortable being alone, and I am attracted to things I can do on my own.
- I prefer to know just a few people well, rather than have a lot of fleeting acquaintances.
- I sometimes spend too much time dwelling on things, and don't move into action quickly enough.
- I sometimes forget to check in with the outside world by spending too much time on my own thoughts and dreams.

In summary, extroverts tend to draw their energy from people and the outside world, while introverts find energy from within. If you are an extrovert, you are likely to be a people-person who enjoys working with others. You will most likely thrive in group settings and enjoy working with others on projects. Extroverts tend to do better when working on a variety of tasks and may be good at motivating others. If you are an introvert, you may be more reserved, and thus be more comfortable working independently. Introverts also tend to think things through very thoroughly and do not act without thinking it through first.

Field 2. Attending: Sensing v. intuition

The second pair of psychological preferences is Sensing and Intuition. Some people pay more attention to the concrete details contained in the information that comes in through their five senses. This is sensing. On the other hand, others pay more attention to the patterns and possibilities that they see in the information they have captured. This is intuition. At the same time, everyone spends some of their time sensing and some of their time using intuition. It is the balance that differs between people. Additionally, people will generally find one of the two approaches more natural, effortless and comfortable. This is their default position, if you like.

Sensing (S)

Sensing types pay attention to physical reality, which is about what they see, hear, touch, taste and smell. The primary concern is what is actual, present, current and real. Sensing types notice facts and remember details that are important to them. They gravitate to the practical use of things and learn best when they doing what they are wishing to learn. Experience speaks to sensing types louder than words and theories.

The following statements generally apply to sensing types:

- I remember events as snapshots of what actually happened.
- I solve problems by working through facts until I understand the problem.
- I am pragmatic and look to the 'bottom line'.
- I start with facts and then form a big picture.
- I trust experience first and trust words and symbols less.
- Sometimes I pay so much attention to facts, either present or past, that I miss new possibilities.

Intuition (N)

Intuitive types pay the most attention to impressions or the meaning and patterns of the information they receive. They would rather learn by thinking a problem through than by hands-on experience. They are interested in new things and what might be possible, so that they think more about the future than the past. They like to work with symbols and abstract theories, and they remember events more as an impression of what it was like rather than as actual facts or details of what precisely happened.

The following statements generally apply to intuitive types:

- I remember events by what I read 'between the lines' about their meaning.
- I solve problems by leaping between different ideas and possibilities.
- I am interested in doing things that are new and different.
- I like to see the big picture, then to find out the facts.
- I trust impressions, symbols and metaphors more than what I actually experience.
- Sometimes I think so much about new possibilities that I never look at how to make them a reality.

In summary, the attending personality trait refers to what catches a person's attention or how that person focuses their thoughts, and whether they rely on sensory or intuitive information. People who identify with the sensing category are likely to be visual learners who prefer to rely on tangible things. In the workplace, they tend to work through problems one piece at a time. They may rely more on those who have proven themselves through past actions rather than on people who talk about what they can accomplish. If they relate more closely to intuition, they tend to solve problems by brainstorming different possibilities and solutions.

They usually view the entire picture before considering the specific items that make up the picture.

Field 3. Deciding: Thinking v. feeling

This third preference pair describes how people go about making decisions. They may put more weight on objective principles and impersonal facts. This is thinking. Or, they may emphasize personal concerns and the people involved. This is feeling. But feelings should not be confused with emotion; everyone has emotions about the decisions they make. And thinking should not be confused with intelligence; everyone uses thinking for some decisions and feeling for others

Thinking (T)

When thinkers make decisions, they like to find the basic truths or underlying principles, regardless of the specific situation involved. They like to analyse pros and cons and then come to a rational and logical conclusion. They aim to be impersonal and not let their personal desires – or other people's wishes for that matter – influence their decisions.

The following statements generally apply to thinkers:

- I enjoy technical and scientific fields where logic is important.
- I notice inconsistencies.
- I look for logical explanations or solutions to almost everything.
- I make decisions with my head and want to be fair.
- I believe telling the truth is more important than being tactful.
- Sometimes I miss or don't value the 'people' part of a situation.
- I can be seen as too task-orientated, uncaring or indifferent.

Feeling (F)

Feelers believe they can make the best decisions by weighing up what people care about and the points of view of persons involved in a situation. They are concerned with values and what is the best for the people involved. They will go out of their way to establish order and maintain harmony. In their relationships, they aim to be caring, warm and tactful.

The following statements generally apply to feeling types:

- I have a people or communications orientation.
- I am concerned with harmony and nervous when it is missing.
- I look for what is important to others and express concern for others.
- I make decisions with my heart and want to be compassionate.
- I believe being tactful is more important than telling the 'cold' truth.
- Sometimes I miss seeing or communicating the 'hard truth' of situations.
- I am sometimes experienced by others as too idealistic, mushy or indirect.

In summary, the deciding personality trait relates to how a person makes decisions. Thinkers tend to leave considerations about people and emotions out of their decision-making calculus.

Thinkers may be perceived as cold, because they are more concerned with what's right or what should happen than with the effects on people or with being polite. Thinkers prefer to have rules and policies applied across the board, regardless of any other factors involved. Feelers, on the other hand, tend to consider the people involved when making any decisions: they want to avoid actions that disrupt harmony, and may not be direct when communicating with others. However, they are warm and tactful when it comes to interpersonal relationships.

Field 4. Living: Judging v. perceiving

The last personality trait is living, and it refers to a person's lifestyle preferences. It describes how people like to live their *outer life*, and focuses on the behaviours of *others*. Judging types prefer a more structured and decided lifestyle, while perceiving types adopt a more flexible and adaptable lifestyle.

Judging (J)

Judgers use their decision-making preference in their outer life. To others, they seem to prefer a planned or orderly way of life, like to have things settled and organized, feel more comfortable when decisions are made and like to bring life under control as much as possible. But since this trait only describes what they prefer in the outer world, they may, inside, feel flexible and open to new information.

The following statements generally apply to judging types:

- I like to have things decided.
- I appear to be task-orientated.
- I like to make lists of things to do.
- I like to get my work done before playing.
- I plan work to avoid rushing just before a deadline.
- Sometimes I focus so much on the goal that I miss new information.

Perceiving (P)

Perceivers use their perceiving function when acting out their outer life. To others, they appear to prefer a flexible and spontaneous way of life, and like to understand and adapt to the world rather than organize it. Others see them being open to new experiences and information. The following statements generally apply to perceiving types:

- I like to stay open to respond to whatever happens.
- I appear to be loose and casual. I like to keep plans to a minimum.
- I like to approach work as play, or mix work and play.
- I work in bursts of energy.
- I am stimulated by an approaching deadline.
- Sometimes I stay open to new information so long that I miss making decisions when they are needed.

In summary, judgers prefer things to be orderly, organized and under control at all times. They like to have plans and do not like to have a lot of things left up in the air. They may use to-do lists to track their progress towards completing tasks. Perceivers, on the other hand, are often spontaneous and flexible. They work with what is handed to them rather than trying to diligently plan for things, work well under pressure and may work better with deadlines.

UNDERSTANDING PERSONALITY: BIG 5 PERSONALITY TRAIT MODEL

An alternative lens for viewing personality is the Big 5 Personality Trait model. It focuses on five broad personality traits and, like the Myers Briggs model, begins with extraversion. The other four traits are agreeableness, openness, conscientiousness and neuroticism.

These five categories can be described as follows.

1. Extraversion

Extraversion is characterized by excitability, sociability, talkativeness, assertiveness and high amounts of emotional expressiveness. People who are high in extraversion are outgoing and tend to gain energy in social situations. People who are low in extraversion (or introverted) tend to be more reserved and have to expend energy in social settings.

2. Agreeableness

This personality dimension includes attributes such as trust, altruism, kindness, affection and other prosocial behaviours. People who are high in agreeableness tend to be more cooperative, whereas those low in this trait tend to be more competitive and even manipulative.

3. Conscientiousness

Standard features of this dimension include high levels of thoughtfulness, with good impulse control and goal-directed behaviours. Those high on conscientiousness tend to be organized and mindful of details.

4. Neuroticism

Neuroticism is a trait characterized by sadness, moodiness and emotional instability. Individuals who are high in this trait tend to experience mood swings, anxiety, moodiness, irritability and sadness. Those low in this trait tend to be more stable and emotionally resilient.

5. Openness

This trait features characteristics such as imagination and insight, and those high in this trait also tend to have a broad range of interests. People who are high in this trait tend to be more adventurous and creative. People low in this trait are often much more traditional and may struggle with abstract thinking.

It is important to note that each of the five personality factors represents a range between two extremes. For example, extraversion represents a continuum between extreme extraversion and extreme introversion. In the real world, most people lie somewhere in between the two polar ends of each dimension.

Based on extensive research into the Big 5 model of personality, many psychologists now believe that these five personality dimensions are not only universal, but also have biological origins. These beliefs have been used to conclude that the above traits represent the key qualities that shape our individual emotions and behaviours, and explain the ways we move through our social landscape.

At the same time, it should be remembered that behaviour involves an interaction between a person's underlying personality and situational variables. The situation in which a person finds themselves plays a major role in how the person reacts. However, in most cases, people offer responses that are consistent with their underlying personality traits. Also, these dimensions represent broad areas of personality. Research has demonstrated that these groupings of characteristics tend to occur together in many people. For example, individuals who are sociable tend to be talkative. However, these traits do not always occur together. Personality is complex and varied, and each person may display behaviours across several traits and personality dimensions.

PERSONALITY AND JOB PERFORMANCE

Research into the application of the Myers Briggs and the Big 5 personality model traits to the workplace suggests that certain personality traits frequently predict not only the profiles of people found in certain occupations and positions, but also their job performance. Take, for example, the following findings:

- *Sales*: In sales positions, conscientiousness is the best predictor of future performance, followed by extraversion.
- *Customer service*: Again, conscientiousness is the best predictor. Agreeableness and openness to experience are also correlated with customer-service job performance. When looking specifically at Call Centre employees, conscientiousness, emotional stability and agreeableness are significantly related to productivity. This unusual mix indicates a complex pattern of personality for jobs that involve complicated and/or demanding interpersonal interactions.
- *Skilled and semi-skilled jobs*: Conscientiousness was once again the strongest predictor, followed by emotional stability, which is lower but significant.
- *Professional occupations*: In professional occupations, conscientiousness is the only Big 5 trait that significantly predicts performance.
- *Leadership roles*: Leadership can be thought of in two ways: (1) how employees 'emerge' as leaders; and (2) how they perform once they are in managerial roles. Conscientiousness and extraversion are associated strongly with leadership emergence, and significantly, but less strongly associated with leadership effectiveness and managerial performance. In other words, these traits may help you be noticed as a leader but are less important once you're in a leadership position. This is because of the complex and context-specific

nature of leadership roles, where different skill sets and personality traits are needed for different positions in the organizational hierarchy.

Such findings provide evidence that supports the use of personality in employee selection for specific job categories, but they also need to be treated with caution.

OTHER PREDICTORS

Managers are frequently enthusiastic about the idea that if they populate their staff functions with appropriate personalities and other good-fit factors, their staffing and employee-performance problems will be resolved. Unfortunately this will not happen, since personality represents only one piece of a much bigger employee-performance jigsaw. The fact is that overall job performance is a multidimensional issue. These dimensions include cognitive ability, motivation, emotional intelligence, past experience and various other job-specific skills and abilities. There are now seen to be six key factors that predispose people to high level job performance. They are:

- General mental ability;
- Job experience and job knowledge;
- A personality embedded with conscientiousness;
- A positive view of one's ability, and a general sense of sense of control; and
- A personality that includes emotional stability.

CASE STUDY

As noted in the introduction to this chapter, everyone has a personality. It is embedded in our psyches. Moreover, each individual has their own unique personality, which is expressed through their emotions, beliefs, attitudes and conduct. Additionally, all people bring their personality to the workplace. Particular types of personality are valued in sport and, stereotypically, officials and players can make their mark by projecting personalities that are larger than life on one hand or eccentric and quirky on the other. In sport, just like in show business and the theatre, a bland personality delivers the worst of all outcomes. At the same time, research undertaken over the last 40 years has shown that every type of personality not only has its weaknesses, but also has its strengths. There is also mounting evidence that certain personality types may be better suited to some work roles than other personality types.

Take, for example, the case of Theo Thickskin. Theo has just been appointed as the Chief Executive Officer for the Boxing Control Board (BCB) for a province in the heartland of Canada. One of Theo's first tasks was to appoint several boxing commissioners, who, as it turned out, were more appropriately positioned as boxing industry liaison officers. Their key role was to act as a conduit among the boxing managers, trainers, medial support staff and the boxers themselves, as well as the Government. As representatives of the Government, they were responsible for ensuring the regulations governing the conduct of boxing were adhered to. Specifically, they were required to keep a register of all bouts and the results, and ensure that all bouts were properly supported by appropriate measures and medical services. They were also responsible for setting up a range of educational programmes that had risk management front and centre. And, in addition, they were responsible for resolving disputes and monitoring the behaviour of managers, making sure bouts were not fixed, and generally maintaining the sometimes dubious reputation of boxing. These were seen as challenging tasks since they not only required knowledge of the legislative parameters surrounding boxing, but also needed finely crafted interpersonal skills whereby they could move between a diverse range of social classes and ethnic cultures.

The question Theo kept asking himself was: 'What personality type best fits this complex set of job responsibilities?' He reminded himself that sociability was an important trait; the job demanded far more than an easy-going manner.

Questions

1   What personality traits appear to be most relevant in work settings in general, and the sport sector in particular?
2   For the above case study, what were the key job requirements?
3   Based on your knowledge of personality and its broad range of types, what four personality traits do you think would be most appropriate for the above position?
4   What problems do you think Theo will face if he uses personality traits as the dominant selection criteria?

Case exercise

Sepp Blatter was the long-time President of FIFA, the world governing body for world football. He had an international reputation and was always in the media spotlight, was a highly political operator and a consummate negotiator. Go to the FIFA website (www.fifa.com) and see how much you can find on the personal attributes of Blatter. Having completed a scan of the site, decide what personality type he appeared to exhibit. Having also looked at his career highlights, was his personality a good fit for the position of President?

SUMMARY

This chapter examined the ways in which the personality of staff, volunteers, players and members can impact on their conduct and job performance. Different personality theories were used to demonstrate the broad range of traits that exist, and the ways in which different traits influence individual conduct. Special attention was given to the strengths and weaknesses of different traits, and how to best match traits to job requirements. It was concluded that although personality can clearly influence job performance, its role should not be overestimated, especially in sport enterprise settings. There are other factors that can also impact on how well people perform in their jobs.

WEBSITE

Bailey, S. (2014). Can personality predict performance? Available from www.forbes.com/sites/sebastianbailey/2014/07/08/can-personality-predict-performance/#3091a7051fa0. See this site for a succinct summary of the relationship between personality and job performance.

REFERENCES AND BIBLIOGRAPHY

Carlstedt, R. (2012). *Evidence-based applied sport psychology*. New York: Springer.

Cervone, D. and Pervin, L. (2016). *Personality: Theory and research* (13th edn). Hoboken, NJ: John Wiley & Sons.

Cooper, C. (2010). *Individual differences and personality* (3rd edn). New York: Oxford University Press.

Cox, R. (2012). *Sport psychology: Concepts and applications* (7th edn). New York: McGraw-Hill.

McCrae, R. and Terracciano, A. (2005). Universal features of personality traits from the observer's perspective: Data from 50 cultures. *Journal of Personality and Social Psychology*, 88(3), pp.547–561.

Silva, J. and Stevens, D. (2002). *Psychological foundations of sport*. Brockport, NY: Brockport Bookshelf.

Silva, J. and Weinberg, R. (1984). *Psychological foundations of sport*. Champaign, IL: Human Kinetics.

Weinberg, R. and Gould, D. (2014). *Foundations of sport and exercise psychology* (6th edn). Champaign, IL: Human Kinetics.

Chapter 9

Perceptions

OVERVIEW

This chapter addresses the issue of perception and, in particular, the often radically different ways in which people in sport enterprises interpret and understand similar events. Special attention is given to the concept of perceptual sets, and how they are shaped by individual values, beliefs and experiences. Additional discussion will centre on perceptual errors, especially those arising from stereotyping and bias.

LEARNING OBJECTIVES

Having interrogated this chapter, readers will be able to:

1   Explain the essential features of perception;
2   Discuss the factors that lead people to frequently perceive the same social phenomena in quite different ways;
3   Explain the concept of a perceptual set;
4   Identify the factors that lead to perceptual error;
5   Explain how perceptual error can undermine the effective management of sport enterprises;
6   Discuss situations where people exhibiting perceptual error can be identified; and
7   Explain how counselling and training can assist sport enterprise staff to reduce levels of dysfunctional perceptual error.

PERCEPTUAL PROCESS

Perception is our sensory experience of the world around us and involves both the recognition of environmental stimuli and actions in response to these stimuli. Through the perceptual process, we gain information about properties and elements of the environment that are critical to our survival. Perception not only creates our experience of the world around us, but also allows us to act in some sort of purposeful and decisive manner within our physical, social and cultural environment.

The perceptual process thus allows us to make sense of the multitude of stimuli we absorb relentlessly. At any given moment we see familiar objects and spaces, feel the touch of objects, animals and people against our skin, smell the aroma of home-cooked meals, and hear the sound of music playing in our neighbour's lounge. All of these things constitute our conscious experience, provide the cues for interacting with others, adjust our immediate behaviour and shape our subsequent conduct.

PERCEPTUAL SETS

At the same time, we are continually organizing our experiences within our own personal frame of reference. We sift and prioritize in all sorts of ways, and as result, the way we see the world is heavily influenced by our own past experiences, expectations, motivations, beliefs, emotions and even our culture. The other important point to note is that not everyone perceives the world in the same way. There is a high degree of subjectivity and personal bias. Sport is the perfect space for revealing the subjectivity of perception. In professional sport's new-player drafting programmes, where clubs can prioritize draft picks, there is only occasional agreement on how recruits will be ranked on their potential to perform at the elite level. Some recruiters may have a preference for a particular body type, and arbitrarily dismiss anyone who does fit the perceptual mould. Others may place a high value on tactical know-how, and fail to see other attributes that may deliver an equivalent level of performance.

The above case is an example of how a perceptual set operates. The term 'perceptual set' refers to the tendency to perceive objects or situations from a particular frame of reference. We have all sorts of ways for constructing perceptual sets, but in the end they involve the creation of schemas, conceptual models and mental frameworks. Perceptual sets allow us to compile diverse amounts of information and interpret this information with a view to understanding its form and meaning. For example, people have a strong schema for faces, making it easier to recognize familiar human faces in the world around them. It also means that when we look at an ambiguous image, we are more likely to see it as a face than some other type of object. Perceptual sets usually lead us to reasonably accurate conclusions, and this is why we use them over and over again. They enable us to act purposively and decisively, but they also lead us astray and cause us to deliver both poor and unfair judgements.

FORCES THAT INFLUENCE PERCEPTUAL SETS

Motivation

Motivation can play an important role in perceptual sets and how we interpret the world around us. If we are supporting our favourite sports team, we might be motivated to view members of the opposing team as overly aggressive, incompetent and always look at ways of securing an unfair advantage. Alternatively, we will view our team as highly skilled, creative and never going outside the rules to secure a competitive edge. In one classic experiment, researchers deprived participants of food for several hours, and they consequently became extremely hungry. When they were later shown a set of ambiguous images, those who had been food-deprived were far more likely to interpret the images as food-related objects: because they were hungry, they were more motivated to see the images in a particular certain way.

Expectations

Expectations also play an important role. If we expect people to behave in certain ways in certain situations, these expectations can influence how we perceive these people and their roles. One of the classic experiments on the impact of expectation on perceptual sets involved showing participants either a series of numbers or letters. Then, the participants were show an ambiguous image that could either be interpreted as the number 13 or the letter B. Those who had viewed the numbers were more likely to see it as a 13, whereas those who had viewed the letters were more likely to see it as the letter B.

Culture

Culture also influences how we perceive people, objects and situations. Surprisingly, researchers have found that people from different cultures even tend to perceive perspective and depth cues differently. The ways in which culture shapes behaviour is discussed in detail in Chapter 3.

Emotions

Emotions can have a dramatic impact on how we perceive the world around us. For example, if we are angry, we might be more likely to perceive hostility in others. One experiment demonstrated that when people came to associate a nonsense syllable with mild electrical shocks, they experienced physiological reactions to the syllable even when it was presented subliminally.

Attitudes

Attitudes can also have a powerful influence on perception. Many studies have shown that attitudes, both positive and negative, can shape the perception of individuals and lead them to build very strong beliefs about an issue. In sport there are many instances of fans directing racist slurs against dark-skinned players of opposition teams. The racist slur is rarely the result of a specific grievance, but is rather the result of an ingrained bias or prejudice. In this instance, the fan is operating under the influence of a perceptual set which rates all black people as inferior or problematic. Additionally, the fan will use this particular perceptual set to form the same attitude about all black people, no matter what the context is, or what this black person happens to be doing. The same principle will apply to prejudices against other people with different ethnic practices or sexual preferences.

SELECTIVE PERCEPTION

Selective perception is the tendency not to notice and more quickly forget stimuli that cause emotional discomfort and contradict our prior beliefs. For example, a teacher may have a favourite student because of a particular personality trait, and thus ignore the student's learning difficulties and poor attainment. Conversely, they might not notice the progress of their least favourite student, who is progressing splendidly. Selective perception is not only interpersonal; it can also involve processes by which individuals perceive what they want to in media messages, while ignoring opposing viewpoints. It is a broad term to identify the behaviour all people exhibit: to tend to see things based on their particular frame of reference. It also describes how we categorize and interpret sensory information in a way that favours one category or interpretation over another. Privileging physical appearance over fundamental skill levels is a case in point. In other words, selective perception is a form of bias because we interpret information in a way that is congruent with our existing values and beliefs.

COGNITIVE BIASES

Cognitive biases are tendencies to think in certain ways that can lead to systematic deviations from a standard of rationality or good judgement, and are often studied in psychology and behavioural economics. Although the reality of these biases is confirmed by replicable research, there are often controversies about how to classify these biases or how to explain them. Some are effects of information-processing rules (i.e. mental shortcuts), called 'heuristics', that the brain uses to produce decisions or judgements. Such effects are called cognitive biases.

PERCEPTUAL ERRORS

Selective perception and cognitive bias inevitably leads to perceptual errors. The most common errors are as follows.

Halo effect

The halo effect refers to the tendency to immediately rate attractive or charismatic individuals more favourably for their personality traits, dispositions and related characteristics than those who are less attractive or charismatic. The halo effect is also used in a more general sense to describe the global impact of likeable personality, or some specific desirable trait, in creating biased judgements about all facets of a person's temperament and general demeanour. Thus, when the halo effect operates, feelings generally overcome cognition when people we like are being appraised for specific traits and capabilities.

Leniency effect

The leniency effect refers to situations where people are treated favourably in order to avoid conflict or disputation. In these instances, a possible criticism is recast as a comment about a positive trait.

Central tendency effect

The central tendency effect refers to situations where people feel uncomfortable making severe judgements about others and, as a result, are unlikely to make either extremely favourable or highly unfavourable comments about their values, beliefs or conduct.

Recency effect

The recency effect involves the tendency to not only remember more recent information about others, but also to use this information to make judgements about their character. This is especially true for information that paints a negative picture. In these situations valuations are often high critical and disproportionately severe.

Similarity effect

The similarity effect involves gravitating towards people who have similar values, beliefs and attitudes. In simple terms, we like people who are like us. On the other hand, we tend to avoid people who do not share our view of the world, or who have different lifestyles and interests.

Perceptual defence effect

Perceptual defence involves the tendency of people to protect themselves against ideas, objects or behaviours that threaten their current belief systems. It is a function of selective perception which protects the individual from threatening or contradictory stimuli. Perceptual defence occurs when a person's value orientations act as a barrier to stimuli that are threatening. For example, an alcoholic athlete may avoid anti-drinking and driving campaigns for fear of what could happen to their image and reputation if they admitted to the problem. In general, perceptual defence can cause people to avoid or misinterpret otherwise important messages.

STEREOTYPING

Stereotyping is the act of ascribing a set of traits to a person or group of people based on cultural preconceptions. Stereotyping is a widespread problem in the workplace, and can reveal itself in a wide variety of interactions and incidents. For instance, candidates for promotion may be overlooked, and work teams may not include the best performing staff. Dealing with stereotyping in the workplace should include education of and interaction with all employees, as well as a clear directive to treat every worker on their individual professional merits. A selection of problematic stereotyping is discussed below.

Gender

Gender stereotyping occurs with men and women. A common preconception about female workers is that emotion overrides logic and reason. When females are comparatively rare in a work environment, the expectation may be that they will be overly assertive in an effort to compete with their male counterparts. Male stereotyping involves the idea that males are inherently stoic and unemotional. More harmful stereotypes imply cronyism among male workers, known as the 'old boys' network'. This stereotype asserts that promotions and perks go to friends of the boss as opposed to more qualified – and often female – workers. The sexual preferences of both genders may be questioned when a certain gender is rare in a given field, such as female truck drivers or male hair stylists.

Race and ethnicity

Racial stereotypes have existed throughout human history. The multinational and multicultural nature of global business demands a broad understanding of race and ethnicity in the face of persistent misconceptions. For example, racial stereotypes commonly ascribed to African-American and Hispanic workers include laziness, distrust and incompetence. Muslim employees may suffer from the perception that they are inherently dangerous and threatening owing to their religion. Even positive stereotypes can be counterproductive. For example, the assumption that decisions and efforts made by Asian workers are inherently better owing to perceptions of higher intelligence and work ethic may cause supervisors to ignore actual output. Although not necessarily insulting, stereotypes may prove harmful when a certain level of competence is assumed rather than proven individually.

Age

Age-based stereotyping affects all groups. Young workers may be viewed as having a sense of entitlement in that recent graduates expect a high grade of employment; young employees may be considered incompetent owing to lack of experience. This unfair thought process works against individuals who have true drive and a strong work ethic. Conversely, older workers may be seen as 'lifers' or simply counting the days towards retirement without putting in much effort. This stereotype ignores years of hard work performed by these employees, along with the experience and leadership these dedicated professionals can provide to younger generations.

MANAGING THE PROBLEM OF STEREOTYPING

Although stereotyping is usually ingrained – based on decades of dubious humour, racism and lack of exposure to people of different ethnic groups – proper training can offset it. No business can change what people think outside the workplace, but every business can establish zero-tolerance policies against discrimination. Human resources and management should address individual violations in private. Group meetings, role-playing and training seminars should be mandated, in addition to punitive policies for those who violate stated policies. Group sessions can educate employees and help workers get to know each other personally. Once individuals are viewed independently of their demographics, the impetus to lump them together diminishes. Work groups and teams may be organized specifically to mix people of different races and genders in an effort to break down inaccurate perception barriers.

PERCEPTUAL ERRORS IN THE WORKPLACE

In the work setting, the halo effect is most likely to show up in a supervisor's appraisal of a subordinate's job performance. In fact, the halo effect is probably the most common bias in performance appraisal. Think about what happens when a supervisor evaluates the performance of a subordinate. The supervisor may give prominence to a single characteristic of the employee, such as enthusiasm, and allow the entire evaluation to be coloured by how they judge the employee on that one characteristic. Even though the employee may lack the requisite knowledge or ability to perform the job successfully, if the employee's work shows enthusiasm, the supervisor may very well give them a higher performance rating than is justified by knowledge or ability.

A second common error in the workplace is known as the leniency error. As already noted, this error is often made in an attempt to avoid conflict. Performance appraisals are an uncomfortable situation for both managers and employees. Managers do not always enjoy giving negative feedback and employees do not like receiving negative feedback. To avoid the awkward situation, some managers will not rate employees accurately. Instead, managers give high ratings to all employees to avoid looking like the bad guy, or creating a reputation as a punitive bully. Although performance appraisal meetings induce anxiety on both the manager and the employee, giving an employee high ratings when they are not deserved does not help employees improve their performance. A poor performer who receives high ratings will not change their behaviour because areas of improvement are not addressed.

Central tendency error occurs when a person rating another does not give high or low ratings, but tends to stay in the middle of the rating scale. Similar to the leniency error, managers who rate employees in the middle do so to avoid conflict with employees. Rather than rate a poor performer at the lowest spectrum of the scale, many managers feel they are being fairer if they rate the individual in the middle of the scale. Again, employees are not getting a true sense as to how their performance is rated.

Similarity error can have a very negative impact on certain employees. Social psychology tells us that we tend to gravitate towards people who are similar to us; that is, birds of a feather flock together; we like people who are like us. In conducting performance ratings, managers may give higher ratings to employees who are similar to them rather than giving an accurate rating. Another way this error can be interpreted is through in-groups and out-groups. In-groups can form based on personality similarities or common interests. Out-groups are those individuals that do not seem to fit into the norm or in-group. A manager may unknowingly rate a member of their in-group higher compared to a member of the out-group.

CASE STUDY

As the above discussion suggests, perception is a critically important aspect of organizational behaviour, since it allows us to understand and interpret the world around us. This is especially important for people working in sport enterprises, since sport is not only diverse, but also requires a broad range of interpersonal skills where quick responses need to be made and sound judgements determined. However, perception is a double-edged sword: whereas it allows us to absorb and evaluate information, and use it to make decisions, it is also subject to distortions and biases. As a result, the objectivity and accuracy of our perceptions can be easily contaminated by highly subjective feelings, emotions and judgements. At the extreme, our perceptions can be shaped dramatically by bias and prejudice.

Consider the following case. The International Council for Disc Golf – where frisbees are substituted for golf balls – has undertaken a performance evaluation of its organization. Two divisions were identified for special analysis: first, the finance department; and second, the public relations department. The finance department was managed by a very capable and well-credentialled officer. He had previous experience with the International Olympic Committee (IOC) as a financial controller, and had also written extensively on the topic of financial transparency in sport organizations. His office was well managed and he had a very loyal staff. At the same time, he was a stickler for following rules and procedures, and this attention to detail was reflected in the annual accounts. This extreme concern for protocols had many strengths, but some senior staff found his conduct obsessive and obstructive. He was also apolitical and found the cut and thrust of office politics difficult to handle. He was not overtly assertive, and preferred to let his professional capabilities do the talking.

The public relations (PR) department was managed by an experienced female who came to the job via the Nike Corporation. She was very adept at managing difficult situations and was highly accomplished at writing persuasive press releases that put the organization in a positive light. She possessed a broad array of marketing and sales skills, but did not have a professional qualification in the area. She was highly ambitious and used her finely tuned interpersonal skills to build a strong network of professional relationships, especially with senior management. Her extravert personality won her many professional friendships, but her sometimes-abrasive personality frequently created discontent among her subordinates. She had a highly crafted ability to take the credit for the PR department's successes, while quickly passing blame to her subordinates when things went wrong.

An independent consultant was invited to undertake a performance review of each department. The finance department was found to have an exemplary record in producing accurate, timely and detailed documentation of the organization's financial affairs. Unfortunately, this highly rated capability had the effect of highlighting in stark detail the financial weaknesses of the organization. The most recent accounts revealed that the most recent World Cup had been a financial disaster and that a major sponsor – a large multinational supplement manufacturer – had discontinued its relationship with the Council.

The consultant also took a detailed look at the PR department. His initial impression was highly positive. The office space was perfectly laid out, staff were energetic and highly articulate and there appeared to be a climate of action, initiative and self-motivation. However, when he dug a little deeper into the operation of the PR department he found pockets of dysfunction. This was especially evident in the relationships the manager had with her subordinates. At the same time, the growing level of dissatisfaction was camouflaged by the contrived exuberance of the manager and a few of her associates. The consultant also noted that the PR department had been unable to effectively manage a corruption scandal involving some members of its governing council. A number of members had taken bribes in return for supporting the bid of a particular host city.

Having completed his evaluation of each department, the consultant rated the performance of the finance department slightly below the PR department. Based on the above case material, this is a surprising outcome. On the other hand, when the problem of perceptual bias is taken into account it is easier to explain the judgement.

Questions

1 Identify, as you see them, the strengths and weaknesses of the finance department.
2 Identify, as you see them, the strengths and weaknesses of the PR department.
3 What factors might lead you to underrate the performance of the finance department?
4 What factors might lead you to underrate the performance of the PR department?
5 What factors might lead you to overrate the performance of the finance department?
6 What factors might lead you to overrate the performance of the PR department?

Case exercise

Look at the websites for the international governing bodies for synchronized swimming (www.fina.org) and cycling (www.uci.ch). Having scanned both sites, how would you rate the significance of each sport and the contribution they make to world sport? Come back to this case a day or so later and reflect on what you said. Examine your responses critically, and identify the perceptual sets you used to make your assessments of each sport.

SUMMARY

This chapter addressed the issue of perception, and in particular, the often radically different ways in which people in sport enterprises interpret and understand similar events. Special attention was given to the concept of perceptual sets and how they are shaped by individual values, beliefs and experiences. Additional discussion centred on perceptual errors, especially those arising from stereotyping and bias.

WEBSITE

Lee Merkhofer Consulting (n.d.) Priority Systems: Part 1: Errors and bias in judgment. Available from: www.prioritysystem.com/reasons1.html. See this site for additional discussion on the ways in which perceptual bias shapes the way people respond so subjectively to many workplace situations.

REFERENCES AND BIBLIOGRAPHY

Cox, R. (2012). *Sport psychology: Concepts and applications* (7th edn). New York: McGraw-Hill.

Lane, A. (2015). *Sport and exercise psychology: Topics in applied psychology* (2nd edn). London: Routledge.

Williams, A., Davids, K. and Williams, J. (1999). *Visual perception and action in sport*. London: E & FN Spon.

Chapter 10

Motivation

OVERVIEW

This chapter examines the ways in which sport enterprise managers can motivate staff, volunteers, members and players to ensure optimal performance. Discussion will focus on structural and operational factors that enable people to feel good about their workplace, be comfortable with their roles and responsibilities, commit themselves to their primary tasks and engage enthusiastically with their work mates.

LEARNING OBJECTIVES

Having engaged critically with this chapter, students will be able to:

1 Explain what is meant by motivation;
2 Understand the importance of motivation in securing staff, volunteer, player and member commitment;
3 Distinguish between higher and lower level motives;
4 Understand the difference between hygiene and job satisfying factors;
5 Understand the importance of rewards in motivating staff, volunteers, players and members; and
6 Explain the relationship that generally exists among motivation, engagement, satisfaction, morale and job performance.

MYSTERY OF MOTIVATION

In life and work, rarely a day goes by without someone saying – or more precisely, complaining – that a friend or colleague lacks motivation. This assertion is usually accompanied by an aside that implies the person is essentially lazy. These types of assertions can be colourful, but they are also simplistic. Motivation is a complex notion and is determined by a broad range of variables. Motivation is situational, which means that someone can be highly motivated in one type of social or work setting, but close to inert in another.

Motivation is essentially about being sufficiently energized to engage in some form of activity. This activity can be passive, but it can also be highly physical. This activation may be stimulated by an outside event, but the activation comes from an internal state or condition. This internal state or condition is often expressed in terms of a desire or a want. The desire might be basic, like the need to eat, or it may be very esoteric, like the need to attend a concert of classical music, or visit a museum. The final point about motivation is that it is goal-directed; that is, motivation also involves the seeking out of a particular experience. In short then, motivation can be expressed as a desire or want that energizes and directs goal-orientated behaviour. The only thing missing here is a reference to the longevity of motivation. There is now broad acknowledgement that the factors that energize behaviour in the first instance are likely to be different from the factors that provide for its persistence. The workplace provides numerous examples of this problem. When the excitement and glamour wears off, and the routine demands of the job take over, the reservoir of energy that drove the high work rate can quickly dissipate.

WHAT MOTIVATES?

There are different ways of managing staff and coordinating different sorts of group-based tasks, and the evidence and research suggests that some approaches will work consistently better than others. At the same time, there is always a balance to be struck between task-centred management and person-centred management, and this is a theme running through this unit of study.

So, what are these so-called 'better' management approaches, and how might we find out the best ways of motivating staff to work hard and commit themselves to the organization's values, mission and strategic direction? What exactly are people looking for when they take up a job offer, and what can sport enterprise managers do to ensure their staff are motivated to do the very best they can? The research says that people are motivated by the following factors:

- Pay and other monetary rewards;
- Job security;
- A positive social environment;
- The opportunity to work autonomously, which means not having 'close' and 'strict' supervision;
- Recognition for work done well; and
- Sense of achievement.

Although a list like this provides a useful guide to motivating staff, it does not take into account the experiences and skills of employees, nor the nature of the task being completed. What works for a seasoned CEO of a professional football club may not suit the demands of a novice track-and-field coach.

MODELS OF WORKPLACE MOTIVATION

There are many models of 'motivation in the workplace'. Some are based around goal attainment, whereas others are concerned with fairness, equity and distributive justice. They are all useful, but there are also models that attend to the satisfaction of various needs. These needs-based models will provide the focal point of this chapter, and are very useful in understanding the behaviour of people working in sport enterprises. They were constructed more than 50 years ago, but have stood the test of time, and can be comfortably implemented in nearly every type of sport-related setting.

MASLOW'S HIERARCHY OF NEEDS MODEL

Abraham Maslow proposed his psychology theory, the Hierarchy of Needs, in 1943, and it is frequently used in the business world in a number of ways, particularly in functions that deal with people. To gain a better understanding of how Maslow's concepts apply in today's business environment, it is important to first understand what the Hierarchy of Needs is. The concept is most often demonstrated with a pyramid that illustrates each need and its relative importance. The base of the pyramid consists of the most basic needs, whereas more complex human needs make up the top of the structure.

Basic physical requirements such as water, food, sleep and warmth are at the bottom of the pyramid, and once those needs are satisfied, an individual can move to the next level of need, which is safety and security. As people satisfy each level of need, more increasingly complex needs are introduced, which are also more social and psychological. For example, we move from the need for friendship, intimacy and love to the need for self-esteem and having feelings of accomplishment as the primary needs to be addressed.

There are five levels on the pyramid. The base is physiological needs, which we've already discussed, but it's important to remember that unless these needs are met, nothing else matters. Safety and security needs are the next level of the pyramid, and although they are important for survival, they aren't nearly as crucial as physiological needs. Some examples of safety and security needs include shelter from the environment, safe neighbourhoods and a steady means of income.

The third level in the pyramid is social needs, or the need to belong and be liked or loved. The social level addresses the need for companionship and acceptance. Next up on the pyramid are the esteem needs. Once the first three types of needs are satisfied, the need for esteem is increasingly vital. This need includes anything that creates personal worth, social recognition, self-esteem and a sense of accomplishment.

Finally, at the top of the pyramid are self-actualizing needs. People who are self-actualizing are concerned with personal growth and less concerned with securing the approval of others.

Maslow classified the five levels of needs into two categories. They are first, deficiency needs, which include the physiological, security, social and esteem needs. The second category includes growth needs. These are different in that they don't stem from a lack of something. Instead, they stem from a desire to develop both professionally and personally.

Maslow's theory has some important considerations for management, including insights into the best way to motivate employees, members, clients and customers. For example, managers can use Maslow's Hierarchy of Needs to find and create ways to motivate employees by carefully considering how needs play into job design, compensation, management style and so forth. For example, managers can harness the power of physiological needs by providing wages that are sufficient for employees to purchase their basic needs, with enough cash left over to place into a savings account. Safety needs can be addressed by providing job security, retirement benefits and a safe working environment. Social needs are addressed by developing a team atmosphere, making sure that employees know that they are a part of something bigger, and they can count on their team members just as their team members should be able to count on them.

MCGREGOR'S BILATERAL MODEL

Douglas McGregor proposed two theories about employee motivation, based on two very different sets of assumptions that managers hold towards workers. McGregor was fascinated with what it was that motivated people do a great job when they go to work, and to commit themselves to their profession. He wanted to find out why some people cared about the goals of the organization and how they could contribute to them, and why others viewed work in instrumental terms. What made some people go beyond the call of duty, and others be solely concerned with securing a getting a regular pay cheque? Douglas McGregor studied these questions and proposed two different views of employee motivation in his 1960 book *The Human Side of Enterprise*. These views are known as Theory X and Theory Y.

Theory X is based on a pessimistic view of employee motivation and behaviour. Theory X assumes that employees dislike work, are not ambitious, want to avoid responsibility, dislike change and are self-centred. Managers who hold these assumptions believe that employees can only be motivated by money, promotions and job security. Such managers are likely to use more of a command-and-control approach with their employees. Employees will cooperate if they feel their basic needs for income and security will be met.

Theory Y is based on an optimistic view of employee motivation and behaviour. Theory Y assumes that employees enjoy work that is meaningful, are willing to take on responsibility and are willing to work for organizational goals or causes they believe in. Theory Y also assumes that employees are capable of creativity, ingenuity and self-direction. Managers who hold these assumptions believe that employees are motivated not just by material needs, but also by higher-level needs, such as self-esteem and a sense of fulfilment. Since these are continuous needs throughout life, managers should address these needs when seeking to motivate employees. Giving employees more authority, broadening the scope of their jobs and allowing them to have a say in decision-making can all motivate employees to work hard for the organization.

ATKINSON AND MCCLELLAND'S NEED FOR ACHIEVEMENT THEORY

This model of motivation is not highly original, but it encapsulates all the strengths of a needs-based model, while conceding its limitations. Unlike other need-based theories, which try to interpret every need, a single drive for achievement allows us to concentrate on what leads people to immerse themselves in their work. Achievement motivation can be broken down into three types:

119

1   *Achievement*: seeks position advancement, feedback, and sense of accomplishment.
2   *Authority*: need to lead, make an impact and be heard by others.
3   *Affiliation*: need for friendly social interactions and to be liked.

Because most individuals have a combination of these three types, an understanding of these achievement-motivation characteristics can be a useful assistance to management in job placement, recruitment and professional development in a wide range of sport-management and sport-delivery roles.

The theory is highly optimistic, since it proposes that, if given the chance, everyone will strive to achieve their goals and advance the organization's vision. It also assumes they tend to be dedicated to their work and strive hard to succeed. Such individuals will also demonstrate a strong desire for increasing their knowledge and for feedback on their performance, often in the form of performance appraisal.

HERZBERG'S TWO-FACTOR THEORY OF MOTIVATION

Frederick Herzberg had close links with Maslow and believed in a two-factor theory of motivation. He argued that there were certain factors that a business could introduce that would directly motivate employees to work harder. These were the 'motivators'. However there were also factors that would demotivate an employee if not present, but would not in themselves actually motivate employees to work harder. These were the 'hygiene' factors.

Motivators are more concerned with the actual job itself; for instance, how interesting the work is and how much opportunity it gives for extra responsibility, recognition and promotion. Hygiene factors are factors which 'surround the job' rather than the job itself; for example, a worker will only turn up to work if a business has provided a reasonable level of pay and safe working conditions, but these factors will not make them work harder at their job once they are there.

Herzberg believed that businesses should motivate employees by adopting a democratic approach to management and by improving the nature and content of the actual job through certain methods. Some of the methods managers could use to achieve this are:

- *Job enlargement*: workers being given a greater variety of tasks to perform (not necessarily more challenging), which should make the work more interesting.
- *Job enrichment*: involves workers being given a wider range of more complex and challenging tasks surrounding a complete unit of work rather a small part of it. This should give a greater sense of achievement.
- *Empowerment*: which involves delegating more power to employees to make their own decisions over areas of their working life.

The Herzberg model of motivation is displayed in Figure 10.1 opposite.

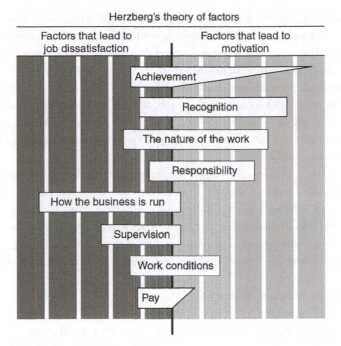

Figure 10.1 Key points of Herzberg's model of job motivation

Source: Herzberg (1959).

Herzberg's model of motivation was underpinned by two core principles:

1 Workers are motivated to work harder by motivators; e.g. more responsibility, more interesting work and more praise for good work; and
2 Workers can become demotivated if hygiene factors are not met; e.g. pay, working conditions and relationships with colleagues are problematic.

Both the Maslow and Herzberg models are more 50 years old, but they have stood the test of time and are still seen as excellent frameworks for enabling staff to work at their very best, and with full commitment to the organization's goals and aspirations.

REWARDS AND INCENTIVES

The idea that people will work harder when offered rewards has become a psychological axiom. However, some rewards are more influential than others, and a reward that works in one setting may not work as well in another. Employee rewards systems are more complex than meets the eye, and when discussing rewards, a useful starting point is to distinguish between intrinsic and extrinsic factors.

Extrinsic rewards – usually financial – are the tangible rewards given to employees by managers, such as pay raises, bonuses and benefits. They are called 'extrinsic' because they are external to the work itself, and other people control their size and whether or not they are granted. In contrast, *intrinsic rewards* are psychological rewards that employees get from doing meaningful work and performing it well.

121

Extrinsic rewards played a dominant role in earlier eras, when work was generally more routine and bureaucratic, and when complying with rules and procedures was paramount. This work offered workers few intrinsic rewards, so that extrinsic rewards were often the only motivational tools available to organizations.

Extrinsic rewards remain significant for workers, of course. Pay is an important consideration for most workers in accepting a job, and unfair pay can be a strong demotivator. However, after people have taken a job and issues of unfairness have been settled, we find that extrinsic rewards are now less important, as day-to-day motivation is more strongly driven by intrinsic rewards.

To identify intrinsic rewards, it is important to examine the nature of work in neo-liberal economies. Basically, most of today's workers are asked to self-manage to a significant degree: to use their intelligence, capabilities and experience to direct their work activities to accomplish important organizational purposes. This is how today's employees add value: innovating, problem-solving and improvising to better meet customers' needs.

In turn, it was found that the self-management process involves four key steps:

1   Committing to a meaningful purpose;
2   Choosing the best way of fulfilling that purpose;
3   Making sure that one is performing work activities competently; and
4   Making sure that one is making progress to achieving the purpose.

Each of these steps requires workers to make a judgement, about the meaningfulness of their purpose, the degree of choice they have for doing things the right way, the competence of their performance and the actual progress being made towards fulfilling the purpose. These four judgements are the key factors in workers' assessments of the value and effectiveness of their efforts – and the contribution they are making.

In an ideal work setting – which may involve a dream job in a sport event business – these judgements are usually accompanied by a positive emotional charge. These positive charges are the *intrinsic* rewards that employees get from work, ranging in size from quiet satisfaction to an exuberant sense of significant achievement. They are the reinforcements that keep employees actively self-managing, motivated and fully engaged in their work.

The following are descriptions of the four intrinsic rewards and how workers view them:

1   *Sense of meaningfulness.* This reward involves the meaningfulness or importance of the purpose staff are trying to fulfil. They feel they have an opportunity to accomplish something of real value; something that matters in the larger scheme of things. They sense they are on a path that is worth their time and energy, giving them a strong sense of purpose or direction.
2   *Sense of choice.* They feel free to choose how to accomplish their work; to use their best judgement to select those work activities that deliver the most rewards, and perform them in ways that are purposeful and committed. In short, they feel ownership of their work, believe in the approach they are taking and feel responsible for making it all work.
3   *Sense of competence.* They feel they are handling their work activities well, that the performance of these activities meets or exceeds their personal standards, and that they

are doing good, high-quality work. They feel a sense of satisfaction, pride or even artistry in how well they handle these activities.

4   *Sense of progress*. They understand that that their efforts are accomplishing something. They feel that their work is on track and meets the vision of the enterprise.

CASE STUDY

As already noted, motivation is a thorny concept. At first glance it appears to be a simple notion that explains what it is that makes some people highly energized and others less so. However, when we dig below the conceptual surface, we find a highly complex range of issues to deal with. While there is an agreed-upon set of factors that appears to motivate people to act, the distribution of these factors between people is remarkably different.

The following case demonstrates these issues. Let's look at the case of Ursula Upstart. Ursula has just secured her dream job. She has just been appointed as an integrity officer with the New Zealand National Football Association. Her job has a number of requirements. The first is to research cases of sport organization malpractice, which range from match-fixing and illegal drug use to incidents of spectator and player-related racism, sexual abuse (especially cases involving adult coaches and adolescent players) and, more generally, player violence in domestic, club and public settings. The second is to produce detailed case reports that provide not only a full description of the incidents, but also a range of policy and disciplinary options. The third is to work with relevant associations and clubs to introduce pro-integrity policies and programmes.

Ursula was led to believe that her role would be highly autonomous and, as a result, would require her to show ongoing initiative when tackling the above three job requirements. However, soon after taking on the position, she found that her autonomous position was being undermined at nearly every turn; it was not the dream job she had initially anticipated.

As it turned out, her immediate supervisor – the general manager for integrity issues – was obsessed with tightly controlling the work of his subordinates. To use the vernacular, he was a 'control freak'. In many cases, especially those involving serious match-fixing issues, he would insist on his own attendance at all meetings and briefing sessions. But it didn't stop there. He would also demand to see drafts of her reports even before she had completed them, and in nearly every situation would require her to foreshadow her movements prior to doing her fieldwork. Ursula became so distressed she had to resign. Her dream job was no more.

Questions

1   What makes motivation such an important workplace issue?
2   Having read the above case study and reflected on the ways in which sporting workplaces might be organized, what motives can best drive employees' behaviour and maximize their performance?
3   In Ursula's case, what motivated her to commit herself to work?
4   In what ways did Ursula's boss stifle her motivation and eagerness at the highest professional level in her new dream job?

5   What could Ursula's supervisor do to secure her motivation and commitment to the job?
6   Do you think a 20 per cent increase in Ursula's salary would have been sufficient to regain her motivation and secure her commitment to the job? Why? Or why not?

Case exercise

Take a look at the Tennis Australia website (www.tennis.com.au) and scan the site for discussion of the use of casual staff at the Australian Open Tennis Championships. What incentives are put in place for ball kids and line umpires? What else attracts these people to participate in the first place? What are the key factors at work here? Are they motivators or hygiene factors?

SUMMARY

All of the above models work on the assumption that, in any workplace, people will only contribute effectively and properly, and do it enthusiastically, if they are motivated to do so. This means that the capacity to engender high levels of job satisfaction is an important part of any sport enterprise manager's motivational toolkit. The motivational models discussed above are also highly adaptable and can therefore cover a broad range of sport spaces and experiences. Take, for example, the following workplace positions:

- CEO of a major community active recreation centre
- Community-based sports club coach
- Professional sport club coach
- Outdoor adventure leader
- Youth worker
- Aerobics instructor
- Personal trainer
- Volunteer committee member with a local tennis.

The above are all positions of responsibility, and all offer experiences that are challenging but rewarding; that is, they offer the opportunity to meet a number of important personal and social needs. Many of these needs are deep-seated and enriching, which also means that these positions will attract committed people who will be highly motivated and prepared to do all that it takes to deliver the best possible outcome. This is why motivation is such a key issue in the field of organizational behaviour.

WEBSITE

Farzalipour, S., Ghorbanzadeh, B., Akalan, C., Kashef, M. and afroozeh, S. (2012). Motivation, satisfaction and burnout of volunteers in sport. Available from: http://scholarsresearchlibrary.

com/ABR-vol3-iss1/ABR-2012-3-1-684-692.pdf. See this site for further advice on how to motivate volunteers.

REFERENCES AND BIBLIOGRAPHY

Barbuto, J. (1998). Motivation sources inventory: Development and validation of new scales to measure an integrative taxonomy of motivation. *Psychological Reports*, 82(3), p.1011.

Carlstedt, R. (2012). *Evidence-based applied sport psychology*. New York: Springer.

Cox, R. (2012). *Sport psychology: concepts and applications* (7th edn). New York: McGraw-Hill.

Farzalipour, S., Ghorbanzadeh, B., Akalan, C., Kashef, M. and Afroozeh, S. (2012). Motivation, satisfaction and burnout of volunteers in sport. *Annals of Biological Research*, 3(1), pp.684–692. Available at: http://scholarsresearchlibrary.com/ABR-vol3-iss1/ABR-2012-3-1-684-692.pdf.

Herzberg, F. (1959). *The motivation to work*. New York: Wiley.

Herzberg, F., Mausner, B. and Snyderman, B. (2010). *The motivation to work* (12th edn). New Brunswick, NJ: Transaction.

Lane, A. (2015). *Sport and exercise psychology: Topics in applied psychology* (2nd edn). London: Routledge.

Maslow, A. (1954). *Motivation and personality* (2nd edn). New York: Harper.

Mellalieu, S. and Hanton, S. (2009). *Advances in applied sport psychology*. London: Routledge.

Pelletier, L., Fortier, M., Vallerand, R., Tuson, K., Briere, N. and Blais, M. (1995). Toward a new measure of intrinsic motivation, extrinsic motivation, and motivation in sports: The Sport Motivation Scale (SMS). *Journal of Sport and Exercise Psychology*, 17, pp.35–53.

Silva, J. and Stevens, D. (2002). *Psychological foundations of sport*. Brockport, NY: Brockport Bookshelf.

Silva, J. and Weinberg, R. (1984). *Psychological foundations of sport*. Champaign, IL: Human Kinetics.

Weinberg, R. and Gould, D. (2014). *Foundations of sport and exercise psychology* (6th edn). Champaign, IL: Human Kinetics.

Williams, J. (ed.) (1993). *Applied sport psychology: Personal growth to peak performance* (2nd edn). Mountain View, CA: Mayfield.

Chapter 11

Attitudes, emotions and job satisfaction

OVERVIEW

This chapter examines the factors that shape people's attitudes to work, their emotional responses to work and their levels of job satisfaction. Special attention is given to the relationship between job satisfaction and employee productivity. Strategies for delivering satisfying work experiences in a sport enterprise setting will also be examined.

LEARNING OBJECTIVES

Having engaged critically with this chapter, readers will be able to:

1 Explain the concept of job satisfaction;
2 Identify the main causes of job satisfaction in sport-related work;
3 Identify the main causes of job dissatisfaction in sport-related work;
4 Associate specific emotional states with different levels of job satisfaction;
5 Explain how job satisfaction can lead to positive emotional states and superior organizational performance; and
6 Formulate strategies for delivering satisfying work experiences in sport enterprises and providing positive work attitudes.

DO SPORT ENTERPRISES OFFER INTERESTING JOBS?

Not everybody enjoys their job, and there many reasons for people being unhappy with their workplace experiences. One of the most frequently cited reasons is a poor supervisor relationship, followed closely by interpersonal conflict. The views that people have about their job are revealed in their attitudes. Attitudes go beyond beliefs and values, and are far more subjective and opinionated. This is because they give weight to feelings and enable people to say what is positive about their job, on one hand, and what is negative about their job, on the other hand.

A job attitude is thus a set of evaluations of one's job that constitute one's feelings towards, beliefs about and attachment to one's job. Additionally, job attitude can be specific and focus on factors like pay, conditions, opportunities for advancement or, alternatively, be more of a generalized statement about the psychological value of the job, the benefits it delivers, the self-esteem it builds and the overall levels of affective job satisfaction it provides. (These areas are also discussed in Chapters 4 and 5.)

THEORIES OF JOB SATISFACTION

A key component of a committed and productive workforce is job satisfaction. Job satisfaction can be defined as a pleasurable or positive emotional state resulting from the appraisal of one's job or job experiences. Job satisfaction is a multifaceted construct, with emotional, cognitive and behavioural components. The emotional component refers to job-related feelings such as boredom, anxiety, acknowledgement and excitement. The cognitive component of job satisfaction pertains to beliefs regarding one's job of whether it is respectable, mentally demanding/challenging and rewarding. Finally, the behavioural component includes people's responses to their work situations and the actions that follow. These can range from highly negative to demonstrably positive, and include tardiness, working slowly, faking illness and undermining the productivity of others, at one end of the job-satisfaction continuum, to working late, providing support to colleagues, delivering high-quality work and a positive attitude to work, at the other.

There are many theories of job satisfaction, but they all have common themes. The first is that job satisfaction comes from working in positions that offer an array of rewards. Additionally, these rewards go well beyond monetary incentives and include powerful psychological feelings around recognition, achievement and autonomy. These issues were raised in Chapter 10.

HERZBERG REVISITED

Frederick Herzberg's work was discussed briefly in Chapter 10 (Herzberg 1959; Herzberg *et al.* 2010), but in light of its broad impact on the analysis of workplace functions, motivation, job satisfaction and productivity, it will be discussed in more detail here. The first point to note is that Herzberg published the two-factor theory of work motivation in 1959, well over 50 years ago. The theory was highly controversial at the time, but it has become one of the most replicated studies in this area, and has provided the foundation for numerous other theories and frameworks in organizational behaviour and human-resource development. The theory states that job satisfaction and dissatisfaction are affected by two different sets of factors; namely, Herzberg developed an initial hypothesis that satisfaction and dissatisfaction could not be measured reliably on the same continuum. Herzberg and his colleagues next conducted an empirical study to test the hypothesis. After two pilot programmes, the design and hypothesis were developed further and expanded. The main hypothesis stated that factors leading to positive attitudes and those leading to negative attitudes would differ. The second hypothesis stated that factors and effects involved in long-range sequences of events would differ from those in short-range sequences.

The major study used the critical incident technique and was conducted in and around Pittsburgh in the USA. More than 200 accountants and engineers were studied. Participants were led through semi-structured interviews in which they were asked to describe any time when they felt either exceptionally good or bad about their job. After describing the story in detail, they were asked for another story at the other end of the continuum. Participants were then asked to rate their experience on a scale of 1 to 20, with 1 indicating that the experience hardly affected their feelings, and 20 indicating that it was an experience with seriously important impacts. These stories were then examined and the feelings attached them were weighted. Strong feelings had a strong impact on job attitudes, and low feelings had minimal impact on job attitudes. Additionally, it was found that a great many things could be a source of dissatisfaction, but only certain factors could contribute to positive satisfaction.

From this data, the original hypothesis was restated and became the two-factor theory of job satisfaction. Factors that affect job satisfaction are divided into two categories. *Hygiene* factors surround the doing of the job, and include supervision, interpersonal relations, physical working conditions, salary, company policy and administration, and job security. *Motivation* factors lead to positive job attitudes because they satisfy the need for self-actualization. Motivation factors are achievement, recognition, the work itself, responsibility and advancement. The opposite of satisfaction is no satisfaction; the opposite of dissatisfaction is no dissatisfaction. The satisfaction of hygiene needs can prevent dissatisfaction and poor performance, but only the satisfaction of the motivation factors will bring the type of productivity improvement sought by business in general, and sport enterprises in particular.

ADDITIONAL FACTORS IMPACTING ON JOB SATISFACTION

One of the more challenging critiques of Herzberg's model suggested that the background, experiences and personality of the workers themselves might also impact on job satisfaction; that is, the worker's overall characteristics may play a part. This is described as the 'worker dispositional factor'.

Internal disposition is the crux of the latest method of explaining job satisfaction, which hints that some people are inclined to be satisfied or dissatisfied with their work, irrespective of the nature of the job or the organizational environment. Simply put, some people are genetically positive in disposition (the glass half-full view of life), whereas others are innately negative in disposition (the glass half-empty way of looking at the world). For instance, a study of twins who were reared apart (same genetic characteristics but different experiences) found that 30 per cent of job dissatisfaction was accredited to genetic factors.

Significant amounts of research have been conducted on the dispositional source of job satisfaction, and have presented strong evidence that job satisfaction, to some extent, is based on a person's overall disposition. This 'dispositional affect' is the tendency to experience relatively stable emotional moods over time. Accordingly, this approach assumes that an employee's attitude about their job originates from an internal mental state. Positive affect is a predisposition favourable to positive emotional experience, whereas negative affect is a predisposition to experience a wide array of negative emotions. Positive affective people feel enthusiastic, active, alert and optimistic, whereas negative affective people feel anger, contempt, disgust, guilt, fear and nervousness.

IMPORTANCE OF JOB SATISFACTION

As mentioned in the overview, job satisfaction has been linked to many variables, including performance, absenteeism and turnover, which will be discussed further in this section. Job satisfaction is significant because a person's attitude and beliefs may affect their behaviour. Attitudes and beliefs may cause a person to work harder or work less. Job satisfaction also impacts a person's general well-being for the simple reason that people spend a good part of the day at work. Consequently, a person's dissatisfaction with work could lead to dissatisfaction in other areas of life.

JOB SATISFACTION AND EMPLOYEE PERFORMANCE

The relationship between job satisfaction and job performance has a long and controversial history. Researchers were first made aware of the link between satisfaction and performance through the 1924–1933 Hawthorne Studies, at the General Electric Plant in the USA. Since the Hawthorne Studies, numerous researchers have critically examined the idea that a happy worker is a productive worker, and research has found a weak connection between job satisfaction and job performance. But when the definition of job performance includes behaviours such as organizational citizenship (the extent to which one's efforts contribute to the success of an organization), the relationship between satisfaction and performance improves. It is also important to note that the connection between job satisfaction and job performance is higher for more difficult and challenging jobs than for less difficult and less challenging jobs.

Although there appears to be a link between job satisfaction and job performance, it is not as strong as one would intuitively expect. The weak link may be attributed to factors such as job structure or economic conditions. For example, some jobs are designed so that a minimum level of performance is required, providing no scope for greater satisfaction. Moreover, in times of high unemployment, dissatisfied employees will perform well, choosing unsatisfying work over unemployment. It has also been found that the more satisfied we are with our life in general, the more productive we are in our jobs.

JOB SATISFACTION AND EMPLOYEE ABSENTEEISM

One of the more widely researched topics in Industrial Psychology is the relationship between job satisfaction and employee absenteeism. It is only natural to assume that if individuals dislike their jobs then they will often call in sick, or simply look for a new opportunity. Yet again, the link between these factors and job satisfaction is weak. It is likely that a satisfied worker may miss work owing to illness or personal matters, whereas an dissatisfied worker may not miss work because they do not have any sick time and cannot afford the loss of income. When people are satisfied with their job they are more likely to attend work even if they have a cold. However, if they are not satisfied with their job, they are more likely to call in sick, even when they are well enough to work.

JOB SATISFACTION AND EMPLOYEE RETENTION

Employee retention is one of the most difficult operational areas for human resources managers to determine exactly why employees leave the organization, and what they should do to retain them. This is of primary importance because organizations invest significant resources in training, developing, tangible and intangible compensation and taking the time to build organizational citizenship and buy-in to goals and objectives. In difficult economies and highly competitive markets, both organizations and employees want the best resources. Job dissatisfaction leads to job turnover. This dissatisfaction can be from intrinsic or extrinsic factors. Job turnover can result from various conditions such as job satisfaction. Job satisfaction is multifaceted, implying that one can be satisfied in one area but this does not necessarily mean satisfaction in all areas; likewise, dissatisfaction in one area does not mean complete job dissatisfaction. Job turnover can also be related to work–life conflict.

In addition, the work life and personal life of individuals are forever being renegotiated and rebalanced. There is an ongoing tension between these two lifestyle options. There is also a high level of mutual inter-independence. An imbalance or dissatisfaction in work often leads to dissatisfaction in one's personal life. This can lead to not only a reduction in morale, but also to increased levels of job turnover. For organizations to remain effective, they need to understand and address the issues around work–life balance to maintain job satisfaction among employees. To support this idea, there is evidence to say that people who are happy with life are happier employees and show better organizational citizenship, courtesy and conscientiousness.

CASE STUDY

In any workplace there will be some staff who enjoy their job intensely and have a strong emotional commitment to it, whereas there will be other staff whose emotional commitment is slight and their level of satisfaction low. The Rolling Meadows Football Club (RMFC) is a case in point. RMFC is a large multipurpose sports club that also offers programmes in basketball, field hockey and tennis. However, most of its revenue is generated from its participation in an elite national football competition. It is a well-serviced club, with a large and loyal member base, but is also a highly competitive club that is tightly controlled by its management committee, especially its chief executive officer (CEO).

Barry Beefcake is the CEO and came to the job very well credentialed. He worked for the Government as a sport policy analyst and had additional experience in the private sector as a public relations (PR) and customer relations divisional manager. Barry came to the job with a commitment to build on the club's previous successes, and to secure not only on-field success with the football team, but also off-field success with its social club and membership-servicing arrangements. Barry was also driven by a strong need to monitor his staff closely. This was not altogether problematic since he developed a raft of operating protocols and practices that set up very clear behavioural expectations and performance standards. Barry was also assertive and exceptionally opinionated. While, in principle, he encouraged staff to share their ideas with him, he rarely acted on them and, for the most part, made it clear that his instructions were not to be challenged, but instead to be acted on precisely and immediately.

Barry was particularly interventionist when working with the PR and customer relations staff. Four of the six staff were female, one of whom was the manager. Betty Bootlace, the PR director was, like Barry, highly experienced and energetic. But unlike Barry, her supervisory style was very much at arm's length and provided space for significant staff initiative. However, unfortunately for Betty, Barry imposed his views on what he thought were PR not only on Betty, but also on her subordinates. After a few months of enduring Barry's highly interventionist and rigidly mechanistic management style, Betty resigned. Her emotional attachment to the club and her job had been extinguished by Barry's relentless interventions. Additionally, Betty's resignation had a domino effect and the other three female PR staff also left the club. Barry was oblivious to the problems he had created. His philosophy on management was very similar to his philosophy to competitive sport: first, if you are not competitive you will not succeed; and second, staff like most athletes and players will only perform at their best when given very clear and precise instructions with no room for subsequent manoeuvre. In short, staff – like athletes – perform best when bound by unambiguous and highly prescriptive instructions. Barry rationalized the departure of most of the PR staff by stating that none of them were able to take the pressure, and were not only poorly skilled, but also emotionally unstable.

Questions

1   What relationship do you think exists between emotional attachment to a job and the ability to perform the job satisfactorily?
2   Can a dissatisfied worker be a productive worker?
3   In the case of the RMFC, how much emotional commitment would staff have had to their job?
4   From your perspective, what effect did Barry's management style have on the level of job satisfaction at RMFC?
5   Did Barry provide anything that could be used by staff to enhance their job satisfaction?
6   If you were the CEO of RMFC, and you wanted to establish a working environment with the potential for staff to achieve high levels of satisfaction, what would you do?
7   Having reflected on this case, is there anything about the structure and conduct of sporting clubs in general that leads you to think the RMFC problem might exist in many other similar clubs as well?

Case exercise

Take a look at the Formula 1 Grand Prix website (www.formula1.com/en/latest.html). Pay particular attention to the vast array of jobs coming out of this large-scale series of major events. Then, reflect on the negative comments made about the Grand Prix, especially its environmental impact, the noise it creates on street circuits, the costs of running the events, the massive levels of commercial involvement, and the excessive glamour and celebrity that comes with it. In the light of these problems, see if you can explain what it is about the Grand Prix circuit that gives its workers – both paid and voluntary – a feeling of achievement and strong sense of a job well done.

SUMMARY

Employee satisfaction is of utmost importance for employees. It not only delivers happiness, but also creates the desire to work hard and help achieve the goals of the enterprise. Satisfied employees are extremely loyal towards their organization and stick with it even in the worst scenarios. The first benefit of employee satisfaction is that individuals rarely think of leaving their jobs. The second benefit of employee satisfaction is that it leads to high levels of work commitment and productivity. In addition, satisfied employees adjust more comfortably to change, and handle work pressures with relative ease. Dissatisfied employees – especially when situated in sport enterprises – are more prone to tardiness, absenteeism and low levels of productivity. But it is also important to understand that job satisfaction is heavily dependent on the ways in which jobs are structured and supervised. Jobs that provide autonomy and reward staff for taking the initiative and overcoming risk lead to high levels of satisfaction. Jobs that are tightly supervised and deny people the opportunity for creativity will usually produce an unhappy and indifferent workforce.

WEBSITE

Hurd, A.R, Barcelona, R.J. and Meldrum, J.T. (2008). Excerpt on 'Reward systems'. In A.R. Hurd, R.J. Barcelona, and J.T. Meldrum. (2008). *Recreation managers can use rewards to improve employee motivation, retention*, Cloth Pass/Kycd (online). Available from: www.humankinetics.com/excerpts/excerpts/recreation-managers-can-use-rewards-to-improve-employee-motivation-retention. See this site for more information on job satisfaction in the recreation sector.

REFERENCES AND BIBLIOGRAPHY

Carlstedt, R. (2012). *Evidence-based applied sport psychology*. New York: Springer.
Cox, R. (2012). *Sport psychology: concepts and applications* (7th edn). New York: McGraw-Hill.
Herzberg, F. (1959). *The motivation to work*. New York: Wiley.
Herzberg, F., Mausner, B. and Snyderman, B. (2010). *The motivation to work* (12th edn). New Brunswick, NJ: Transaction.
Lane, A. (2015). *Sport and exercise psychology: Topics in applied psychology* (2nd edn). London: Routledge.
Mellalieu, S. and Hanton, S. (2009). *Advances in applied sport psychology*. London: Routledge.
Richards, R. (2009). *Contemporary sport psychology*. New York: Nova Science.
Robbins, S. and Judge, T. (2012). *Essentials of organizational behavior* (15th edn). Upper Saddle River, NJ: Prentice Hall.
Saari, L. and Judge, T. (2004). Employee attitudes and job satisfaction. *Human Resource Management*, 43(4), pp.395–407.
Silva, J. and Stevens, D. (2002). *Psychological foundations of sport*. Brockport, NY: Brockport Bookshelf.
Silva, J. and Weinberg, R. (1984). *Psychological foundations of sport*. Champaign, IL: Human Kinetics.
Weinberg, R. and Gould, D. (2014). *Foundations of sport and exercise psychology* (6th edn). Champaign, IL: Human Kinetics.
Williams, J. (ed.) (1993). *Applied sport psychology: Personal growth to peak performance* (2nd edn). Mountain View, CA: Mayfield.

Part D

Communication systems and social processes

Chapter 12

Group behaviour

OVERVIEW

This chapter discusses the dynamics of group behaviour in group enterprises. The chapter begins by describing the various types of groups that exist, followed by reasoning for why people join groups. The five-stage group-development model (forming, storming, norming, performing, adjourning) is then discussed. Next, there is an examination of the roles, norms and status of groups and group members. The chapter ends with a conversation about various aspects of group decision-making.

LEARNING OBJECTIVES

Having read the chapter, students will be able to:

1. Be able to define and classify groups;
2. Comprehend the reasons behind why people join groups;
3. Learn the five stages of group development: forming, storming, norming, performing, and adjourning;
4. Understand the group properties of roles, norms and status; and
5. Recognize group decision-making and the techniques used by groups to make decisions in sport enterprises.

INTRODUCTION TO COMMUNICATION AND SOCIAL PROCESSES

Communication is a social process that produces changes in the knowledge, attitudes and behaviours of individuals and groups, by providing factual and technical information, using motivational or persuasive messages, and by facilitating the learning process and social environment. All of this makes it clear that communication is a social process. Social processes are the ways in which individuals and groups interact, adjust and readjust and establish relationships and patterns of behaviour which are again modified through social interactions. The concept of social process refers to some of the general and recurrent forms that social interaction may take. Interaction or mutual activity is the essence of social life. Interaction between individuals and groups occurs in the form of social process. Social processes refer to forms of social interaction that occur again and again. The social character of communication processes can be analysed from two different perspectives. One is the social relation between the two positions in the communication process: the communicator and the recipient. The second perspective focuses on the other relevant social relations of the communicator or the recipient, and their influence on the origins or results of communication. When we participate in communication processes, we are not only communicators or recipients, but we are also members of different social groups and still integrated in a relevant network of social relations.

DEFINING AND CLASSIFYING GROUPS

A group is defined as two or more individuals, interacting and interdependent, who have come together to achieve particular objectives. Groups can be either formal or informal. By formal groups, we mean those defined by the organization's structure, with designated work assignments establishing task. If formal groups, then the behaviours that one should engage in are stipulated by and directed towards organizational goals. The six members making up an airline flight crew are an example of a formal group. In contrast, informal groups are alliances that are neither formally structured nor organizationally determined. These groups are natural formations in the work environment that appear in response to the need for social contact: three employees from different departments who regularly eat together are an example of an informal group.

It is possible to further subclassify groups as command, task, interest or friendship groups. Command and task groups are dictated by the formal organization, whereas interest and friendship groups are informal alliances. A command group is determined by the organization chart. It is composed of the individuals who report directly to manager. A Director of Coaching and their 12 coaches form a command group. Task groups, also organizationally determined, represent those working together to complete a job task. However, a task group's boundaries are limited to its immediate hierarchical superior. It can cross command relationships. For instance, if a college athlete is accused of a campus crime, it may require communication and coordination among the dean of academic affairs, the dean of students, the registrar, the director of security and the student's adviser. Such a formation would constitute a task group. It should be noted that all command groups are also task groups, but because task groups can cut across the organization, the reverse need not be true. People who may or may not be aligned into common command or task groups may affiliate to attain a specific objective with which each is concerned. This is an interest group. Employees who bond together to have their holiday schedules altered to support a peer who has been fired, or to seek improved working conditions, represent a united body to further their common interest.

There is no single reason why individuals join groups. Individuals join groups for a number of reasons. For instance, it could be for security, to: reduce the insecurity of 'standing alone'; feel stronger; have fewer self-doubts; and be more resistant to threats. It could be for status, as inclusion in a group is viewed by outsiders as important, and it provides recognition and status. Groups provide a sense of self-esteem by providing feelings of self-worth to group members, in addition to conveying status to outsiders. It could be for reasons of affiliation; accommodating social needs through regular interaction can be primary source for fulfilling need for affiliation. Groups provide a source of power that cannot be achieved individually, but in a group there is 'power in numbers'. Finally, groups can facilitate goal achievement, as some tasks require more than one person. There is a need to pool knowledge or power to complete the job. In such instances management may rely on the use of a formal group for this to happen.

Groups, however, go through a process of development. Group development is a dynamic process and most groups are in a continual state of change. The evidence is that groups pass through a standard sequence of five stages. These stages are:

1   Forming: the first stage in group development, characterized by much uncertainty;
2   Storming: the second stage in group development, characterized by intragroup conflict;
3   Norming: the third stage in group development, characterized by close relationships and cohesiveness;
4   Performing: the fourth stage in group development, when the group is fully functional; and
5   Adjourning: the final stage in group development for temporary groups, characterized by concern with wrapping up activities rather than task performance.

Some studies confirm that groups do not develop in a universal sequence of stages; however, the timing of when groups form and change the way they work is highly inconsistent. The first meeting sets the group's direction, the first phase of group activity is one of inertia, then a transition takes place which initiates major changes, then a second phase of inertia follows the transition, and finally, the group's last meeting is characterized by markedly accelerated activity. The punctuated equilibrium model characterizes groups as exhibiting long periods of inertia interspersed with brief revolutionary changes, triggered primarily by their members' awareness of time and deadlines.

Work groups are not disorganized gangs; rather they have structure that shapes the behaviour of members and the group itself. These structural variables include the designation of roles. A role within a group is a set of expected behaviour patterns attributed to someone occupying a given position in a social unit. When we think of a role we associate it with:

■   Role identity: certain attitudes and behaviours consistent with a role;
■   Role perception: an individual's view of how they are supposed to act in a given situation;
■   Role expectations: how others believe a person should act in a given situation; and
■   Role conflicts: a situation in which an individual is confronted by divergent role expectations.

Some group efforts are more successful than others because of a number of complex variables such as the ability of the group's members, the size of the group, the level of conflict and the internal pressures on the members to conform to the group norms. Norms are acceptable standards of behaviour within a group that are shared by the group's members. Group norms provide parameters for acceptable group behaviour. They therefore impose limitations on behaviour and deliver guidelines for corralling the conduct of group members and signalling appropriate interpersonal behaviour. This is done to set the tone of the group; if the group is going to be serious and goal-orientated, discipline and rules are a must. If the tone of the group is casual and lively, then the norms are more lenient. In this manner, group norms have an effect by setting the boundaries and the tone of the role of each individual within the group. Adjusting your behaviour to align with the norms of the groups requires conformity. Conformity is the term used for the convergence of individuals' thoughts, feelings and behaviour towards a group's norms. Private conformity occurs when people truly believe that the group is right, and even occurs in the absence of group members. Public conformity occurs when people are pressured and feel that they do not have a choice other than to conform to group norms. When publicly conforming, people pretend to agree, but privately think that the group is wrong. At times, however, the need to conform to group norms can lead to 'Groupthink'. Groupthink is a phenomenon in which the norm for consensus overrides the realistic appraisal of alternative courses of action.

A socially defined position or rank given to groups or group members by others is termed 'status'. Status also constitutes the chain of command that enforces group norms and sets and maintains the group tone. The upper ranking members of an organization evaluate performance, and confirm whether the organizational mission is being carried out or not. They also should serve as supporters and models to their peers, as well as examples to those below their own status in the group. In this way, status affects individual behaviour because status represents leverage within the organization: the more leverage someone has, the more influential their control. Therefore, more evident boundaries are created from person to person once a role becomes delineated. These boundaries ultimately affect the dynamics and interaction within the group.

Status characteristics theory predicts the emergence and structure of power and prestige orders in task groups from the members' status attributes. Status and group interactions – behaviour based on an established set of norms – may have a positive effect on the group, its functioning and interactions among members. It may improve the group's productivity, but it may also lead to the isolation and rejection of deviant members and can lead to negative employee deviant behaviours. Employee deviance is defined as voluntary behaviour that violates significant organizational norms and in so doing threatens the well-being of an organization, its members, or both. Employee deviance is voluntary in that employees either lack the motivation to conform to normative expectations of the social context or become motivated to violate those expectations (Kaplan 1975). Negative workplace deviant behaviours include employee delinquencies such as not following the manager's instructions, intentionally slowing down the work cycle, arriving late, committing petty theft, as well as not treating co-workers with respect, and/or acting rudely with co-workers. Unlike unethical behaviour that violates societal rules, negative deviant behaviour focuses on the violation of significant organizational norms.

At times there may also be a tendency for group members to do less then than they are capable of individually, resulting in an inverse relationship between group size and individual performance. In small groups, people are more likely to feel that their efforts are more important and will therefore contribute more. The larger the group, however, the less individual effort people will extend. This is known as *social loafing*. Social loafing is the phenomenon of people exerting less effort to achieve a goal when they work in a group than when they work alone. This means that if all members of the group are pooling their effort to achieve a common goal, each member of the group can contribute less than they would if they were individually responsible. This can have a serious impact on group productivity.

GROUP COHESIVENESS AND DECISION-MAKING

Should management seek cohesive groups? Cohesive groups can be defined as the degree to which group members are attracted to each other and share common goals. You can think of group cohesion as the social glue that binds a group together. Many people believe that work teams that demonstrate strong group cohesion will function and perform better in achieving work goals. However, you should note that the research results on this claim are mixed. Group cohesion is not caused by one single factor, but the interaction of more than one factor. Whereas group cohesion may have an effect on group performance, group performance may create or increase group cohesion. This makes sense – everyone wants to be on a winning team and no one wants to be on a losing team. However, members of highly cohesive groups may be motivated to accomplish more, which may not necessarily align with the organization's interest in performance. Thus, group cohesion can actually have a negative effect on group task performance.

Cohesiveness is a measure of the attraction of the group to its members (and the resistance to leaving it), the sense of team spirit and the willingness of its members to coordinate their efforts. Compared with members of a low-cohesive group, those in a high-cohesive group will, therefore, be keen to attend meetings, be satisfied with the group, use 'we' rather than 'I' in discussions, be cooperative and friendly with each other, and be more effective in achieving the aims they set for themselves. The low-cohesive group will be marked by absenteeism, the growth of cliques and factions, and a sense of frustration at the lack of attainment.

At times there may also be a tendency for group members to do less then than they are capable of individually, resulting in an inverse relationship between group size and individual performance. Large groups facilitate the pooling of information about complex tasks. Large groups have strengths and weaknesses. The strengths include the fact that they can deliver more complete information, can allow for an increased diversity of views, there is the possibility for higher quality of decisions and an increased acceptance of solutions. The weaknesses are that they are more time-consuming, there is increased pressure to conform, there can be domination by one or a few members, and they can create ambiguous responsibility. Smaller groups are better suited to coordinating and facilitating the implementation of complex tasks.

Large and small groups need to employ group decision-making techniques. The most common form of group decision-making takes place in face-to-face interacting groups. Interacting groups often censor themselves and pressure individual members towards conformity of opinion. Once a manager has determined that a group-decision approach should be used, they can determine the technique best suited to the decision situation.

Brainstorming is a good technique for generating alternatives. The idea behind brainstorming is to generate as many ideas as possible, suspending evaluation until all of the ideas have been suggested. Participation is encouraged to build upon the suggestions of others, and imagination is emphasized. Brainstorming is meant to overcome pressures for conformity in the interacting group that retard the development of creative alternatives. Groups that use brainstorming have been shown to produce significantly more ideas than groups that do not. In a typical brainstorming session, about six to ten people sit and discuss the problem. The group leader states the problem in a clear manner, so that all participants understand it. No criticism is allowed, and all the alternatives are recorded for later discussion and analysis.

The nominal group technique (NGT) restricts discussion or interpersonal communication during the decision-making process, hence the term 'nominal'. Group members are all physically present, as in a traditional committee meeting, but members operate independently. NGT has the following discrete steps: (1) individuals list their ideas silently; (2) ideas are written on a chart one at a time until all ideas are listed; (3) discussion is permitted, but only to clarify the ideas, and no criticism is allowed; and (4) a vote is taken by ballot or other recordable means. NGT is a good technique to use in a situation where group members fear criticism from others. The chief advantage of the NGT method is that it permits the group to meet formally but does not restrict independent thinking, as does an interacting group.

CASE STUDY

Bob Wallace from Thompson Coburn's Sport Law group noted that the first week of November 2013 was a particularly interesting period in the National Football League (NFL), especially as it applied to what was acceptable group behaviour between football team mates and in a professional locker room. Richie Incognito, an eight-year veteran offensive lineman for the Miami Dolphins, was accused of harassing and/or bullying teammate Jonathan Martin, a second-year offensive tackle from Stanford, who played next to Incognito on the offensive line. According to voicemails and text messages released to the media, Incognito levied extensive verbal abuse on Martin. The harassment apparently continued over a period of at least a few months.

As a result of the alleged actions by Incognito and Martin's reaction to these behaviours, a firestorm engulfed the football world and garnered the attention of commentators, as well as current and former football players. The controversy also spread to others in the sports world; shortly after the Incognito story broke, the National Basketball Association (NBA) issued guidelines on 'hazing', reminding members that no form of 'hazing' of its players would be tolerated and encouraging players to report any violations they witnessed or were exposed to. Hazing is an entrenched group practice and usually occurs as a part of a group initiation process. It is often defined as 'any activity expected of someone joining a group that humiliates, degrades, abuses or endangers, regardless of the person's willingness to participate'. As a form of team activity, hazing tends to be destructive to group cohesion.

Miami Dolphins right tackle Jonathan Martin left the team after he claimed he had been mentally harassed. A voicemail was released that showed the Dolphins' offensive guard Richie Incognito threatening Martin and abusing the second-year player with racial epithets. The incident opened up the discussion of hazing in sports, so it makes sense that the NBA would want to jump in and ensure the safety of its players. Some called for the League to expel Incognito or levy a lifetime ban. Some said that Martin wasn't tough enough and should have handled the situation 'man to man'. Others defended Incognito's actions as a rite of passage that Martin, like many rookie players, had to endure. It's argued that such 'trials by fire' build teamwork and serve as an essential part of the testosterone-driven culture of the NFL. However, others suggest the argument falls short when you consider the racially charged and threatening nature of Incognito's messages. That part of the incident contributed significantly to what took this incident well across the line of acceptable hazing, indoctrination or team-building.

As a result of this incident, sports organizations quickly realized that certain group behaviours were unacceptable in the workplace. Sporting organizations do not operate under a different set of rules, and academics and media commentators suggested that the sooner they came to this realization the better. Just after the incident Boston Globe columnist Christopher Gasper wrote, when discussing the Incognito hazing allegations: 'The insular and Darwinian culture of the NFL locker room is not yet ready to join the rest of society in open acknowledgment of the seriousness of bullying and hazing', and that culture seems 'more interested in protecting locker room sanctity'. Instead, Gasper suggested that what the NFL 'should be concerned about is its players creating an environment that is openly hostile to the next player reporting bullying or harsh hazing'. Teams 'must evolve past the idea that hazing, intimidating, or belittling teammates is a necessary part of NFL team building'.

A more productive strategy would be for teams and the leagues to change the culture of their locker rooms and to stress to their workforce that the behaviours of the past will no longer be acceptable or tolerated. Ben James of Law 360, suggested several steps that sport organizations could take to change their toxic workplace cultures, including creating a written policy, articulating the importance of appropriate and safe workplaces, and putting in place formal procedures to handle complaints. If the Dolphins had taken these steps, they might not have found themselves in this position. They could have created a culture where Incognito's boorish ways were not greeted with appreciative laughter or a blind eye. They could have built an organizational institution where team mates and staff members were educated and aware about what was appropriate workplace behaviour. They could have created a team where players felt empowered to stand up to so-called hazing bullies.

Source: adapted from: www.thompsoncoburn.com/news-and-information/publications/
publication/13-11-18/but-it-s-our-locker-room-what-is-acceptable-behavior-
in-the-sports-workplace.aspx

Questions

1   What is hazing and why is it a negative form of group behaviour?
2   Why do you think hazing is more prevalent in sporting organizations?
3   What do you think the consequences for the Miami Dolphins could be for allowing this behaviour to continue?
4   Develop anti-hazing guidelines for a professional sporting organization.

5   Compare and contrast command, task and interest groups.

6   What might motivate an individual to join a group?

7   How could you use the punctuated equilibrium model to better understand group behaviour?

8   Identify how group norms develop.

9   High cohesiveness in a group leads to higher group productivity. Do you agree or disagree? Explain.

Case exercise

Review the YouTube clip *Group dynamics and performance in team sports* (www.youtube.com/watch?v=mqj3U0lpQ6Y). Discuss how the principles that underpin the theory of group dynamics can provide competitive advantage.

SUMMARY

This chapter discussed the dynamics of group behaviour. The chapter began with describing the various types of groups that exist, followed by reasoning for why people join groups. The five-stage group-development model (forming, storming, norming, performing, adjourning) was then discussed. Next, an examination commenced of the roles, norms and status of groups and group members. The chapter ended with a conversation about various aspects of group decision-making.

WEBSITE

MindTools.com (n.d.). Improving Group Dynamics: Helping your team work more effectively. Available from: www.mindtools.com/pages/article/improving-group-dynamics.htm. See this site for tips on how to manage high-performance teams more effectively.

REFERENCES AND BIBLIOGRAPHY

Delia, E. (2015). The exclusiveness of group identity in celebrations of team success. *Sport Management Review*, 18, pp.396–406.

Kantor, D. (2012). *Reading the room: Group dynamics for coaches and leaders*. San Francisco, CA: Jossey-Bass.

Kaplan, R. (1975). Some methods and strategies in the prediction of preference. In E.H. Zube, R.O. Brush and J.G. Fabos (eds) *Landscape assessment: Values, perceptions, and resources* (pp.118–129). Stroudsburg, PA: Dowden, Hutchinson & Ross.

National Football League. Adapted from: Wallace, B. (2013). But it's our locker room: What is acceptable behaviour in the sports workplace? Available at: www.thompsoncoburn.com/news-and-information/publications/publication/13-11-18/but-it-s-our-locker-room-what-is-acceptable-behavior-in-the-sports-workplace.aspx.

Oja, B.D., Bass, J.R. and Gordon, B.S. (2015). Conceptualizing employee identification with sport organizations: Sport employee identification. *Sport Management Review,* 18, pp.583–595.

Robinson, S.L. and Bennett, R.J. (1995). A typology of deviant workplace behaviors: A multidimensional scaling study. *The Academy of Management Journal,* 38(2), pp.555–572.

Chapter 13

Team dynamics

OVERVIEW

This chapter extends the discussion on groups by focusing on team dynamics. Teams differ from groups as they are designed to achieve a goal. This chapter distinguishes the various types of teams. The composition of teams is detailed in the chapter before discussion of how to create effective teams in sport enterprises. The chapter then explores team-management processes and factors for developing team effectiveness. The chapter ends with an examination of the contextual factors surrounding team effectiveness.

LEARNING OBJECTIVES

Having read the chapter, students will be able to:

1   Understand the differences between groups and teams;
2   Identify the various types of teams within sport enterprises and the composition of those teams, and how team roles are differentiated;
3   Comprehend the processes in creating effective teams through training, communication, empowerment and rewards;
4   Learn the processes of managing effective teams, especially through team players and team trust; and
5   Understand the organizational contextual factors that can constrain or improve team performance in sport enterprises.

INTRODUCTION TO TEAM DYNAMICS

There is a difference between groups and teams. A team is a group of people who share a common understanding of their mission and work together to accomplish it. Teams can be temporary or permanent. Managing a team will reflect the nature and composition of that team. Teams bring several benefits to organizations, including greater levels and depth of expertise. They are more productive than individuals, can deliver large projects successfully and build a workplace community, thus boosting morale.

There is some confusion about the difference between a group and a team. Traditionally academics, communication and management theorists use the terms group, group working, group interaction, group structure, etc. to refer to the dynamics of people working together towards a common cause. The word 'group', however, has a broader meaning: a group of passengers on a sporting tour has a common characteristic – to travel to watch sport – but they are not necessarily working towards a common cause. Groups do not even need to refer to people; for example, a group of products in a sport equipment store. In this case, the group is arbitrary and could be defined by any number of variables.

A team is generally more specific. We would not refer to our sport tourists as a team, unless they crashed on a desert island and needed to work together to survive. The distinction is that a team works together for a common cause. A *group* of schoolchildren may be in the same class, whereas a team of schoolchildren may be working together on a specific project within the class. When we talk about groups and teams we use the terms interchangeably – it is possible to have a group without a team, but not a team without a group. We use the following points to define of group:

- A group can consist of any number of people.
- People in groups interact, engage and identify with each other, often at regular or pre-determined times and places.
- The group members share beliefs, principles and standards about areas of common interest, and they come together to work on common tasks for agreed purposes and outcomes.
- People in groups are defined by themselves and by others as group members; in other words, individuals are aware that they are part of a group.

TYPES OF TEAMS

A team is a collection of individuals organized to accomplish a common purpose, who are interdependent and can be identified by themselves and by observers as a team. Teams exist within a larger organization and interact with other teams and with the organization. Teams are one way for organizations to gather input from members, and to provide organization members with a sense of involvement in the pursuit of organizational goals. Furthermore, teams allow organizations flexibility in assigning members to projects and allow for cross-functional groups to be formed. Teams can be classified according to their objective. The four most common forms of teams you are likely to find in an organization are: problem-solving teams; self-directed teams; cross-functional teams; and virtual teams.

Problem-solving teams are usually temporary and focus on solving a specific issue. For example, after the 2008 financial crisis, several organizational task-force teams and governmental committees were created to come up with solutions to help the country climb out of a steep recession. Once guidelines were set in place and plans were formed, the task forces and committees were disbanded. In sport enterprises they are typically composed of

5–12 employees from the same department who meet for a few hours each week to discuss ways of improving quality, efficiency and the work environment. Sport enterprises rely increasingly on problem-solving teams to help solve organizational problems. In problem-solving teams, members share ideas or offer suggestions on how work process and methods can be improved. Rarely, however, are these teams given the authority to implement any of their suggested actions unilaterally.

Self-directed teams are given autonomy over deciding how a job will be done. These teams are provided with a goal by the organization, and then determine how to achieve that goal. Frequently there is no assigned manager or leader and very few, if any, status differences among the team members. These teams are commonly allowed to choose new team members, decide on work assignments and may be given responsibility for evaluating team members. They must meet quality standards and interact with both buyers and suppliers, but otherwise have great freedom in determining what the team does. Teams form around a particular project and a leader emerges for that project. The team is responsible for carrying out the project, recruiting team members and evaluating them. These types of teams in Great Britain and Sweden emerged in the 1950s, and in organizations are generally composed of 10–15 people.

In *cross-functional teams*, workers across functions or specialties of the organization make up these types of teams. People with separate areas of expertise work together; they are usually at about the same hierarchical level and can often make decisions without management. Often, these are temporary. Cross-functional teams are an effective means of allowing people from diverse areas within an organization to exchange information, develop new ideas, solve problems and coordinate complex projects. The general goals of using cross-functional team include some combination of innovation, speed and quality that come from early coordination among the various specialties.

Virtual teams are composed of members who are not located in the same physical place. They may be in different cities, states or even countries. Technology is impacting how teams meet and function. Collaborative software and conferencing systems have improved the ability for employees to meet, conduct business, share documents and make decisions without ever being in the same location. They use technology and specific skills to achieve a common goal, and tend to be more task- and project-orientated and less concerned with social interaction. Although the basic dynamics of other types of teams may still be relevant, the dynamics and management of virtual teams can be very different. Issues can arise with a lack of facial or auditory clues; participants must be taken at their word, even when video-conferencing tools are used. Accountability is impacted by making a team virtual. Each member is accountable for their tasks and to the team as a whole, usually with minimal supervision. Key factors in the success of a virtual team are effective formation of the team, trust and collaboration between members, and excellent communication. It is important for sport-management students to master virtual skills early on in their academic career, as conference calls and WebEx presentations have become ubiquitous in the workplace.

Research and Development (R&D) departments are common in many larger companies, especially those working with newer products or technologies subject to important shifts. Whereas research and development teams can be instrumental in creating new products or adding features to old products, the work that these teams undertake is more complex than simple innovation, and is connected to marketing, cost management and other parts of business strategy.

TEAM COMPOSITION

Team composition has been identified as a key factor that influences team performance (Senior 1997; Belbin 2010). Team composition not only questions what individual members bring to the group in terms of skill, ability, experience role etc., but also whether these individual capabilities combine to result in higher performance for the team as a whole, thus forming a synergy. Let's look at those key factors that can influence a team's performance.

To begin, part of a team's performance depends on the knowledge, skills and abilities of its individual members. A team's performance is not merely the summation of its individual members' abilities. However, these abilities set limits on what members can do, and how effectively they will perform in a team.

Many of the dimensions identified in the Big 5 Personality Trait model have been shown to be relevant to team effectiveness (for greater discussion on the Big 5 Personality Trait model, see Chapter 8). Research has also provided a good idea about why these personality traits are important to teams: for example, conscientious people are good at backing up other team members, and are also good at sensing when their support is truly needed. One study found that specific behavioural tendencies, such as personal organization, cognitive structuring, achievement orientation and endurance, were all related to higher levels of team performance. Open team members communicate better with one another and throw out more ideas, which make teams composed of open people more creative and innovative

The degree to which members of a work unit (group, team or department) share a common demographic attribute, such as age, sex, race, educational level or length of service in the organization, is the subject of organizational demography. Organizational demography suggests that attributes such as age or the date of joining should help to predict turnover. The logic goes like this: turnover will be greater among those with dissimilar experiences because communication is more difficult and conflict is more likely. Increased conflict makes membership less attractive, so employees are more likely to quit. Similarly, the losers in a power struggle are more apt to leave voluntarily or be forced out. Demographic diversity, however, is essentially unrelated to team performance overall. One qualifier is that gender and ethnic diversity have more negative effects in occupations where diversity is less.

The optimal size and composition of teams (team size) will vary depending on the team's purpose and goals. The optimal size and composition of teams depends on the scope of the team's goals and should take into account the scope and complexity of required tasks and activities. As a whole, team members should bring all the necessary skills and knowledge to meet the team's goals. Team size and composition can affect team processes and outcomes. With too few people, a team will not have the resources and skills it needs to complete its tasks; too many members can make communication and coordination difficult and lead to poor team performance. Research shows that teams perform best with between five and nine members. Dr Meredith Belbin (1991) did extensive research on teams prior to 1990 in the UK that suggested the optimum team size is eight roles, plus a specialist as needed. Fewer than five members resulted in decreased perspectives and diminished creativity. Membership in excess of twelve resulted in increased conflict and greater potential for subgroups forming that could disrupt team cohesion.

Not every employee is a team player. Given the option, many employees will select themselves out of team participation. When people who would prefer to work alone are required to team up, there is a direct threat to the team's morale and to individual member satisfaction. This suggests that, when selecting team members, managers should consider individual preferences along with abilities, personalities and skills (Robins *et al.* 2014).

CREATING EFFECTIVE TEAMS

Teams have different needs and people should be selected for a team to ensure that there is diversity and that all various roles are filled. Sport managers need to understand the individual strengths that each person can bring to a team, select members with their strengths in mind and allocate work assignments accordingly. Put your most able, experienced and conscientious workers in the most central roles in a team (see Figure 13.1).

When faced with employees who lack team skills, sport managers can put those employees through team-building activities. Many people are not inherently team players and many

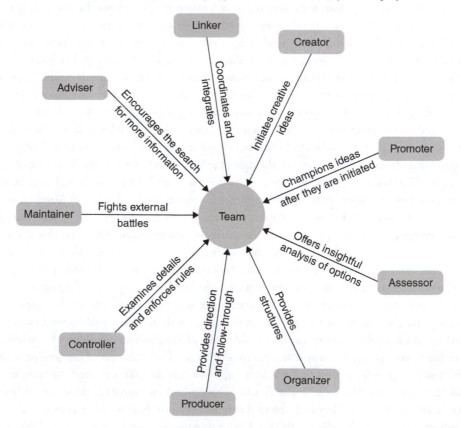

Figure 13.1 Role options for team members

Source: Margerison and McCann (1990).

organizations have, historically, nurtured individual accomplishments so team-building exercises can be useful for addressing these issues. Team-building activities that use high-interaction group activities to increase *trust* and openness among team members can improve coordinative efforts and increase team performance (Robin *et al.* 2014).

When trust is established among team members it has been shown that performance will improve. The highest level of trust is achieved when there is an emotional connection between the parties. It allows one party to act as an agent for the other and substitute for that person in interpersonal transactions. This is called 'identification-based trust'. Trust exists because the parties understand each other's intentions and appreciate the other's wants and desires. This mutual understanding is developed to the point that one person can effectively act for the others. Management controls are minimal at this level as the other party does not need to be monitored because unquestioned loyalty exists. The best example of identification-based trust is the happily married couple: a husband comes to learn what's important to his wife and anticipate those actions; she, in turn, trusts that he will anticipate what's important to each other without having to ask. Increased identification enables each to think like the other, feel like the other and respond like the other. Broken promises have led to a breakdown in what was, at one time, a bond of unquestioned loyalty, which is likely to have been replaced with knowledge-based trust.

Most organizational relationships are rooted in knowledge-based trust; that is, trust is based on the behavioural predictability that comes from a history of interaction. It exists when you have adequate information about someone to understand them well enough to be able to accurately predict their behaviour. Knowledge-based trust relies on information rather than deterrence. Knowledge of the other party and predictability of their behaviour replaces the contracts, penalties and legal arrangements more typical of deterrence-based trust. This knowledge develops over time largely as a function of experience that builds confidence of trustworthiness and predictability. The better you know someone, the more accurately you can predict what they will do. Predictability enhances trust even if the other is predictably trustworthy, because the ways that the other will violate the trust can be predicted. The more communication and regular interaction you have with someone else the more this form of trust can be developed and depended on. In an organizational context, most manager-employee relationships are knowledge-based. Other parties have enough experience working with each other that they know what to expect. A long history of consistently open and honest interaction is not likely, for instance, to be permanently destroyed by a single violation.

Calculus-based trust draws on deterrence theory as a mechanism to preserve trust. This form is grounded not only in the fear of punishment for violating trust, but also in the rewards for preserving it. Trust is based on a calculation comparing the costs and benefits of creating and sustaining a relationship versus the costs and benefits of severing it. For deterrence to be an effective threat, the potential loss of a relationship must outweigh the gain created by defecting from it. There must be monitoring and reporting between the parties. The person who has been harmed must also be willing to follow through on threats of punishment. Management control of another person's behaviour is central to calculus-based trust. A metaphor for the growth of calculus-based trust is tactical climbing, as in scaling ladders or mountains. Parties coordinate their actions as they increasingly take risks and reveal their vulnerability to each other.

Team-building typically includes goal-setting, development of interpersonal relations among team members, role analysis to clarify each member's role and responsibilities and team-process analysis. It may emphasize or exclude certain activities, depending on the purpose of the development effort and the specific problems with which the team is confronting. Training specialists conduct exercises that allow employees to experience the satisfaction that teamwork can provide. If your organization relies on cohesive and well-functioning teams to achieve organizational goals, it is necessary to invest in building and enhancing this capacity. Workshops to help employees improve their problem-solving, communication, negotiation, conflict-management and coaching skills are useful. Teams can also empower employees. Employees with a high level of job involvement identify strongly with and really care about the kind of work they do. Psychological empowerment is the degree to which employees' beliefs influence their work environment, their competence, the meaningfulness of their hob and their perceived autonomy. High levels of both job involvement and psychological empowerment are positively related to organizational citizenship and job performance.

A sport enterprise's reward system needs to be reworked to encourage cooperative efforts rather than competitive ones. Because cooperation is important, teams select new members carefully so that they will contribute to effectiveness and thus team bonuses. It is usually best to set a cooperative tone as soon as possible in the life of a team. Teams that switch from a competitive to a cooperative system do not share information and make rushed, poor-quality decisions. The low trust typical of a competitive group will not be readily replaced by high trust with a quick change in reward systems. These problems are not seen in teams that have consistently cooperative systems. Promotions, pay increases and other forms of recognition can be given to individuals who work effectively as team members, by training new colleagues, sharing information, helping resolve team conflicts and mastering needed new skills. This does not mean that individual contributions should be ignored; rather, they should be balanced with selfless contributions to the team.

Finally, do not forget the intrinsic rewards like camaraderie that employees can receive from teamwork. It is exciting and satisfying to be part of a successful team. The opportunity for personal development of self and teammates can be a very satisfying and rewarding experience (Robins *et al.* 2014; for greater discussion on reward systems, see Chapter 6).

CONTEXTUAL FACTORS RELATED TO TEAM PERFORMANCE

Teams are part of a larger organization system. As such, all work teams rely on resources outside the group to sustain them, and a scarcity of resources directly reduces the ability of the team to perform its job effectively. As one set of researchers concluded, after looking at 13 factors potentially related to group performance, perhaps one of the most important characteristics of an effective work group is the support the group receives from the organization. This support includes timely information, proper equipment, adequate staffing, encouragement and administrative assistance. Teams must receive the necessary support from management and the larger organization if they are going to succeed in achieving their goals.

Team members must agree on who is to do what and ensure that all members contribute equally in sharing the workload. In addition, the team needs to determine how schedules will be set, what skills need to be developed, how the group will resolve conflicts, and how the group will make and modify decisions. Agreeing on the specifics of work and how they fit together to integrate individual skills requires team leadership and structure. This can be provided directly by management or by the team members themselves. Leadership, of course, is not always needed. For instance, the evidence indicates that self-directed work teams often perform better than teams with formally appointed leaders, as leaders can obstruct high performance when they interfere with self-directing teams. In self-directing teams, team members absorb many of the duties typically assumed by managers. In traditionally managed teams, we find that two factors seem to be important in influencing team performance: the leader's expectations; and their mood. Leaders who expect good things from their team are more likely to get them. For instance, military platoons under leaders who hold high expectations perform significantly better in training than control platoons. In addition, studies have found that leaders who exhibit a positive mood get better team performance and lower turnover.

Members of effective teams trust each other, and they also exhibit trust in their leaders. Interpersonal trust among team members facilitates cooperation, reduces the need to monitor each other's behaviour, and reassures team members around the belief that others on the team will not take advantage of them. Team members, for instance, are more likely to take risks and expose vulnerabilities when they believe they can trust others in their team. Trust in leadership is important in that it allows the team to be willing to accept and commit to their leaders goals and decisions.

MULTICULTURAL TEAMS

Multicultural teams are made up of people from different social and professional cultures who work together for a common project goal. Managing cross-functional teams (discussed previously in this chapter) is a complex skill and process, and it becomes even more challenging when the multicultural component is included in the team mix. Multicultural teams encourage adaptation. Some teams find ways to work with or around the challenges they face, adapting practices or attitudes without making changes to the group's membership or assignments. Adaptation works when team members are willing to acknowledge and name their cultural differences, and to assume responsibility for figuring out how to live with them. It's often the best possible approach to a problem, because it typically involves less managerial time than other strategies. And because team members participate in solving the problem themselves, they learn from the process. When team members have this mindset, they can be creative about protecting their own substantive differences while acceding to the processes of others.

When multicultural teams do encounter problems there may be a need for direct management intervention. When a manager behaves like an arbitrator or a judge, making a final decision without team involvement, neither the manager nor the team gains much insight into why the team has stalemated, but it is possible for team members to use managerial intervention effectively to sort out problems (Brett *et al.* 2006). Problems may occur for other reasons. A challenge inherent in multicultural teamwork is that by design, teams have a rather flat structure. However, team members from some cultures, in which people are treated differently according to their status in an organization, are uncomfortable in flat teams. If they defer to higher status team members, their behaviour will be seen as appropriate when most of the team comes from a hierarchical culture, but they may damage their stature and credibility – and even face humiliation – if most of the team comes from an egalitarian culture. In cases such as this there may be a need for structural intervention.

CASE STUDY

Sport volunteers are an important component of a modern mega sport event. The temporary assembly and allocation of roles that are endowed to volunteers enables an event to progress smoothly and successfully. Take 2012 London Olympic Games as an example: Over 70,000 volunteers who worked along with 130,000 paid staff and contractors set an great example of how to work as 'one team' to deliver a great Games. Naming themselves the 'Games Makers', these 200,000 participants aimed to have the right workforce in the right roles, in the right place and at the right time. In other words, how to effectively manage such a massive and more often specialized team was pivotal for them to make sure the Games were a great success.

Starting with volunteer recruitment, in order to set realistic expectations to filter out those not willing to make the necessary commitments, a specialized IT volunteer team was assembled by the Games planning team to design a website that facilitated clear messaging, an effective welcome, efficient application handling and a IT system that did an initial sift, aligning preferences expressed by applicants before actual invitations to selection meetings were sent out. Then, these volunteers were trained separately in different functional areas, according to their roles and preferences, in accordance with an overall training framework. Such training programmes enabled volunteers to understand their shared goals and what should they bring to the team as a team member; what tasks they were up for and what information or knowledge they needed to gain to accomplish the tasks, and finally, how to solve problems with the support and coordination within a team. To make sure that superb customer service was delivered and that volunteers were motivated, volunteers were encouraged by their leaders and managers to operate within their roles as they saw best, and to allow their personalities to shine through their volunteering. In addition, volunteers' birthdays were celebrated during the Games and there were regular prize draws, recognition items such as badges reflecting the number of hours of shifts worked, certificates, letters, etc. Through the effort of the whole team, everyone felt so engaged that they had an unbreakable connection to the Games to inspire passion and support.

Source: adapted from: www.metavalue.co.uk/wp-content/uploads/2015/07/Volunteer-programme-best-practice-London-Olympics.pdf

Questions

1   How can you make people feel part of a team?
2   What are the characteristics of this highly effective volunteer team?
3   What competencies should an effective team-builder and leaders possess?

4   What strategies were used to create an effective volunteer team for the London 2012 Olympic Games?

5   Discuss the different types of team, and the advantages and disadvantages of each.

6   Discuss the importance of trust in building effective teams, and outline the different forms of trust.

7   Research some examples of how effective teams are used in sport organizations.

8   Using Figure 13.1 as a reference, identify and justify the three roles you are most suited to.

9   Identify other contextual factors you feel may impact on team performance.

Case exercise

Review the website on 'Great examples of sports teamwork to grow your business' (www.inc.com/john-boitnott/business-lessons-from-the-most-amazing-sports-teamwork-moments.html). Discuss how the principles of teamwork in sport can be applied to business. Do the principles of team dynamics apply in these examples?

SUMMARY

This chapter extended the discussion on groups by focusing on team dynamics. Teams differ from groups as they are designed to achieve a goal. This chapter distinguished the various types of teams. The composition of teams was detailed in the chapter before discussing how to create effective teams. The chapter then explored team-management processes and factors for developing team effectiveness. The chapter ended with an examination of the contextual factors surrounding team effectiveness.

WEBSITES

McLean, A. (2015). 6 simple steps to enhancing team dynamics and effectiveness. Available from: www.unchainpotential.com/6-simple-steps-to-enhancing-team-dynamics-and-effectiveness/. See this for an overview of six steps to enhance team dynamics.

Williams, K.L. (2013). What is team dynamics? Helping your team work more effectively. Available from: www.livestrong.com/article/354170-what-is-team-dynamics/. See this for more information and insights into team dynamics

REFERENCES AND BIBLIOGRAPHY

Belbin, M. (1991). Design innovation and the team. *Design Management Journal*, 2(3), pp.38–42.

Belbin, R.M. (2010). *Management teams: Why they succeed or fail* (3rd edn). Oxford: Butterworth-Heinemann.

Brett, J., Behfar, K. and Kern, M.C. (2006). Managing multicultural teams, *Harvard Business Review*, 84(11), pp.84–91.

London 2012 Olympic Games. Work as one team for the success of 2012 London Olympic Games. Adapted from: www.metavalue.co.uk/wp-content/uploads/2015/07/Volunteer-programme-best-practice-London-Olympics.pdf.

Margerison, C. and McCann, D. (1990). *Team management: Practical new approaches.* London: Mercury Books.

Robins, S.P., Judge, T.A., Millet, B. and Boyle, M. (2014). *Organizational behaviour* (7th edn). Frenchs Forest, NSW, Australia: Pearson.

Senior, B. (1997). Team roles and team performance: Is there 'really' a link? *Journal of Occupational and Organizational Psychology,* 70(3), pp.241–258.

Chapter 14

Interpersonal communication

OVERVIEW

This chapter discusses interpersonal communication within sport enterprises. The chapter begins with a discussion of the communication process, progressing to a discourse on the direction and modes of communication. The chapter continues with an exploration of encoding and decoding messages. Next, the chapter discusses the strengths and weaknesses of different communication methods, and then provides strategies for improving communication, ending with a discussion of ethical considerations and tools for removing barriers to effective communication.

LEARNING OBJECTIVES

Having read the chapter, students will be able to:

1 Understand the communication process;
2 Learn the various modes of communication, including verbal, non-verbal, written and electronic;
3 Comprehend the encoding and decoding process for effective communication;
4 Identify the best communication channels for different contexts;
5 Learn how to improve interpersonal and organizational communication; and
6 Identify the barriers to effective communication.

INTRODUCTION TO INTERPERSONAL COMMUNICATION

Interpersonal communication is the process by which people exchange information, feelings and meaning through verbal and non-verbal messages: it is face-to-face communication. Interpersonal communication is not just about what is actually said – the language used – but how it is said and the non-verbal messages sent through tone of voice, facial expressions, gestures and body language. Most of us engage in some form of interpersonal communication on a regular basis, and how well we communicate with others is a measure of our interpersonal skills. Interpersonal communication is a key life skill, and can be used to:

- Give and collect information;
- Influence the attitudes and behaviour of others;
- Form contacts and maintain relationships;
- Make sense of the world and our experiences in it;
- Express personal needs and understand the needs of others;
- Give and receive emotional support;
- Make decisions and solve problems;
- Anticipate and predict behaviour; and
- Regulate power.

UNDERSTANDING THE COMMUNICATION PROCESS

Communication serves four main functions within an organization:

1 *Control*, both formally and informally, is maintained by communicating, sometimes very explicitly, the norms that are to be followed.
2 *Motivation* is fostered through communication by clarifying to employees what is to be done, how well they are doing, and what can be done to improve performance.
3 *Emotional expression* of feelings and fulfilment of social needs.
4 *Information* is provided to assist the decision-making process.

For any communication to occur there must be at least two people involved. It is easy to think about communication involving *a sender* and *a receiver* of a message. However, the problem with this way of seeing a relationship is that it presents communication as a one-way process, where one person sends the message and the other receives it: when one person is talking, another is listening. In fact, communications are almost always complex, two-way processes, with people sending and receiving messages to and from each other simultaneously. In other words, communication is an interactive process: while one person is talking the other is listening, but while listening they are also sending feedback in the form of smiles, head nods and the like.

A sender composes the message in their mind. In composing the message, they may take into account such things as the reason for the message, such as to persuade or inform. This involves *encoding*, which is the transfer of mental thoughts for the message into words. Sport managers must encode messages in words and symbols that are meaningful to the receiver. The message not only means the speech used or information conveyed, but also the non-verbal messages exchanged, such as facial expressions, tone of voice, gestures and body language. Non-verbal behaviour can convey additional information about the spoken message. In particular, non-verbal behaviour can reveal more about emotional attitudes that may underlie the content of speech. If the encoding is done carelessly, the message decoded by the sender will have been distorted.

The communication message then travels through a medium known as the 'channel', which refers to the physical means by which the message is transferred from one person to another. In a face-to-face context the channels that are used are speech and vision. However, during a telephone conversation the channel is limited to speech alone.

The next stage of the communication is when the receiver of the message processes the information into understanding, called *decoding*. The *receiver* is the one to whom the information is sent. Decoding is retranslating a sender's communication message. For example, you decode a written message by interpreting the meanings of the symbols (letters and punctuation), including their arrangement (sentence and paragraph structure), on a printed page.

Throughout this process the message may be distorted by *noise*. Noise has a special meaning in communication theory, and refers to anything that distorts the message, so that what is received is different from what is intended by the speaker. While physical 'noise' (for example, background sounds or a low-flying jet plane) can interfere with communication, other factors are considered to be 'noise'. The use of complicated jargon, inappropriate body language, inattention, disinterest and cultural differences can be considered 'noise' in the context of interpersonal communication. In other words, any distortions or inconsistencies that occur during an attempt to communicate can be seen as noise.

The final link in the communication process puts the message back into the system as a check against misunderstandings. Feedback consists of messages the receiver returns, which allow the sender to know how accurately the message has been received, as well as the receiver's reaction. The receiver may also respond to the unintentional message, as well as the intentional message. Types of feedback range from direct verbal statements – for example, 'Say that again; I don't understand' – to subtle facial expressions or changes in posture that might indicate to the sender that the receiver feels uncomfortable with the message. Feedback allows the sender to regulate, adapt or repeat the message in order to improve communication. An overview of the 'communication process' is shown in Figure 14.1.

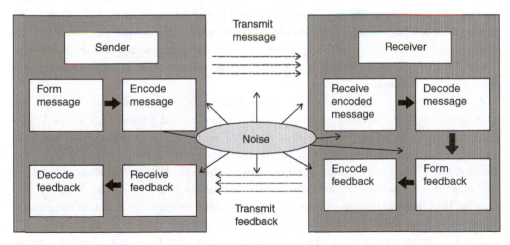

Figure 14.1 Communication processes in organizations

Source: Mitchell and Arnold (2010).

DIRECTION OF COMMUNICATION

Formal communication is designed by the management team. It is an official communication that takes place through the line of authority or chain of command. The basic purpose of designing such communication is to connect various subsystems of the organization and coordinate their functioning to achieve organizational goals. Such communication is official and part of formal organization that operates through a formal relationship of superior and subordinate.

Communication is typically initiated at the top of the organizational hierarchy and flows directly to subordinates. This is commonly known as *downward communication*. That is why, traditionally, this direction has been highlighted or emphasized. It is based on the assumption that the people working at higher levels have the authority to communicate with people working at lower levels. This direction of communication strengthens the authoritarian structure of the organization. This is also called 'downstream communication' and does have its limitations. Quite often the communication originating at the highest level is *distorted* or *diluted* on the way to the lower levels. Sometimes the messages may be lost. It has to be ensured that the receiver fully understands the purport/ instructions/directions coming from above. This requires an efficient feedback system. Another drawback of downward communication is that it is often time-consuming. The more levels the communication has to pass through, the greater the chances of *delay*. That is why sometimes managers choose to send their messages directly to the person concerned.

Sometimes managers may withhold some valuable information and *filter* the information they only wish to convey to employees. Filtering information is a sender's manipulation of the information so the receiver will see it more favourably. In such a situation the employees become frustrated, confused and powerless. This may spoil the employer–employee relationship. Sometimes, however, the receiver can filter information. This is known as 'selective perception', and refers to filtering what the receiver sees and hears to suit their own needs. This process is often unconscious. Small things can command our attention when we're visiting a new place ; a new city or a new company. Over time, however, we begin to make assumptions about the way things are on the basis of our past experience. Often, much of this process is unconscious. 'We simply are bombarded with too much stimuli every day to pay equal attention to everything so we pick and choose according to our own needs' (Pope 2008). Selective perception is a time-saver; a necessary tool in a complex culture. But it can also lead to mistakes.

Upward communication is also an essential component of organizational communication, and its function is to send information, suggestions, complaints and grievances from the lower-level workers to the managers above. It is, therefore, more participative in nature. It was not encouraged in the past, but modern sport managers encourage upward communication, as a direct result of increasing democratization. This is also called 'upstream communication'. However, it is not without its limitations. Many managers do not like to be 'told' by their juniors. They may not be patient enough to listen to them or may even suppress the message sent to them from below. In such a situation the employees may feel let down.

Lateral communication is a type of communication can be seen taking place between people operating at the same level or working under the same executive. Functional managers operating at the same level, in different departments, through their communication, present a good example of lateral communication. The main use of this dimension of communication is to maintain coordination and review activities assigned to various subordinates. Occasions for lateral communication arise during committee meetings or conferences, in which all members of the group, mostly peers or equals, interact. The best example of lateral communication can be seen in the interaction between sport production and marketing departments.

Finally, there is external communication. This is communication that takes place between a sport manager and external groups such as suppliers, vendors, banks, financial institutes etc. For instance, to raise capital the managing director of a sport enterprise would interact with the bank manager.

COMMUNICATION MODES

Communication can take a number of forms. The first is oral communication, which involves the spoken word. It includes individuals conversing with each other, be it direct conversation or telephonic conversation. Speeches, presentations, discussions are all forms of oral communication. Oral communication is generally recommended when the communication matter is of a temporary nature, or where direct interaction is required. Face-to-face communication (including meetings, lectures, conferences and interviews) can often be time-absorbing, but if conducted in reasonable and non-threating ways, can build a rapport and trust.

Written communication also has great significance in today's sports world. At best, it is an innovative activity of the mind. Effective written communication is essential for preparing worthy promotional materials for business development. Whereas speech came before writing, writing is more unique and formal than speech. Effective writing involves the careful choice of words, in the correct order, in sentence formation, as well as the cohesive composition of sentences. Also, writing is more valid and reliable than speech. However, while speech is spontaneous, writing causes delay and takes time as feedback is not immediate.

Non-verbal communication involves messages conveyed through body movements, the intonations or emphasis we give to words, facial expressions (i.e. kinesics) and the physical distance between the sender and receiver. Non-verbal communication can influence the meaning of verbal symbols and it is less rule-bound than verbal communication, Non-verbal communication can also assist in decoding hidden messages as it provides continuous feedback to the speaker, and increases the receiver's emotional understanding of the other person's experience.

Electronic communication and the Internet are also vital tools for communicating ideas, messages, instructions and policies. It doesn't just mean new tools for communication; it means new ways to communicate. Today sport organizations interact with their various constituents differently – employees, board members, customers, partners and others – depending upon the nature of the message, the goals they are trying to achieve and the strengths (and weaknesses) of the available media such as telephones, voicemail, fax machines and print.

Email is now the preferred medium for coordinating work and tends to increase communication volume. It significantly alters communication flow but communicates emotions poorly, and reduces politeness and respect. It can be inefficient for ambiguous, complex, novel situations and lead to information overload. Text messaging as in instant messaging is now a common form of organizational communication. Instant messaging allows employees to send text messages to people on their PCs by logging in to the messaging server and sending messages to their group. Some messaging services such as MSN Explorer will even let you talk to your group using a microphone. Phone messaging lets you send short text messages up to a maximum of 160 characters. These are stored on central computer systems and then forwarded to pagers, mobile phones and palmtop computers with mobile phone connections.

SOCIAL NETWORKING AND ONLINE COMMUNITIES

Networking has become an essential aspect of daily life. It starts with interpersonal connections being established and can end with a sophisticated array of business contacts being developed. This has become an established part of social media. As a result, sport fans, clients, suppliers and participants will immediately judge the quality of an enterprise by the images presented on its website, its blogging features, and by what is posted on social media sites. Facebook, Twitter and LinkedIn are prime examples and represent the leading publicly traded social network stocks. Social networks like Facebook, Twitter and LinkedIn are now seen to be essential avenues for meeting fans, community stakeholders, sponsors and potential clients. They also allow more intensive socialization with professional colleagues. Regardless of which social media sites are utilized, they all have the potential to grow the networks of sporting enterprises. (Pritchars and Stinson 2014).

Online discussion forums are also useful as a social networking strategy. A discussion board (known also by various other names such as discussion group, discussion forum, message board and online forum) is a general term for any online 'bulletin board', where participants can leave their contributions and inevitably receive an array of responses to their messages. Alternatively, participants may just wish trawl the board for updates, professional gossip and the latest sporting announcements. Discussion boards were initially available on bulletin board systems. However, as the Internet has expanded, many discussion systems have been introduced. One example is Usenet, which provides thousands of discussion boards; these can now sometimes be viewed from a web browser.

Online forums provide a highly time-efficient tool for accessing information and exchanging views; for example, they can provide a platform that allows sport affinity groups to communicate freely. Many websites offer discussion boards so that users can share and discuss information and opinions. Special software is available that provides discussion board capability for a website. These types of forums are becoming increasingly popular to facilitate fan engagement.

Avatar sites have gained prominence in certain industries such as 'gaming'; an industry that is reaching deeper and deeper into the sport industry. Generally speaking, an avatar is the embodiment of a person or idea. However, in the computer world, an avatar refers specifically to a character that represents an online user. Avatars are commonly used in multiplayer sport gaming, online communities and web forums. Avatars are also used in online communities. These avatars can be custom-designed to create a truly unique appearance for each player.

Once a user has created an avatar, they become part of an online community filled with other users' avatars. Players can interact with other avatars and talk to them using text or voice chat. It's no surprise that 'Second Life' refers to a virtual life that players live through their avatars. Finally, avatars may also be seen in web forums. Online discussion boards typically require users to register and provide information about themselves, and many give users the option to select an image file that represents the user's persona. This image, combined with a made-up username, serves as a person's avatar. For example, a user may select a picture of a Pac-Man and choose the name 'pac32' for their avatar. This avatar typically appears next to each posting the user contributes in an online forum.

Wikis in sports currently discuss members of a team, share ideas, educate the world about the game, soft-sell a product or team, and serve as a soapbox for contributors to the wiki. By design, a wiki's content changes rapidly, no matter what its purpose. Blogs, and in particular live blogging, are a synthesis of traditional journalism and contemporary digital technologies that are changing the way news is produced, presented and consumed online. News publishers worldwide have adopted the format, including *The New York Times*, Al Jazeera and the BBC. The live blogs that Britain's second-most popular newspaper website, the Guardian.co.uk publishes (Marcovici 2013), receive more visitors for longer periods of time than conventional articles or picture galleries on the same subject. It is increasingly the default format for covering major breaking sport news stories.

The smartphone has changed the way we live and the way businesses operate. It is also changing how people attend sporting contests. Chip Suttles, Vice President of technology for the Seattle Seahawks, noted how his team has been testing 75 beacons at all entry points and around attractions at CenturyLink Field like the Twelfth Man flag wall. The beacons, which are also being tested by Major League Baseball's Seattle Mariners at Safeco Field, push out notifications to smartphone owners and provide relevant information like digital game-day guides.

IMPROVING INTERPERSONAL COMMUNICATION

Getting a message across requires active listening. Active listening means listening with intensity, empathy, acceptance and a willingness to take responsibility for completeness. Listening is not the same as hearing; learn to listen not only to the words being spoken but how they are being spoken, and the non-verbal messages sent with them. Use the techniques of clarification and reflection to confirm what the other person has said and avoid any confusion. Try not to think about what to say next while listening. Instead, clear your mind and focus on the message being received. Your colleagues will appreciate good listening skills.

As an effective sport manager you should follow up after communication and attempt to determine whether the intended meaning was actually received. This is also where your active listening skills of empathy can be important. Empathy is trying to see things from the point of view of others. When communicating with others, try not to be judgemental or biased by preconceived ideas or beliefs. Instead view situations and responses from the other person's perspective. Stay in tune with your own emotions to help enable you to understand the emotions of others. If appropriate, offer your personal viewpoint clearly and honestly to avoid confusion. Bear in mind that some subjects might be taboo or too emotionally stressful

161

for others to discuss. For example, athletes may find it difficult to discuss concerns about their sexuality and its implications for not only themselves but also for the team and the club. Dealing with circumstances such as this requires mutual trust. Offer words and actions of encouragement, as well as praise. In a general sense, when establishing trust through communication, make people feel welcome, wanted, valued and appreciated. If you let others know that they are valued, they are much more likely to give you their best. Try to ensure that everyone involved in an interaction or communication is included through effective body language and the use of open questions.

Ethical communications need to be considered in communications. We often differentiate between 'real lies' and 'white lies', with the latter considered acceptable and even necessary in social interaction. As an ethical sport manager you need to ask yourself if a sound purpose justifies intentionally distorting information. Most of us will face dilemmas in the sport business world where evasive, distorted and outright lying to others may come into play. You need to be guided by your ethical standards in these situations.

BARRIERS TO GOOD COMMUNICATION: INFORMATION OVERLOAD

One of the key barriers to good communication is information overload, which canan be defined as 'occurring when the information processing demands on an individual's time to perform interactions and internal calculations exceed the supply or capacity of time available for such processing' (Pope 2008). Messages reach us in countless ways every day. Some are societal: advertisements that we may hear or see in the course of our day. Others are professional: emails, and memos, voicemails, and conversations from our colleagues. Others are personal: messages and conversations from our loved ones and friends. Add these together and it is easy to see how we may be receiving more information than we can take in. This state of imbalance is known as information overload. Experts note that information overload is:

> [a] symptom of the high-tech age, which is too much information for one human being to absorb in an expanding world of people and technology. It comes from all sources including TV, newspapers, and magazines as well as wanted and unwanted regular mail, e-mail and faxes. It has been exacerbated enormously because of the formidable number of results obtained from Web search engines.
>
> (Pope 2008)

Other research shows that working in such fragmented fashion has a significant negative effect on efficiency, creativity, and mental acuity.

Emotional disconnects also act as a barrier to communication. This happens when the sender or the receiver is upset, whether about the subject at hand or about some unrelated incident that may have happened earlier. An effective communication requires a sender and a receiver who are open to speaking and listening to one another, despite possible differences in opinion or personality. One or both parties may have to put their emotions aside to achieve the goal of communicating clearly. A receiver who is emotionally upset tends to ignore or distort what the sender is saying. A sender who is emotionally upset may be unable to present ideas or feelings effectively.

Cultural barriers are factors that influence how a person interprets words. The less we consider our audience, the greater our chances of miscommunication will be. When communication occurs in the cross-cultural context, extra caution is needed given that different words will be interpreted differently across cultures, and different cultures have different norms regarding non-verbal communication. Eliminating jargon is one way of ensuring that our words will convey real-world concepts to others. Speaking to our audience, as opposed to about ourselves, is another.

Gender differences in communication have been documented by a number of commentators and business consultants. At the same time, many of these differences are based on stereotyped views of male and female behaviour. For example, it is often argued that while men and women work together every day, their different styles of communication can sometimes work against them. Generally speaking, women like to ask questions before starting a project, while men tend to 'jump right in'. Another difference that has been noticed is that men often speak in sports metaphors, whereas many women use their home as a starting place for analogies. Women who believe men are 'only talking about the game' may be missing out on a chance to participate in a division's strategy and opportunities for teamwork, and 'rallying the troops' for success. 'It is important to promote the best possible communication between men and women in the workplace,' notes gender policy adviser Dee Norton, who provided the above example. As we move between the male and female cultures, we sometimes have to change how we behave (speak the language of the other gender) to gain the best results from the situation. Clearly, successful organizations of the future are going to have leaders and team members who understand, respect and apply the rules of gender culture appropriately. Being aware of these gender differences can be the first step in learning to work with them, as opposed to around them. It is often argued, for instance, that in general men tend to focus more on competition, data and orders in their communications, whereas women tend to focus more on cooperation, intuition and requests. Both styles can be effective in the right situations, but understanding the differences is a first step in avoiding misunderstandings based on them.

CASE STUDY

Managing a meaningful and long-term relationship with customers is always an important task for companies to maintain brand loyalty and novelty. As the world's leading sportswear company, Nike has certainly set a good example of establishing an effective interpersonal communication system with its customers.

In 2010, Nike launched a new business division called Nike Digital Sport (NDS). The objective of NDS was to develop technologies and devices to allow users to track their personal performance, while Nike collected and stored data relating to customer trends and needs. Through NDS, Nike has been able to communicate openly and effectively with customers about their needs. Nike also has its own social networking service called Nike+. This social networking service focuses on building social networks and social relationships among people and communities, and has enabled the company to build a relationship with its customers by understanding the customers' needs and preferences.

In addition, a programme called Nike Fuel is also implemented by Nike to build and maintain customer relationships. Nike Fuel enables customers to record their progress through the use of Nike+ devices. These devices are designed to update customers on the latest Nike sports trends and insights, and allow them to communicate with Nike. Nike also developed its Nike+ Connect app. This is a free app that uploads customers' Nike+ data from Plus devices to their nikeplus.com accounts. Finally, the Nike+ running app enables customers to share their experiences on social media sites such as Twitter and Facebook.

Nike reaches over 200 million fans every day in an interactive dialogue, rather than having to rely on big sponsored events to reach this number. The massive volumes of freely shared user data produce meaningful brand insights, lead to product innovations and allow the brand to get closer to consumers. Effective interpersonal communication systems have enabled Nike to collaborate with customers, drive business processes, maximize return on investment and support brand development.

Source: adapted from: https://nikebuzzjstewart.wordpress.com/

Questions

1 Why is maintaining effective communication with customers so important to Nike?
2 If you were the CEO of Nike, how would you communicate your brand message internally; i.e. to your employees?
3 How can Nike make sure its customers value the information received via its communication systems?
4 How can Nike encourage feedback from its employees and customers on its interpersonal communication strategies?
5 Is external communication or internal communication more important to Nike? Why?
6 Describe the communication process in the above case study, then identify its key components and give an example of how this process operates in both oral and written communication.
7 Identify the key elements associated with active listening.
8 What can you do to improve the likelihood that your communications will be received and understood as you intend?

Case exercise

Go to Manchester United's home page (www.manutd.com). Review the page and discuss if the layout is user-friendly for communicating with its fans and clients. Identify the different communication tools that are available on the website, and discuss if the communication tools allow the club to engage with fans, drive potential and existing business, support brand development and maximize its return on investment.

SUMMARY

This chapter discussed interpersonal communication within a sport enterprise. The chapter began with a discussion of the factors and methods of the communication process, progressing to a discourse on the direction and modes of communication. The chapter continued with an exploration of encoding and decoding messages. Next, the chapter discussed choosing the best communication method, succeeding to specific communications within organizations. The chapter then expressed ideas for improving communication, and ended with ethical considerations and barriers to effective communication.

WEBSITE

Soper, T. (2015). How smartphones will change the experience of watching sports in a stadium. Available from: www.geekwire.com/2015/smartphones-will-change-experience-watching-sports-stadium/. See this for a discussion on how smartphones will communicate information that will change the stadium viewing experience.

REFERENCES AND BIBLIOGRAPHY

Marcovici, M. (2013). *The wealthy blogger: How to make money with your blog.* Germany: Books on Demand.

Mitchell, D. and Arnold, K. (2010). *4-Communication Process Model.* University of Illinois at Chicago. Retrieved from: https://uic.blackboard.com/bbcswebdav/institution/classes/dhd547/Katie/Week10B-LB-Communication/Week10B-LB-Communication4.html.

Nike. Establish Effective Communication with Customers. Adapted from: https://nikebuzzjstewart.wordpress.com/.

Pope, R.R. (2008). *Selective perception.* Illinois State University. Retrieved from http://lilt.ilstu.edu/rrpope/rrpopepwd/articles/perception3.html.

Pritchars, M. and Stinson, J.L. (eds) (2014). *Leveraging brand in sport business.* New York: Routledge.

Wenner, L.A. (2016). *Communication and sport.* London: Sage.

Chapter 15

Leadership

OVERVIEW

This chapter explores the many aspects of leadership. It begins with a brief comparison of managers and leaders. The chapter then details traditional leadership styles. This is followed by a discussion of substitutes for and neutralizers of leadership. The chapter concludes with a discussion of unique aspects of leadership in sport, and provides examples of the leadership styles in the commercial sport environment.

LEARNING OBJECTIVES

Having read the chapter, students will be able to:

1   Understand the difference between managing and leading;
2   Comprehend how approaches to leadership have evolved;
3   Gain knowledge of the traditional theories of leadership, and how they underpin society's view of what a leader should be; and
4   Understand the unique circumstances that leaders must navigate in sport.

INTRODUCTION TO LEADERSHIP

Many problems that have confronted international sporting organizations over recent times are a consequence of poor leadership. One only has to think of FIFA and the entrenched corruption within the organization, the International Association of Athletics Federation's (IAAF) performance-enhancing drug scandal and, previously, the scandals surrounding the IOC. It could be argued that if these sport enterprises had good leadership then these problems might not have occurred.

As a potential leader it is important to understand if leadership can be distinguished from management. Zaleznik (1977) suggested that managers are concerned with how things get done, whereas leaders are more concerned with what things mean to people. Bennis and Nanus (1985) suggested that managers are people who do things right, and leaders are people who do the right thing. It is generally accepted that leadership and management are different. This suggestion begs the question 'What should leaders be able to do that might be different from managers?' The literature tells us that effective leaders: provide a clear sense of direction by defining goals in a strategic way; communicate clearly inside and outside the organization; provide flexibility when guiding tasks; take risks while being responsible; listen with humility and recognize the importance of the views of others; build trust as they see it as an essential resource; act with courage as they have faith in success; build a team around them and see teams as interdependent systems; and distribute the leadership function as leaders create leaders. There are nearly as many definitions of leadership as there are people who have attempted to define the concept (Bass 1990). As far back as 1959, Bennis suggested 'the concept of leadership eludes us or turns up in another form to taunt us again with its slipperiness and complexity. So we have invented an endless proliferation of terms to deal with it...and still the concept is not sufficiently defined' (Bennis 1959:121). So let's address the theories that have shaped our understanding of leadership.

LEADERSHIP THEORIES

Traditional theories of leadership have tended to focus on specific attributes that make a good leader. Trait theory or the trait model of leadership is based on the characteristics of many leaders – both successful and unsuccessful – and is used to predict leadership effectiveness. Many of the traits emerged from the notion of the 'Great Man Theory'. Great men were seen to have certain traits, as shown in Figure 15.1.

As trait theory gathered greater momentum resulting lists of traits were compared to those of potential leaders to assess their likelihood of success or failure. Scholars taking the trait approach attempted to identify physiological (appearance, height and weight), demographic

Figure 15.1 Components of effective leadership

Source: Swanson (2015).

(age, education and socioeconomic background), personality (self-confidence and aggressiveness), intellective (intelligence, decisiveness, judgement and knowledge), task-related (achievement drive, initiative and persistence), and social characteristics (sociability and cooperativeness) with leader emergence and leader effectiveness.

Successful leaders definitely have interests, abilities and personality traits that are different from those of less effective leaders. Research conducted in the last three decades of the twentieth century identified a set of core traits of successful leaders. These traits are not solely responsible for identifying whether a person will be a successful leader or not, but they are essentially seen as preconditions that endow people with leadership potential. These traits create integrated patterns of personal characteristics that foster consistent leader effectiveness, and include: extraversion, agreeableness, conscientiousness, openness, neuroticism, integrity, charisma, intelligence, creativity, motivation, need for power, technical knowledge, communication skills and problem-solving abilities. Table 15.1 outlines the key leadership traits that have been identified since the late 1940s.

In summary, traits were based on identifying the qualities of 'great persons', as well as the impact of other factors, which together resulted in certain traits that were considered critical in effective leadership (see Figure 15.2).

Psychologist Kurt Lewin developed his framework in the 1930s, and it provided the foundation of many of the approaches that followed afterwards. He argued that there are three major styles of leadership: Autocratic, Democratic and Laissez-faire leadership. *Autocratic leaders* make decisions without consulting their team members, even if their input would be useful. This can be appropriate when you need to make decisions quickly, when there's no need for team input, and when team agreement isn't necessary for a successful outcome. However, this style can be demoralizing, and can lead to high levels of absenteeism and staff turnover. *Democratic leaders* make the final decisions, but they include team members in the decision-making process. They encourage creativity and people are often highly engaged in projects and decisions. As a result, team members tend to have high job satisfaction and high productivity. This is not always an effective style to use though, when you need to make a quick decision. *Laissez-faire leaders* give their team members a lot of freedom in how they do their work and how they set their deadlines. They provide support and advice if needed, but otherwise they don't get involved. This autonomy can lead to high job satisfaction, but can be damaging if team members don't manage their time well, or if they don't have the

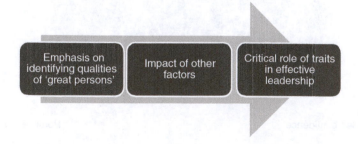

Figure 15.2 Leadership traits and qualities

Source: Swanson (2015).

Table 15.1 Research findings on leadership traits

Stogdill (1948)	Mann (1959)	Stogdill (1974)	Lord, De Vader and Alliger (1986)	Kirkpatrick and Locke (1996)	Zaccaro, Kemp and Bader (2004)
Intelligence	Intelligence	Achievement	Intelligence	Drive	Cognitive abilities
Alertness	Masculinity	Persistence	Masculinity	Motivation	Extraversion
Insight	Adjustment	Insight	Dominance	Integrity	Conscientiousness
Responsibility	Dominance	Initiative		Confidence	Emotional stability
Initiative	Extraversion	Self-confidence		Cognitive ability	Openness
Persistence	Conservatism	Responsibility		Task knowledge	Agreeableness
Self-confidence		Cooperativeness			Motivation
Sociability		Tolerance			Social intelligence
		Influence			Self-monitoring
		Sociability			Emotional intelligence
					Problem-solving

knowledge, skills or self-motivation to do their work effectively. (Laissez-faire leadership can also occur when managers don't have control over their work and their people.) Lewin's framework is popular and useful, because it encourages managers to be less autocratic than they might instinctively be.

In the 1940s and 1950s behaviour and skill became the focus and were used to understand leadership. Many of the leadership studies conducted in the 1950s focused on understanding the distinction between the task and people. Robert Blake and Jane Mouton proposed a graphic portrayal of leadership styles through a managerial grid (sometimes called a leadership grid). The grid depicted two dimensions of leader behaviour – concern for people (accommodating people's needs and giving them priority) on the y axis; and concern for production (keeping tight schedules) on the x axis – with each dimension ranging from low (1) to high (9), thus creating 81 different positions into which the leader's style may fall (see Figure 15.3).

The grid identifies four styles of leadership. First, there are those who have concern for the task. Here leaders emphasize the achievement of concrete objectives. They look for high levels of productivity and ways to organize people and activities in order to meet those objectives. Second, there are leaders who have concern for people. This is the degree to which a leader considers the needs of team members, their interests and areas of personal

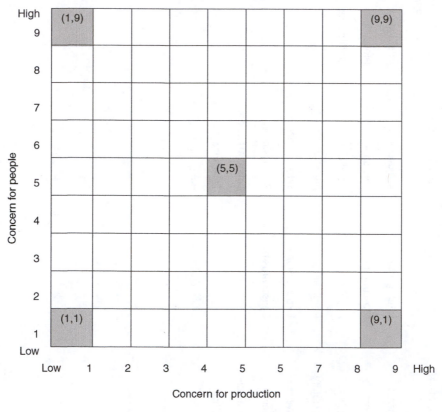

Figure 15.3 Managerial grid

Source: Blake and Mouton (1964).

development when deciding how best to accomplish a task. Directive leadership is the third style identified. This style is characterized by leaders taking decisions for others and expecting followers or subordinates to follow instructions. Finally, Blake and Mouton identified participative leadership, where leaders try to share decision-making with others (Wright 1996).

During this period understanding leadership skills became important. Leadership skills were divided into three main categories: (1) technical; (2) human; and (3) conceptual. Technical skills were associated with specialized knowledge; human skills were identified as the leader's ability to work with people; whereas conceptual skills were seen as the leader's ability to work with ideas and concepts. From this perspective leaders need all three skills but their relative importance changes based on the level of management, as shown in Figure 15.4.

Leadership thinking started to shift to understanding situational factors. The school of thought was that there was no one best way of leading and that a leadership style that was effective in some situations might not be effective in others. In other words, the optimal leadership style was contingent upon various internal and external constraints. These constraints might include the size of the organization, how it adapted to its environment, differences among resources and operational activities, managerial assumptions about employees, organizational strategies and technologies used. This led to the emergence of situational leadership theory. Situational leadership is a leadership style developed by Kenneth Blanchard and Paul Hersey, and refers to when the leader or manager of an organization must adjust their style to fit the development level of the followers they are trying to influence. With situational leadership, it is up to the leader to change their style, not the follower to adapt to the leader's style. In situational leadership, the style may change continually to meet the needs of others in the organization, based on the situation. The model serves as a framework to analyse each situation, based on the amount of guidance and direction (task behaviour) a leader gives, the amount of socio-emotional support (relationship behaviour) a

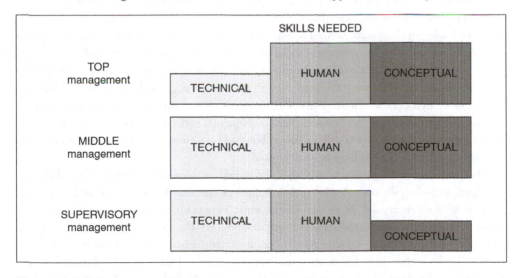

Figure 15.4 Leadership-skill matrix
Source: Swanson (2015).

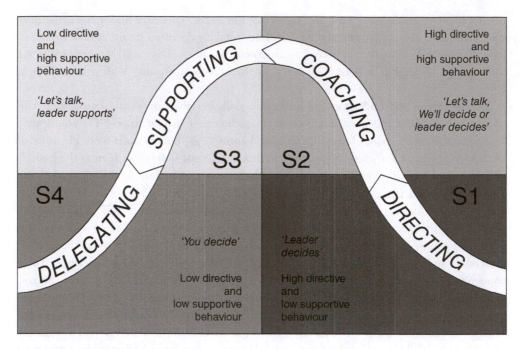

Figure 15.5 Modes of leadership

Source: Hersey and Blanchard (1977).

leader provides, and the readiness level that followers exhibit in performing a specific task, function or objective. An overview of the model is shown in Figure 15.5.

Situational leadership theory has two pillars: leadership style, and the maturity level of those being led. To Hersey and Blanchard (1977) leadership styles stem from four basic behaviours. First, there is *telling*; this behaviour is simply a unidirectional flow of information from the leader to the group. Second is *selling*; the leader attempts to convince the group that the leader should lead by providing social and emotional support to the individual being convinced. There is two-way communication, but it is clear that the leader is leading. The third behaviour is *participating;* the leader shares decision-making with the group, making the system more democratic. There is less of an emphasis on accomplishing an objective than on building human relations. And finally, there is *delegating*, reflected by parcelling out tasks to group members. The leader is still in charge, but there is more of an emphasis on monitoring the ones to whom the tasks have been delegated.

The 1980s saw an explosion of scholarly and popular works on leadership. Several themes emerged, including do as the leader wishes, influence and transformation. Transformational leadership is often argued to be one of the most important ideas in business leadership. Leadership expert James McGregor Burns introduced the concept of transformational leadership in his 1978 book *Leadership*. He defined transformational leadership as a process where 'leaders and their followers raise one another to higher levels of morality and motivation'. Bernard M. Bass, in his book *Leadership and Performance Beyond Expectations*, developed the concept of transformational leadership further. According to Bass (1985), a transformational leader is a model of integrity and fairness. They set clear goals and have high expectations. A transformational leader encourages others while providing support and recognition. This stirs the emotions of people and gets them to look beyond their self-interest, inspiring them to reach for the improbable.

The twenty-first century has led to the recognition that leadership is complex and has different meanings for different people. In recent times it has been suggested that effective leaders have a high level of emotional intelligence, and need to be able regulate emotion in themselves and others. Leaders require an awareness of the emotions of others in way that enables influence and relationships to be managed effectively as leaders construct networks, manage relationships and build rapport across multiple sectors. Leaders need to display empathy and a cognition of others non-verbal emotional signals, feelings and intentions. They need to be attuned to their environment and understand the social world in which they exist. This means they need to be receptive to listening and have high levels of social cognition in order to influence people strategically and favourably. In this way leaders strive for emotional maturity to inhibit impulses, identify emerging challenge or exploit appearing opportunities.

SUBSTITUTES FOR AND NEUTRALIZERS OF LEADERSHIP

Contrary to the arguments made, leadership may not always be important. A theory of leadership suggest that, in many situations, whatever actions leaders exhibit are irrelevant. Certain individuals, jobs and organizational variables can act as substitutes for leadership or neutralize the leader's influence on their followers. Neutralizers make it impossible for a leader's behaviour to make any difference to followers' outcomes. They negate the leader's influences. Substitutes, however, make a leader's influence not only impossible but also unnecessary; they act as a replacement for the leader's influence. For instance, employees' characteristics such as their experience, training, professional orientation or indifference to organizational rewards, can substitute for or neutralize the effect of leadership. Experience and training can replace the need for a leader's support or ability to create structure, and reduce task ambiguity. Jobs that are inherently unambiguous and routine, or that are intrinsically satisfying may place fewer demands on the leadership variable. Organizational characteristics like explicit, formalized goals, rigid rules and procedures and cohesive work groups also replace formal leadership.

LEADERSHIP STYLES OF GREAT COACHES

Mike Carson, in his book *The Manager: Inside the Minds of Football's Leaders* (Carson 2013), draws parallels between the best CEOs and football managers in how they strive to introduce long-term structures and values to foster a culture of success. He suggests that football management is not unlike being a senior executive, where you have to balance the needs of multiple parties: investors, shareholders, committees, customers, clients, consumers and stakeholders in general. No one gets it right all the time and for the managers of the big clubs and national teams, the stakes are very high indeed. He suggests the likes of José Mourinho, Arsène Wenger and Sir Alex Ferguson are under constant press and media scrutiny, and have frequent high-profile and high-impact dealings with press, club owners, agents and top talent, high-priced players. Coaching is very closely aligned with many leadership principles: a number of Fortune 500 companies regularly bring in professional coaches to talk to their companies about teamwork, goal-setting, buy-in, identifying strengths and weaknesses, learning from experience, and fostering humility and trust. Tony Dungy is the model for an authentic, genuine and ethical leader, who truly leads by example and sticks to his personal values, even when the going gets tough. Dungy started out as an NFL player, playing for the Pittsburgh Steelers and the San Francisco 49ers before landing a job as head coach of the Tampa Bay Buccaneers from 1996 to 2001, and then the Indianapolis Colts from 2002 to 2008. He is credited with building up the Buccaneers team that won the 2002 Super Bowl, and led the Colts to the 2007 NFL Championship. Dungy is the model for an authentic, genuine and ethical leader who truly leads by example and sticks to his personal values, even when the going gets tough. Authentic leadership stems from the view that effective leaders need to be aware of and feel comfortable with their values, personality and self-concept. The authentic, individually considerate leader is concerned about helping followers to become more competent, to provide for a more successful succession (Bass 1999).

A 38-year veteran coach in the NFL, it would be remiss not to mention Patriots head coach Bill Belichick. In addition to head coaching duties he also acts as general manager, whereby he makes personnel decisions – a role that has allowed him to establish the 'Patriot Way'. And what a way it is. With five Super Bowl appearances and three Super Bowl rings, he's an expert in team-building and incorporating individuals to buy into a team, even ones coming in with less than stellar reputations. He brings out his player's strengths and doesn't make any excuses. Like Dungy, Belichick is also not without personal struggles; he was fired from his first head coaching job in Cleveland, but has made the most of his opportunities in New England. Belichick exemplifies one of the most important characteristics of a great leader: someone who makes everyone around him better, and who empowers others to become future leaders. Seattle Seahawks coach Pete Carroll also had some failures early in his career. He was fired after one season with the Jets, but he went on to win two national college football championships with the University of South Carolina (USC) and by 2014, lined up two NFC title game appearances, and one Super Bowl appearance with the Seattle Seahawks. He's an example of how if you don't let your failures get you down, you can turn them into positives.

Taking a hard look at what weaknesses you can improve upon can go a long way, both for yourself and for your team. A Hall of Fame coach, Bill Parcels coached the New York Giants to two Super Bowl wins and the Patriots to a Super Bowl appearance during his career. Parcels was more of an authoritarian leadership figure ('you can buy into what we're doing here, or go somewhere else'), but he was very good at finding out what motivated people and bringing out their best. He held a 'team-first' approach that centred on the fact that people wanted to be led. Bill Belichick was one of his understudies and has many of the same leadership philosophies. The namesake of the Super Bowl trophy, Vince Lombardi is widely considered one of the greatest coaches of all time, having won five NFL Championships in seven years with the Green Bay Packers in the 1960s. Although the game was different back then, his leadership qualities were timeless, and he set the standard for excellence in coaching. His players respected him because he was a strict but fair leader, who brought out the best in his team through goal-setting. And when the pressure was on, he knew how to win the big games. The leadership styles of these NFL coaches are summarized in Table 15.2.

Table 15.2 Leadership in practice

Tony Dungy	Bill Belichick	Pete Carroll	Bill Parcels	Vince Lombardi
Authentic, genuine and ethical leader	Expert in team-building	Example of turning failures into positives	Authoritarian leadership	Strict but fair
Leads by example	Brings out player's strengths	Examines weaknesses and improves	Good at finding people's motivators	Brought out the best through goal-setting
Sticks to personal values in times of difficulty	Does not make excuses	Creativity and freedom of expression	Brings out the best in people	Handled pressure well
	Makes everyone around him better		'Team-first' approach	
	Empowers others to become future leaders			

CASE STUDY

John Wooden (1910–2010) is remembered by the world as a successful American basketball coach. His achievements during his tenure as head coach at UCLA included compiling 4 undefeated seasons, winning 88 consecutive games and 10 national championships. He is also very much respected as a great leader by those who worked with him or know about his coaching style.

When Wooden returned from the Navy following World War II to become athletic director and head basketball coach at Indiana State Teachers College, his 1946–47 team received a post-season invitation to the National Association of Intercollegiate Basketball (NAIB) national play-offs. After the coach learned that Clarence Walker, a young African-American second-string guard on his team, would not be allowed to participate in the tournament because of his race, Wooden declined the offer. The college basketball world was stunned. (This was more than two decades before the Civil Rights Act was passed in America.) A considerable amount of criticism and pressure to cave in and go to the tournament was faced by Wooden, as one can imagine.

The following season NAIB officials invited Indiana State again, and this time decided they would allow Clarence to play, provided he didn't stay at the hotel with his team mates and wouldn't be seen publicly with them. Once again, the coach declined. Wooden and his wife Nell thought of all the young men on the team as extended members of their family, who they loved and the coach wasn't about to allow Clarence to be humiliated. But Clarence and his family saw it in a different light. They were excited about the opportunity for him to become the first African-American player in history to participate in the prestigious tournament. So they, along with officials from the National Association for the Advancement of Colored People (NAACP), approached the coach to persuade him that attending the tournament would help, not hurt, Clarence and other African-American players. The coach decided to accept the NAIB's offer, and the team packed up to head to the play-offs in Kansas City.

On their way to the tournament, the team bus stopped for meals. If a restaurant wouldn't serve Clarence, the coach would make the team get back on the bus. Often the team had to pick up food at grocery stores along the way and eat on the bus. When Clarence finally walked onto the basketball court to warm up, he appeared to be nearly paralysed with fear. Many people in the crowd spotted the courageous young man and began to applaud. Clarence Walker became the first African-American player to participate in the NAIB play-offs, and Indiana State made it to the finals, where they lost to Louisville.

Because of Clarence's courage and Wooden's resolve to stand up for what he believed in, the NAIB tournament was finally opened to African-American student-athletes. The following season, three teams brought African-American players with them to the tournament.

Source: adapted from: http://michaelhyatt.com/
john-wooden-and-the-power-of-virtue-in-leadership.html

Questions

1 What leadership traits did John Wooden display?
2 What was the leadership style of John Wooden?
3 Would you call John Wooden a transformational leader?
4 Do you think leaders such as John Wooden are born or made? Explain your position.
5 Develop a table that distinguishes the key differences between management and leadership.
6 Identify the key elements associated with transformational leadership.
7 Explain how emotional intelligence could be useful in the management of sport.
8 Identify a well-known leader in sport and discuss their leadership style. What are the strengths and weaknesses of their style?
9 There is an argument that suggests there are substitutes for and neutralizers of leadership. Discuss if you support or do not support the argument. Support your answer with examples.
10 The charismatic leader has not been discussed in this chapter. Research what defines a charismatic leader and how perceptions of this have changed overtime. Provide examples of sportspeople you feel are charismatic leaders.

Case exercise

Go to the 'Foundation for Leadership through Sport' website (www.flsport.net).

Identify who is involved in the organization, its purpose and the methods it uses to achieve its purpose. Who do you think can benefit from being a member of this organization?

SUMMARY

This chapter explored the many aspects of leadership. It began with a comparison of managers and leaders. The chapter then detailed the evolution of traditional theories of leadership and challenged the need for leadership. The chapter concluded by identifying how teamwork, goal-setting, buy-in, identifying strengths and weaknesses, learning from experience, and fostering humility and trust are all leadership outcomes desired by CEOs and football managers and coaches.

WEBSITE

LeadershipGeek.com. (n.d.). Leadership biographies: Stories of sports leaders. Available from: www.leadership-with-you.com/leadership-biographies.html. See this site for leadership biographies and stories of sport leaders.

REFERENCES AND BIBLIOGRAPHY

Bass, B. (1985). *Leadership and performance beyond expectations*. UK: Free Press.

Bass, B.M. (1999). Ethics, character, and authentic transformational leadership behavior. *The Leadership quarterly*, 10(2), pp.181–217.

Bennis, W.G. (1959). Leadership theory and administrative behavior: The problem of authority, *Administrative Science Quarterly*, 4, pp.259–260.

Bennis, W.G. and Nanus, B (1985). *Leaders: Strategies for taking charge*. London: Collins.

Blake, R. and Mouton, J. (1964). *The managerial grid: The key to leadership excellence*. Houston, TX: Gulf.

Burns, J.M. (1978). *Leadership*. New York: Harper & Row.

Carson, M. (2013). *The manager: Inside the minds of football's leaders*. London: Bloomsbury.

Gentry, W.A. and Eckert, R.H. (n.d.). Integrating Implicit leadership theories and fit into the development of global leaders: A 360-degree approach. *Industrial and Organizational Psychology Perspectives on Science and Practice*, 5, pp.224–227.

Hersey, P. and Blanchard, K.H. (1977). *Management of organizational behavior: Utilizing Human resources*. New Jersey, USA: Prentice Hall.

Kellerman, B. (2010). *Leadership: Essential selections on power, authority, and influence*. New York: McGraw Hill.

Kirkpatrick, S.A. and Locke, E.A. (1996). Direct and indirect effects of three core charismatic leadership components on performance and attitudes. *Journal of Applied Psychology*, 81(1), pp.36–51.

Lord, R.G., De Vader, C.L. and Alliger, G.M. (1986). A meta-analysis of the relation between personality traits and leadership perceptions: An application of validity generalization procedures. *Journal of Applied Psychology*, 71, pp.402–410.

Mann, R.D. (1959). A review of the relationship between personality and performance in small groups. *Psychological Bulletin*, 56, pp.241–270.

Northouse, P. (2013). *Leadership theory and practice* (6th edn). Los Angeles, CA: Sage.

Stogdill, R.M. (1948). Personal factors associated with leadership: A survey of the literature. *Journal of Psychology*, 25, pp.35–71.

Stogdill, R.M. (1974). *Handbook of leadership: A survey of the literature*, New York: Free Press.

Swanson, S. (2015). *Leadership models and practices: Application to a sport context*. London: Loughborough University.

Wooden, J. The power of virtue in leadership. Adapted from: http://michaelhyatt.com/john-wooden-and-the-power-of-virtue-in-leadership.html.

Wright, P.L. (1996). *Managerial leadership*. New York: Routledge.

Zaccaro, S.J., Kemp, C. and Bader, P. (2004). Leader traits and attributes. In Antonakis, J., Caincilio, A. and Sternberg, R. (eds) *The nature of leadership* (pp.101–124). Thousand Oaks, CA: Sage.

Zaleznik, A. (1977). Managers and leaders: Are they different? Retrieved from: https://hbr.org/2004/01/managers-and-leaders-are-they-different.

Part E
Managing problematic structures, operations and behaviours

Chapter 16

Safety and risk

OVERVIEW

This chapter introduces the concepts safety and risk in the workplace. The chapter begins by introducing the concepts of safety and risk in sport. It then identifies three broad areas of responsibility that sport enterprises need to address to manage safety and risk in an increasingly complex sporting world. The chapter will conclude by identifying how to create a safe and risk-conscious sport environment and workplace.

LEARNING OBJECTIVES

Having read the chapter, students will be able to:

1   Understand the importance of managing safety and risk in the sport environment and workplace;
2   Identify the importance of establishing a safety climate and culture to create a safe sport environment and workplace, and manage risk; and
3   Identify the types of attitudes and behaviours required to establish a safe sport environment and workplace.

INTRODUCTION TO SAFETY AND RISK

In few other industries are concerns around safety and risk as evident as in sport. Risk is an integral element of sport. Sport without risk would cease to be sport. This unique aspect of sport must be factored into any discussion of risk management within sport facilities, programmes and events. The business of sport takes place around the boardroom table and today sport organizations have greater responsibilities towards their participants and spectators than ever before. Sport managers require knowledge and skills that they didn't used to need, including knowledge and skills about the law, insurance, information

◼ **Table 16.1** *Risk-management grid*

Impact	Actions		
Significant	Considerable management required	Must manage and monitor risks	Extensive management essential
Moderate	Risks are bearable to certain extent	Management effort worthwhile	Management effort required
Minor	Accept risks	Accept but monitor risks	Manage and monitor risks
	Low	*Medium*	*High*
		Likelihood	

Source: Risk Management Models (2016).

technology, marketing, contracts and safety and risk management. Risk management means more than locking away valuables and taking steps to keep participants from physical harm; it also means managing financial and human resources wisely, governing effectively, making decisions soundly and projecting a positive image towards sponsors, Government funders and the community.

In general terms, risk management is the process of minimizing or mitigating risk. It starts with the identification and evaluation of risk followed by the optimal use of resources to monitor and minimize the same. Risk generally results from uncertainty. In organizations this risk can come from uncertainty in the marketplace (demand, supply and the stock market), failure of projects, accidents, natural disasters and a work environment that may expose employees to potential harmful effects to their health and general well-being. There are different tools to deal with these depending upon the kind of risk. Ideally in risk management, a risk-prioritization process is followed in which those risks that pose the threat of great loss, and have great probability of occurrence, are dealt with first. Table 16.1 provides an example of this practice.

MANAGING SAFETY AND RISK IN SPORT

Corbett (2002) suggests sport enterprises should perform risk management occasionally, but very rarely is there an established routine to perform risk management in an organized and systematic way, or an awareness created within the organization of the importance of risk management. Corbett suggests there are three important areas of responsibility for the sport organization aimed at creating a *safe and risk-conscious environment*. First, sport organizations create policies and standards that promote *safe participation/spectating, safe programmes and safe stadiums/facilities*. Corbett highlights that an injury to an employee, participant or spectator can lead to a lawsuit that will cost the organization money and time and very possibly higher future insurance costs.

The term 'injury' is ambiguous and can relate to short- and long-term consequences associated with the environment in which the injury occurred. However, risks that are inherent in a sport activity and injuries that occur in the normal course of a game rarely give rise to a claim of negligence. Despite that, risks that are not inherent in the sport, that pose an unreasonable risk of danger, that arise out of a deliberate disregard for the rules of the game and that can otherwise be foreseen *may* be the basis of negligence, and are precisely the risks that need to be managed. For example, the debate over concussion has drawn a great deal of public interest, particularly in the United States where class action litigation between former football players and the National Football League (NFL) resulted in a huge out-of-court settlement (Fainaru-Wada and Fainaru 2013). The implications of this case have been felt widely across other codes of heavy contact sports. Player unions have been vocal, as have codes themselves in pushing for improved safety standards, including altering some of the rules around how contact is made and imposing new rules around recovery from concussion. All four of the major professional sports leagues in the United States involve a union that negotiates on behalf of the players. In a typical unionized environment, the union serves as a third party in the negotiation process. Through collective bargaining, unions and firms set a variety of parameters that typically include health and safety regulations. These changes that are being implemented to protect players reflect a growing awareness in sports, as in other industries, of the general principle that employers have a primary duty of care.

Corbett (2002) suggests that to be negligent someone must first have been in circumstances that created a duty of care to ensure the reasonable safety of another person. The circumstance that gives rise to this duty is the existence of a relationship between one person and another. In a general sense, a duty of care is owed to anyone who we can reasonably foresee will be affected by our actions. More specifically, coaches have a duty to athletes (as is the case with the NFL), sport managers have a duty their employees, sports have a duty to their participants, and stadium/facility operators have a duty of care to their spectators.

Occupational Health and Safety (OHS) law imposes a responsibility on clubs as employers, and codes themselves as regulators, to provide a safe working environment in what are inherently dangerous places of work. Although it is absurd to think that risk can be eliminated from contact sports, the principles of OHS demand that risk be managed and minimized as far as it is practicable to do so. OHS risk also arises from issues beyond the contact made between rival players, such as from fan violence (pitch invasions) or from players being injected with substances to enhance performance that perhaps unfolded unwittingly in the Australian Football League (AFL). Although sports are subject to anti-doping regulations these cases also raise OHS matters that pertain to the rights of the parties under the contract of employment, where breaches could result in resignation, termination or legal remedy (Barry *et al.* 2016). The AFL player contracts provide a clear indication of the responsibility it has towards the safety of its players. A clause within the contract states:

> The AFL club shall provide a playing, training and working environment which is, so far as is practicable, free *of any risk to the health, safety and the welfare of the player*. Without limitation, the AFL club shall observe and carry out its obligations under the applicable Occupational Health and Safety Act or its equivalent.
>
> (Clause 7.3, AFL/Essendon/Player Contract)

Safe stadiums and facilities relate to having knowledge of safety standards and guidelines. This is an essential part of managing risk in a stadium/facility setting. Most fundamentally, risk management entails reducing or eliminating the risk of injury and death, and the potential subsequent liability that comes about through involvement with sport and sport services. Decisions pertaining to safety are the most important decisions that sport or stadium/facility managers can make (Spengler *et al.* 2006). Spengler *et al.* (2006) developed a model to assist in identifying and managing risk. By addressing each of the areas in the model, the sport manager is able to make an informed decision on the action required to mitigate the risk. This process is shown in Figure 16.1.

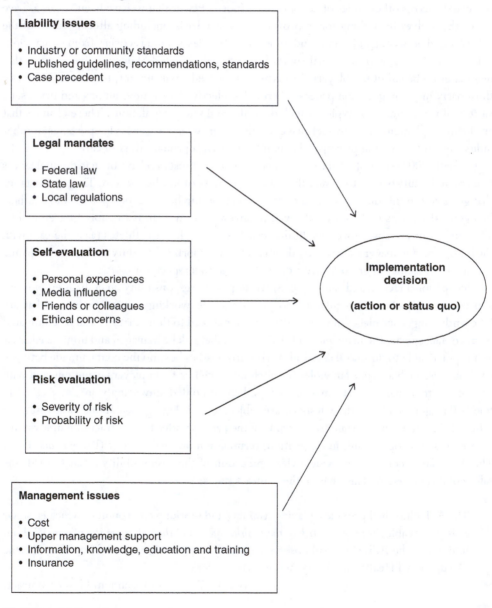

Figure 16.1 Risk-management processes

Source: Spengler *et al.* (2006:7).

The second area Corbett (2002) suggests is the need for sport enterprise's responsibility to have *clear and transparent policies and procedures* for making commercial decisions and handling internal organization disputes. Corbett suggests that poor organizational conflict management can lead to lawsuits that will take an emotional toll on individuals, as well as have significant financial cost. Even if legal action isn't the result of bad decisions, these disputes will harm important relationships and tarnish a sport organization's goodwill and public image. An example of having appropriate polices and procedure may include establishing polices to deal with sexual harassment. Sexual harassment lawsuits have the potential to tarnish the public image of the sport enterprise, accompanied by a significant financial settlement claim. In the sporting world entrenched organizational practices can promote a culture where sexual harassment can occur. For example, skewed gender ratios (e.g. an absence of women in managerial positions), sexualized atmospheres (e.g. scantily clad cheerleaders) and organizational power (e.g. the power held by coaches) have all been found to influence the incidence of sexual harassment. The problem of sexual harassment in sport runs so deep that even students of sporting disciplines are at greater risk of experiencing sexual harassment than students from other disciplines (Moston and Engelberg 2016). Having clearly defined and articulated policies that address sexual harassment can provide clarity around acceptable behaviours, and establish a process that deals with complaints about sexual harassment in the workplace.

Although Corbett (2002) is correct in pointing out that having clear and transparent policies and procedures for dealing with organizational disputes such as sexual harassment claims, the problem with sexual harassment is, however, that there is still no clear consensus as to what sexual harassment is (Moston and Engelberg 2016) and how it is interpreted, particularly in sport. Some of the various interpretations can be seen at three levels. First, at the geographical and cultural level, there are differences in how sexual harassment is defined across countries. Differing perspectives on the issue, as well as different legal systems, inevitably determine that a definition from one country is unlikely to be wholly endorsed in another. Most importantly, cultural variations will also have an important influence on acknowledging whether sexual harassment exists as a social or organizational problem, or is seen as part of the normal courtship process (Moston and Engelberg 2016). As sport is now a global business and operates across international geographical boundaries managing this differing interpretation of what constitutes sexual harassment creates policy challenges.

There are also differences between organizations. Behaviour that is tolerated in one workplace, educational institution or sport setting may be seen as unacceptable in another. This may be evident in several ways, such as differing policies between sport organizations in the same geographical region. Even within a single organization, inconsistencies can be found. For example, language that is permitted on the playing field is not acceptable in an organizational setting, management environment or the boardroom. This can confuse employees and create ambiguity in the workplace. There are also differences at the individual level. One person may find a certain behaviour undesirable and distressing, but to another the same behaviour may be regarded as harmless fun. Psychological research on attitudes towards sexual harassment has shown that in interpreting and defining behaviours as sexual harassment, individuals take into account a large number of factors that are not stipulated in organizational policies, such as prior relationships between the parties concerned (Moston and Engelberg

185

2016). In both these cases the communication of policies that address what constitutes sexual harassment in the sport organization is essential.

Policies may also be required to establish minimum and maximum age limits for participation. There have been repeated calls to introduce a maximum age limit for boxers as a health measure. Comparable restrictions have already been put in place for football referees. Likewise, minimum ages seek to protect the health and safety of young athletes, as in professional North-American-style football in the United States and Canada. Ensuring an athlete's or official's fitness to carry out assigned duties could sufficiently justify the need for policy direction in this area and been seen as a part of risk management.

The third area of responsibility for creating a *safe and risk-conscious environment* that Corbett (2002) identifies is the need for the sport organization to *care for and protect its assets and resources*. This includes finances, equipment, facilities and intangible property such as data, corporate image and marketing rights. She suggests that failure to take care of assets – whether tangible assets such as physical property or intangible assets such as intellectual property – is poor business practice that can lead to short- and long-term harmful financial and legal consequences. For example, sport and intellectual property rights (IP) are becoming more of an issue as innovation and creativity become key drivers for creating competitive advantage. In nearly every sporting organization there are inventors and creators working behind the scenes to push the boundaries, creating new business opportunities and for athletes to better their performance. IP refers to creations of the mind, such as: inventions; literary and artistic works; designs; and symbols, names and images used in commerce. It lies at the heart of the huge commercial opportunities offered by the business of sport. IP rights help to secure the economic value of sport, which in turn stimulates growth of the sports industry, enables sporting organizations to finance high-profile sports events, and provides the means to promote sports development. Business transactions related to sponsorship, merchandising, broadcasting and media deals are all built on IP rights. By acquiring IP rights and then using them strategically, sports organizations can protect and increase their income-generating potential. For example, IP rights are the basis of licensing and merchandising agreements that earn revenues to support the development of the sports industry (WIPO 2016).

Sport enterprises need to protect their IP and they can do this in a number of ways. A patent is an exclusive right granted for an invention, which is a product or a process that provides, in general, a new way of doing something, or offers a new technical solution to a problem. To obtain a patent, technical information about the invention must be disclosed to the public in a patent application. Patents protect technological advances that result in better sporting equipment. Trademarks, brands and designs are capable of distinguishing the goods or services of one sport enterprise from those of other sport enterprises and are IP-protected. Trademarks play a pivotal role in safeguarding the unique character of the Olympic Games and their identification, including the Olympic symbol, Olympic emblems, the flag, the torch and the anthem. Brands are critical for creating business value, and the sports business is no exception. Strong brands such as Nike command customer loyalty and premium prices, constituting valuable assets that drive company revenue and growth. The influence of design in the world of sport is far-reaching. Where image and aesthetics are involved, so too is design, and where new materials emerge, aesthetics or design soon follow. Copyright is a legal term used to describe the rights that creators have over their literary and artistic works.

Works covered by copyright range from books, music, paintings, sculpture and films, to computer programmes, databases, advertisements, maps and technical drawings. Copyright generates the revenues needed for broadcasters to invest in the costly undertaking of broadcasting sports events to fans all over the world. Collectively these forms of IP rights can act together to protect a new product. For example, several IP rights may protect a new sport shoe on the market: patents protect the technology used to develop the shoe; designs protect the 'look' of the shoe; trademarks distinguish the shoe from similar products and protect the 'reputation' of the shoe (and the company/brand making it); and copyright protects any artwork and audio-visual creations used to publicize the shoe (WIPO 2016).

HOW TO CREATE A SAFE AND RISK-CONSCIOUS SPORT ENVIRONMENT AND WORKPLACE

Effective design and implementation of safety programmes can minimize the loss and damage caused to persons and property by reducing risk. Safety programmes can also result in substantial cost savings, increased productivity and can assist in establishing a harmonious sport and workplace environment. Designing and implementing an effective safety plan and risk-management strategy requires a thorough analysis of environmental and workplace conditions to determine the level of protection required. The degree of protection depends upon the degree of risk involved. Sport organizations can reduce the risk in the workplace by identifying the level of risk, modifying the already existing policy and implementing it effectively. Corbett (2002) suggests three practical steps for establishing safety plans and managing risk that can be applied to participants, spectators, stadiums/facilities, technology and other important assets. The practical steps are linked to an organized process of asking the following three questions:

1   What are the possible things that can go wrong (*identifying* risks)?
2   How likely is it these things will go wrong, and what are the consequences if they do go wrong (*measuring* risks)?
3   What can we do to keep things from going wrong (*controlling* risks)?

Corbett (2002) suggests the sport manager can then determine which risks are more important and thus warrant taking measures to control them. Once significant risks are identified, the third step of the risk-management process involves finding practical, affordable and reasonable ways to control these risks. There is no secret formula for controlling risks – the control measures that a sport manager will select and implement will depend on the nature, factors and circumstances of the sport organization, stadium/facility or event.

CASE STUDY

For years, the NFL has denied the link between football injuries – namely, concussions – and brain injury. However in 2016, nearly five years after the first concussion lawsuit was brought against the NFL, the league secured an important court ruling that should mostly end the legal controversy of this still-unresolved health crisis. As expected, a panel of judges on the US Court of Appeals for the Third Circuit unanimously affirmed an April 2015 order by a US District Judge that approved a class action settlement between the NFL and more than 20,000 retired NFL players. The settlement, which could cost the NFL about US$1 billion over 65 years, calls for varying levels of compensation for retired players, depending on their age, injuries and NFL experience. The settlement is expected to pay retired players, on average, around US$190,000 and up to US$5 million. Pending further court review, attorneys who represented the retired players are set to receive US$112.5 million for their work (McCann 2016).

NFL players were also starting to walk away from the game in order to protect their mental and physical health. When the controversy first emerged, Hall of Famer Tony Dorsett and two other former NFL players had been diagnosed with signs of Chronic Traumatic Encephalopathy (CTE) – the degenerative brain disease linked to concussions and repetitive brain trauma. In 2016, stories again began to surface about the dangers of playing football, when it was revealed that 96 per cent of deceased professional football players tested positive for CTE. At Christmas 2015, the major motion picture *Concussion*, which recounted how the NFL initially tried to suppress Dr Bennet Omalu's discovery of CTE, was released in cinemas nationwide. This media exposure reinforced that the NFL needed to create a safer working environment for NFL players.

The NFL still has a responsibility to try to alleviate its concussion crisis and, after years of attempting to squash or downplay research that linked playing football with head trauma, the league has donated US$30 million to the National Institutes of Health in order to help fund further medical research on brain injuries. In addition, the NFL and General Electric have recently partnered up for the US$10 million Head Health Challenge, which awards grants to companies that are studying innovative ways to improve the treatment of concussion.

The NFL has also launched a new website as part of an organizational approach part to keep players safe, during their time on the field and long after. The website is aimed at not only spreading awareness of the dangers associated with these injuries, but also documents the efforts of the league to fund research that will hopefully help to provide a better comprehension of the long-term impacts of these injuries.

That's not to say that some of these attempts to combat head injuries haven't come without scrutiny. Last month, ESPN's *Outside the Lines* reported that the league withheld funding from a Boston University study, sponsored by the National Institute of Health (NIH), that will attempt to track the progress of CTE in living patients, because the lead researcher on the inquiry, Dr Robert Stern, has been critical of the NFL's handling of concussion. Although the NFL denies the story, four congressional Democrats announced they wanted more information about the league's partnership with the NIT.

Despite some of the controversy surrounding some of the research-funding, members of the medical community saw it as a victory for athletes of all ages, at all levels. Imposing stricter rules regarding return-to-play following a head injury has indirectly helped to protect countless kids from similar injuries and even more complicated side effects. Schools and youth sports groups have taken a page from the NFL playbook and have begun to enforce new rules stating that players must be evaluated by a medical professional before returning to the field (Chirban 2011).

The enforcement of these new rules has helped to bring the severity of concussion to light for many coaches, players and parents. Parents now know that they must play a proactive role in protecting their children, both on and off the field, and athletes know that playing through the pain is simply not an option anymore. This alone has probably saved thousands of kids from possible concussion mismanagement. In addition to changing how the game of football is played, or rather enforcing the rules that were there all along, the NFL has been doing extensive research to better understand concussion and its connection to brain damage.

A main focus of some of the NFL's research has involved impact testing; specifically, how they can effectively measure the impact a hit has on a player's brain at the time of the injury. The NFL has updated player helmets, so that they are embedded with impact-sensors. Sensors are placed in the helmet's padding, which are activated when a player is hit with dangerously high force. Upon activation of the sensor, the data is sent to the trainers and coaches on the sideline, who are then able to evaluate the injury immediately.

The use of technology in creating a safer playing environment for NFL players means that NFL players no longer have the opportunity to injure themselves further by returning to the game prematurely after a traumatic blow. Further, the collected data from all the injured players can be studied in the hope of gaining a broader understanding of the impact of these hits. Upon learning more about how the brain reacts to trauma in different areas, helmets can be tailored to better protect players at all levels. Some helmet manufacturers are already building new prototypes, aimed at better protecting the brain and the playing environment of NFL players.

Source: adapted from: www.huffingtonpost.com/sharon-chirban-phd/
nfl-concussions-league-fights-injury_b_809934.html and
www.si.com/nfl/2016/04/18/nfl-concussion-lawsuit-settlement-retired-players

Questions

1 Why do you think the NFL denied a link between playing football and concussion for so long?
2 Do you feel NFL players need to accept the consequences of playing, given that playing football comes with risk? Alternatively, does the NFL have a duty of care to its players and therefore needs to create a safe work environment for players?
3 What else could the NFL do to create a safer and less risky playing environment for its players?

4   How can technology play other roles in establishing a safer and more risk-adverse environment for players and athletes?

5   In today's complex world of sport, business risk can be identified in many ways. Explain the different types of risk sport organizations can be exposed to.

6   Discuss how the model developed by Spengler, Connaughton and Pittman (2006) can be used to manage risk.

7   Explain why sport organizations should protect their intellectual property.

8   Explain some of the challenges in trying to mitigate risk against sexual harassment.

Case exercise

Go to the Australian Sports Commission webpage (www.ausport.gov.au). Search the website and identify the guidelines they provide for how to reduce risk and improve safety in sport enterprises. Do you feel these guidelines cover all areas of risk to which the sport enterprise could be exposed? Discuss what other information you would put on the website to guide the development of risk-management policies in sport enterprises.

SUMMARY

This chapter introduced the concepts safety and risk in the workplace. It discussed the concepts of safety and risk in sport and identified three areas of responsibility that a sport organization needs to address to manage safety and risk. The chapter identified how to create a safe and risk-conscious sport environment and workplace.

WEBSITE

Australian Sports Commission, Australian Institute of Sport (AIS). (n.d.). *Risk Management.* Available from: www.ausport.gov.au/supporting/clubs/resource_library/managing_risks/risk_management. See this site for the resources available to the sport manager to manage risk.

REFERENCES AND BIBLIOGRAPHY

Barry, M., Skinner, J. and Engelberg, T. (2016). Sidelined: The employment relations of professional sport. In M. Barry, J. Skinner and T. Engelberg (eds), *Research handbook of employment relations and sport* (pp.1–17). London: Edward Elgar.

Chirban, S. (2011). NFL concussions: League fights injury with technology. Retrieved from: www.huffingtonpost.com/sharon-chirban-phd/nfl-concussions-league-fights-injury_b_809934.html

Corbett, R. (2002). *Risk management for sport organizations and sport facilities.* Available at: www.sportlaw.ca/2002/08/risk-management-for-sport-organizations-and-sport-facilities/

Fainaru-Wada, M. and Fainaur, S. (2013). *League of denial.* New York: Random House.

McCann, M. (2016). What's next for each side after the NFL's concussion settlement. Retrieved from: www.si.com/nfl/2016/04/18/nfl-concussion-lawsuit-settlement-retired-players

Moston, S. and Engelberg, T. *Hiding in plain sight: Sexual harassment in sport*. In M. Barry, J. Skinner and T. Engelberg (eds) *Research handbook of employment relations and sport* (pp.295–309). London: Edward Elgar.

NFL Concussion Concerns. The role of technology in managing concussion. Adapted from: www.huffingtonpost.com/sharon-chirban-phd/nfl-concussions-league-fights-injury_b_809934.html and www.si.com/nfl/2016/04/18/nfl-concussion-lawsuit-settlement-retired-players.

Risk Management Models (2016). Enterprise PM. Retrieved from www.enterprise-pm.com/pmbasics/risk-management-models.

Skinner, J. Moston, S. and Engelberg, T. (2016). *The evolution of anti-doping policy: Workplace implications for athletes*. In M. Barry, J. Skinner and T. Engelberg (eds) *Research handbook of employment relations and sport* (pp.310–329). London: Edward Elgar.

Spengler, J.O., Connaughton, D.P. and Pittman, A.T. (2006). *Risk management in sport and recreation*. Champaign, IL: Human Kinetics.

Westerbeek, H., Smith, A., Turner, P., Emery, P., Green, C. and Van Leeuwen, L. (2005). *Managing Sport facilities and major events*. London: Routledge.

World Intellectual Property Organization (WIPO). (2016). *Sport and intellectual property*. Retrieved from: www.wipo.int/ip-sport/en/.

Chapter 17

Stress and aggression

OVERVIEW

This chapter discusses the effects of stress and aggression on people working within a sport enterprises. The first part of the chapter focuses on stress, beginning with an introduction to what constitutes stress and aggression. Causes of stress are identified, leading to a discussion of how stress can be managed in the organization. The final part of the chapter focuses on workplace aggression, and describes several types of aggression, including bullying, harassment and violence.

LEARNING OBJECTIVES

Having read the chapter, students will be able to:

1   Understand what stress is, and why it is important to address stress in the workplace;
2   Comprehend the influences and causes of stress in the workplace, and how workplace stress can be managed;
3   Recognize the three types of workplace aggression: hostility, obstructionism and overt aggression; and
4   Recognize the ways aggression is acted out in the workplace, including bullying, harassment and violence.

INTRODUCTION TO STRESS AND AGGRESSION

Stress is often described as an adaptive response to a situation that is perceived as challenging or threatening to the person's well-being. The human body has a natural chemical response to a threat or demand, commonly known as the 'flight or fight' reaction, which includes the release of adrenalin. Once the threat or demand is over the body can return to its natural state. A 'stressor' is an event or set of conditions that causes a stress response. Stress is the body's physiological response to the stressor, and *strain* is the body's longer-term reaction to chronic stress. Occupational stress can affect your health when the stressors of the workplace exceed the employee's ability to have some control over their situation, or to cope in other ways. For example, workers are overburdened with workloads that remain high regardless of their efforts: the workload is the stressor. Employees feel anxious and their heart rate speeds up because they cannot control their workloads; this is stress. Increased blood pressure, insomnia or chronic headache is strain.

In many countries, employers have a legal responsibility to recognize and deal with stress in the workplace so that employees do not become physically or mentally ill. It is important to tackle the causes of stress in the workplace as stress at work can lead to problems for the individual, working relationships and the overall working environment. These issues may include lowered self-esteem and poor concentration skills for the employee. The employer may suffer from increasing customer complaints, staff turnover and days lost to sickness. Managing stress in the workplace is therefore an essential part of both individual and corporate responsibility.

Stress in itself is not necessarily a bad thing, as it can have a positive value. Athletes rise to the occasion, at or near to their maximum. Stress is associated with constraints and demands: the former prevents you from doing what you desire; the latter refers to the loss of something desired. The two conditions are necessary for *potential* stress to become *actual* stress. There must be uncertainty over the outcome and the outcome must be important.

CAUSES OF STRESS

There are no reliable statistics on stress intensity at work or the percentage of the work population suffering from serious stress symptoms. However, a large number of people report they are suffering from stress, and stress-related health problems come at a cost to business and society. The management of stress is therefore important. However, before we can manage stress we need to understand what causes stress. Stress can be caused by a number of different factors, which we can refer to as stressors. However, some of us may be more susceptible to stress than others. Our personality type can be a key indicator of how much stress we manufacture ourselves. Type A personalities can be characterized by their chronic and incessant struggle to achieve more and more in less and less time. At times, this may be against the opposing efforts of others or other things. Individuals with Type A personalities tend to be competitive, impatient, preoccupied with their work and tend to choose stressful lives (Lussier and Kimball 2004). Type B personalities are rarely hurried by the desire to complete an increasing number of tasks, or to participate in an increasing number of organizational activities in an ever-decreasing amount of time. It should be clear, then, that Type A personalities are more susceptible to stress and need to engage in stress-management techniques to reduce the influence of stress on their lives.

Other factors can contribute to creating stress. Your own personal circumstances can create stress in your workplace. Circumstances relating to your personal life or your own economic situation can make you more likely to exacerbate stress at work. This is particularly the case if an employee is experiencing work-overload stress; that is, the extent to which individuals feel that the demands of their workload and the associated time pressures are a source of pressure. This is becoming more common as dramatic changes have taken place in the economy – mergers and acquisitions, increased global competition, new technological innovations, large redundancies and job restructuring – and put pressure on sport managers to work longer hours. Sport managers have to deal with organizational pressures owing to task demands, role demands, interpersonal demands and leadership demands. This can create conflict between work and life roles. Just as your personal life can impact on your work life, so the demands of work have the potential to spill over and affect personal and home life, putting a strain on relationships outside work.

The experience of pressure is strongly linked to perceptions of a *lack of control*. Lack of influence and consultation in the way in which work is organized and performed can be a potential source of pressure, For example, if employees feel they have a lack of control over aspects of the job, a lack of involvement in decision-making, a lack of influence over performance targets, and a lack of time to complete their task, they are more likely to experience stress. Job *conditions* are also potential sources of stress. These relate to the fundamental nature of the job itself. Factors such as the physical working conditions, type of tasks and the amount of satisfaction derived from the job are all potential stressors. Many jobs demand regular contact with other people at work and therefore the need for good interpersonal skills. Poor or *unsupportive relationships* with colleagues and/or supervisors can be a potential source of pressure. In addition, pressure can occur if individuals feel isolated or unfairly treated. Poor work relationships can be a result of an aggressive management style, a lack of support from others, feeling isolated at work and aversive behaviour such as bullying and harassment.

MANAGING WORK-RELATED STRESS

Understanding what stress is and its causes allows an organization to create an environment that facilitates the management of stress. In the UK, the Health and Safety Executive (HSE) has issued a guide entitled *Tackling Stress: The Management Standards Approach* (2005), which outlines six key areas of the workplace that should be monitored in order to assess levels of stress. These key areas are shown in Table 17.1.

Managing work-related stress can also be dealt with at a more practical level. To begin with, the stressor can be removed. One way for organizations to manage stress is to investigate the main causes of stress in their workplace. Audits asking staff to complete confidential questionnaires to identify when and how they experience stress can be conducted. Management can change the corporate culture and reward systems so they support a work–life balance and no longer reinforce dysfunctional *workaholism*. Removing the stressor may be the ideal solution, but it is often unfeasible. An alternative strategy is to remove employees permanently or temporarily from the stressor. Permanent withdrawal occurs when employees are transferred to jobs that better fit their competencies and values. If neither removing the stressor nor the employee is possible, the organization can also change perceptions of the stressor. Employees often experience different levels of stress in the same situation because they perceive it differently. Consequently, changing perceptions of the situation can minimize stress. This does not involve ignoring risks or other stressors. Rather, organizations can look to strengthen employee self-efficacy and self-esteem so that job challenges are not perceived as threatening.

Table 17.1 *Management tools for reducing stress*

Demands	Issues such as workload, work patterns and work environment
Control	How much control the person has in the way they do their work
Support	Includes the encouragement, sponsorship and resources provided by the organization, line management and colleagues
Relationships	Includes promoting positive working to avoid conflict and dealing with unacceptable behaviour
Role	Whether people understand their role within the organization, and whether the organization ensures that the person does not have conflicting roles
Change	How organizational change is managed and communicated within the organization

Some sport enterprises are flexible about the hours, days and amount of time employees want to work. For example, sport enterprises can allow employees the freedom to rearrange their work schedule to accommodate family events, from attending their kids' sports activities to caring for elderly parents. Job-sharing is also an option as it splits a career position between two people. They can then experience less time-based stress between work and family, and typically work different parts of the week with some overlapping work time in the weekly schedule to coordinate activities. Employers with strong work–life values offer extended maternity, paternity and personal leave to care for a new family or take advantage of a personal experience. More governments now offer paid maternity leave and childcare support, and given the ageing population, increasingly, employees require personal leave to care for elderly parents who need assistance.

Social support structures and practices can also be used to manage stress. Social support refers to the perceived comfort, caring, esteem or help the person receives from other people or groups (Cobb 1976). There are five basic types of social support. First, there is *emotional support*. This is the expression of empathy, caring and concern towards the person. Second, *esteem support* occurs through people's expression of positive regard for the person, encouragement or agreement with the individual's ideas or feelings, and positive comparison of the person with others, such as people who are less able or worse off. This kind of support serves to build the individual's feeling of self-worth, competence and of being valued. Esteem support is especially important during the appraisal of stress, when the individual is assessing whether the demands exceed their personal resources. Third, *tangible or instrumental support* involves direct assistance. Fourth, *informational support* includes giving advice, suggestions or feedback. Finally, *network support* provides a feeling of membership in a group of people who share interests. The type of support depends upon the stressful circumstances; for instance, emotional and informational support is particularly important for people who are seriously ill. Employees who received more frequent esteem support tended to report less depression following stressful experiences.

Finally, sport enterprises can look to control the consequences of stress. Coping with workplace stress also involves controlling its consequences. For this reason, an increasing number of corporate organizations have gyms or provide gym memberships that allow employees to keep in shape. Research indicates that physical exercise reduces the physiological consequences of stress by helping employees lower their respiration, muscle tension, heartbeat and stomach acidity. Another way to control the physiological consequences of stress is through relaxation and meditation. Generally, these activities decrease the individual's heart rate, blood pressure, muscle tension and breathing rate. Not managing stress appropriately can lead to distress and work burnout. Burnout results when individuals have an unhealthy relationship with their work. They put more and more energy into their work to the detriment of their personal life, while deriving less and less satisfaction from it. This state manifests itself through emotional or physical exhaustion, reduced productivity at work and a feeling of depersonalization.

WORKPLACE AGGRESSION

Workplace aggression is behaviour that is intended to have the effect of harming a person, yet in sport aggression has long been considered a legitimate a part of the sport domain. In fact, sport is perhaps the only setting in which acts of interpersonal aggression are not only tolerated, but applauded enthusiastically by large segments of society. However, there is more and more aggressive behaviour in sport that is starting to be perceived as violence, which imposes a negative impression on society. Aggressive behaviour in sport is not a new phenomenon; for example, in 1997, during a Manchester United v. Leeds United match, Roy Keane attempted to trip Alf-Inge Haaland by kicking his leg, and in doing so injured himself by tearing his cruciate ligament. Haaland felt Keane was feigning injury and stood over him shouting at him. In 2001, the players met again in the Manchester Derby, when Keane ran towards Haaland putting his studs into the top of Haaland's knee and causing a serious injury that meant Haaland never played a full professional football match again (Gearing 2012). Roy Keane had intended to injure Haaland, but the reason for the act of aggression was in revenge for the abuse he had received from Haaland four years earlier. Keane went on to say he had 'no remorse' for the injury and in his autobiography described his attitude as 'an eye for an eye'.

Sport managers need to be aware of all forms of workplace aggression. However, the two causing growing concern and increasing incidence are workplace violence and workplace bullying and harassment. Workplace violence is violence or the threat of violence against workers. It can occur at or outside the workplace and can range from threats and verbal abuse to physical assaults. As the general level of violence increases in society, workplace violence is a growing concern for employers and employees, must be dealt with immediately and may require involving the police. Workplace bullying is repeated and persistent negative actions directed towards one or more individuals, that involve a power imbalance and create a hostile work environment. Harassment is behaviour that makes someone feel intimidated or offended. Bullying and harassment can happen face to face, or by letter, email, phone or through social media. It can include such things as the spreading malicious rumours, unfair treatment, picking on someone, regularly undermining a competent worker and denying someone training or promotion opportunities. Workplace bullying and harassment needs to be addressed appropriately and cannot be allowed to manifest itself in the organization. If it does it will create a dysfunctional culture that will have significant short- and long-term consequences for the sport enterprise.

Bullying and harassment in a sport environment often go unnoticed as they may be considered historically accepted practice. For example, Lalor (2005) notes with respect to coaches in sport teams:

> Coaches are being dragged, kicking, swearing, and screaming into the modern era. For years the rest of us in our towers and trenches have worked under a strict code of behaviour dictated by anti-harassment legislation, but on the field the fire and brimstone coach has remained in his or her bunker, doing it the only way they know how.
>
> (Lalor 2005:56).

One of the unique challenges for sport managers is to address coaching practices that could be considered a form of bullying or a form of harassment. Practices such as shouting, swearing, bullying, intimidation and public humiliation are still seen by some community and professional coaches as the way to discipline players. The products of an education system that teaches and instils strong personal values and self-worth, modern players are trained to expect to give and receive a high level of interpersonal communication from others, including their coaches.

Sport is one of the last bastions of inappropriate interpersonal behaviour. By its very nature sport involves a degree of on-field physical intimidation, but in the modern sport climate it is now completely unacceptable for players to be subjected to bullying and/or harassment by their coaches off the field. As an example to support these assertions, an English Super League coach was recorded as using 15 profanities in a post-game tirade in which he articulated his feelings on the injuries sustained during his team, St Helen's, win over Hull in August 2003:

> They're all f****** serious. Have you ever played the game at impact? Mate, they were f*****. We had no ball and they were f*****, completely f*****. Every f****** injury. Get out the f****** medical thing and I'll tell you, it's there. John Kirkpatrick is f*****, his body's f*****, he's got a f***** shoulder, f***** ribs, f***** leg, f***** everything. Those blokes are f****** bust big time. I can't believe you didn't see f****** blood, guts everywhere. We did it f****** tough. Do you understand combat, do you understand warfare? It was war out there.
>
> (Lalor 2005:56)

Unfortunately, incidents like this still occur today. In some cases, coaches have used physical aggression towards players and even injured them. Perhaps the most publicized incident is when Sir Alec Ferguson allegedly lost his temper resulting in England Captain David Beckham receiving a cut to his eye from a flying football boot. It may have been coincidence that following frenzied media speculation and a level of public dissatisfaction over the incident, but Beckham subsequently left Manchester United for Real Madrid. The challenge for contemporary sport managers is to work within the parameters of modern anti-bullying/harassment legislation. Modern players have a right to be treated with respect and have a right to be educated in order to fulfil their potential. How can players be expected to behave in socially responsible ways if such actions are not being modelled consistently in their sports enterprises?

197

HARM MODEL OF AGGRESSION

To assist in understanding the relative levels of workplace aggression, Hellriegel and Slocum (2010) conceptualized the Harm Model of Aggression. The model is a continuum that ranges from harassment to aggression, to rage, to mayhem. *Harassment* is the first level of behaviour on the continuum. This behaviour may or may not cause harm or discomfort to the employee, but harassment is generally considered unacceptable in the workplace. Examples include acting in a condescending way to a customer, slamming an office door, glaring at a colleague, or playing frequent practical and cruel jokes. The second level is *aggressive behaviours*. These are behaviours that cause harm to or discomfort for another employee, or for the organization. Such behaviours include shouting at a customer, spreading damaging rumours about a co-worker or damaging someone's personal belongings. The third level on the continuum is *rage*. Rage is seen through intense behaviours that often cause fear in other employees, and which may result in physical or emotional harm to people or damage to property. Rage typically makes the inappropriate behaviours physical and visible. Examples of rage can range from pushing a customer to sabotaging a co-worker's presentation, or leaving hate statements on someone's desk. *Mayhem* is the final stage on the continuum. This stage represents physical violence against employees or customers, or the violent destruction of property. Actions in this category can range from punching a customer or ransacking an office, to physically punching a co-worker or superior to destroying the building.

Employees who engage in workplace violence at the rage and mayhem levels frequently exhibit clear observable warning signs. These warning signs include the following: violent and threatening behaviour; strange behaviour; performance problems; interpersonal problems; and they are generally considered to be at the end of their tether (Hellriegel and Slocum 2010). Rage and mayhem behaviours may occur as a result of triggering events. The triggering event is seen by the violence-prone individual as the last straw that creates a mindset of no way out, or no more options (Hellriegel and Slocum 2010). It is essential to establish organizational practices and procedures to prevent workplace violence. Sport enterprises need to have zero-tolerance violence policies that are enforced fairly and communicated consistently. Employee training around workplace violence is essential, and during the recruitment process careful interviewing and background checks are essential.

CASE STUDY

The inclusion and acceptance of lesbian, gay and bisexual (LGB) people across the English-speaking world has improved dramatically in recent years. However, sporting culture, and particularly team sporting culture, has not seen the same progress that has been observed in broader society. For example, as recently as 2015, an Australian Channel Seven commentator was widely condemned for calling an AFL player a 'big poofter' during a recent broadcast. But preliminary results from the first national study on homophobia in Australian sport reveal such incidents are a common experience in many sporting environments, all the way down to the grassroots level.

Nearly 2,500 players and spectators of many sports, and at all levels, took part in the study, with the most common form of homophobia reported being verbal abuse such as 'fag', 'dyke' and 'poofter'. Of the 1,200 Australian respondents who were lesbian, gay or bisexual (LGB), 84 per cent reported hearing such verbal slurs, while 74 per cent of straight respondents reported the same. This was followed in frequency by reports of homophobic jokes and humour, and casual comments such as 'that's so gay'. Most LGB survey respondents – 64 per cent – agreed, or strongly agreed, that homophobia in the form of comments, jokes, insults or abuse was more common in team sporting environments than in general society. However, heterosexual people were split on this question, with 47 per cent agreeing. Half of LGB respondents reported being a direct target of homophobia. Of those, one in four said they had experienced verbal threats, repeated bullying or had been excluded from social groups. One in four heterosexual men also said they had personally been a target. When the Olympic champion swimmer Ian Thorpe revealed he was gay, one reason he gave for not coming out earlier was that he had feared a negative reaction.

These findings also mirror those of the international 'Out on the Fields' study, on homophobia in sport. The first international study into homophobia in sport casts a light on the prevalence of homophobia in sport around the world. The findings came at a time of increased awareness and heightened interest in the issue of homophobia in sports. For example, in 2013, Michael Sam made international headlines when he became the first American Football player to be drafted into the NFL after very publicly 'coming out of the closet'. His story captivated many and continues to do so simply because he is so rare as an openly gay male professional athlete. Yet contrasting Sam's announcement were the findings made at the 2014 Men's FIFA World Cup that suggested that none of the 736 competitors was openly gay. This would indicate that there are no gay men in international men's football, and yet the 'Out on the Fields' study found that football was one of the most popular sports among gay and bisexual men. The report suggests it is more likely is that none of the players was comfortable revealing their sexuality; something not unique to soccer. The international study discovered that many athletes of all sexualities, playing all sports, choose to remain silent. Very few, particularly in youth sport, feel safe to 'come out of the closet' in the same way as Michael Sam for fear of discrimination and aggressive attitudes towards them: some 30 per cent of gay male participants said they did not come out because they feared discrimination from coaches and officials.

The study also noted that that there had been a series of recent high-profile international incidents of fans shouting or holding signs with homophobic slurs and insults. For example, in 2014, fans at a rugby union match in the UK shouted slurs at internationally respected referee Nigel Owens. The incident made headlines around the world; however, it was unclear whether this incident was isolated and whether this kind of behaviour has any impact on the safety of LGB people who may be spectators. The 'Out on the Field' participants were asked two separate questions about spectator stands, and their answers show overwhelmingly that they feel that homophobia is both very common among those watching sport, and that this behaviour is affecting the safety of LGB people. Participants were first asked to identify the most likely sporting environment for homophobia to occur. Overall, 41 per cent of participants

199

identified spectator stands, which was nearly double the number who chose school physical education classes (21 per cent); the next most commonly selected was location. Interestingly, given the Nigel Owens incident, nearly half (49 per cent) of the participants from the UK (more than any other country) chose spectator stands as the most homophobic sporting environment.

A researcher from the study and senior lecturer in sports ethics, Dr Caroline Symons from Victoria University, said that while gay, lesbian and bisexual people were likely to experience a wide range of homophobic discrimination – particularly in team sports – the results showed that straight people also experienced homophobic attacks. 'The big message is there's still a lot we need to do in sport to make it more inclusive of gender and sexual diversity,' Symons said. She said some positive moves had been made, with peak Australian sporting bodies and high-profile players from rugby league, rugby union, cricket and soccer uniting in a campaign to confront homophobia in sport. 'It's challenging work,' Symons said, 'and it will actually take some resourcing, leadership, education programmes, social marketing programmes and conversations at the grassroots and elite sports levels to explore what clubs are doing well now in addressing homophobia in sport, and what needs to be changed.'

Source: adapted from: www.theguardian.com/sport/2014/jul/16/homophobia-sport-study-abuse-still-widespread and *Out on the fields: Research report into homophobia in sport*, commissioned by REPUCOM (Denison and Kitchen 2014).

Questions

1 Why do you think homophobic behaviour has a greater prevalence in sport than in society in general?
2 Do you consider the use of homophobic slurs by spectators aggressive behaviour, or should it just be considered part of sporting culture? Justify your position.
3 Do you feel it is the responsibility of sport enterprises to punish spectators for such behaviour? Why or why not?
4 If sport enterprises were to prosecute fans that use homophobic slurs, provide examples of what action could be taken.
5 What role can education, training and counselling of athletes play in the elimination of homophobia?
6 Identify strategies you might employ to reduce the negative consequences of homophobia in sport. For example, how would you prevent the Nigel Owens incident from reoccurring?
7 How would you describe your own personality type? Give examples to support you claim.
8 What can individuals and organizations do to reduce stress?
9 Some would argue that living in a large city such as London, Melbourne, New York or Paris creates stresses for employees that don't exist in smaller urban or rural communities. Do you agree or disagree with this statement? Provide reasons to support your claim.
10 Develop an anti-bullying policy for a sport organization.
11 Discuss why the level of workplace violence is increasing and the implications of this for sport managers.

Case exercise

In some cases coaches have used physical aggression towards players, and even injured them, in an attempt to improve their performance or demonstrate their displeasure with a performance. Perhaps the most publicized incident is the when Sir Alex Ferguson allegedly lost his temper resulting in England Captain David Beckham receiving a cut to his eye from a flying football boot. It may have been coincidence that Beckham subsequently left Manchester United for Real Madrid. Search for information about this case and identify the circumstances that led up to these actions occurring. Why do you feel Beckham was the recipient of Ferguson's alleged anger about the performance of the team? Explain why this type of behaviour seems to be tolerated in sport and not in other workplaces.

SUMMARY

This chapter discussed the effects of stress and aggression on the sport organization. The first part of the chapter focused on stress, beginning with an introduction to what constituted stress and aggression. Causes of stress were identified, leading to a discussion of how stress can be managed in the sport organization. The final part of the chapter focused on workplace aggression and described several types of aggression, including bullying, harassment and violence.

WEBSITE

CornerstoneOnDemand.com (n.d.) *Learning how to manage stress in the workplace*. Available from www.cornerstoneondemand.com/learning-how-manage-stress-workplace. See this site for insights into how to manage stress at work.

REFERENCES AND BIBLIOGRAPHY

Cobb. S. (1976). Social support as a moderator of life stress. *Psychosomatic Medicine*, 38, pp.300–314.

Denison, E. and Kitchen, A. (2014). *Out on the fields: Research report into homophobia in sport*. Commissioned by REPUCOM. Available from: www.outonthefields.com.

Gearing, N. (2012). Aggression in football. Retrieved from: http://believeperform.com/performance/aggression-in-football/.

Hellriegel, D. and Slocum, J.W. (2010). *Organizational behavior* (13th edn). Mason, OH: South-Western Centage Learning.

Homophobia and Sport. Adapted from: Davey, M. (2014). Homophobia in sport: Study reveals abuse still widespread. Adapted from: www.theguardian.com/sport/2014/jul/16/homophobia-sport-study-abuse-still-widespread.

Lalor, P. (2005). Sensitive ears are forcing coaches to find the bleep button. *The Week-end Australian*, 14/15 May, p.56.

Lussier, R.N. and Kimball, D.C. (2004). *Applied sport management skills*. Champaign, IL: Human Kinetics.

Pandey S. and Pestonjee, D.M. (2013). *Stress and work: Perspectives on understanding and managing stress*. London: Sage.

Chapter 18

Conflict management and resolution

OVERVIEW

This chapter defines and discusses organizational conflict within a sport enterprise setting. Three viewpoints on conflict are introduced: (1) traditional; (2) managed conflict; and (3) interactionist. The chapter then details the 'Conflict Process Model' that posturizes the intentions of conflict. Next, the sources of conflict are examined, with a discussion of contextual factors such as age, culture and gender leading to a discussion of conflict resolution. The chapter concludes with a discussion on organizational misbehaviour and how it can be managed in sport enterprises.

LEARNING OBJECTIVES

Having read the chapter, students will be able to:

1   Learn what constitutes organizational conflict;
2   Understand the Conflict Process Model, and the different conflict intentions of competing, collaborating, avoiding, accommodating and compromising;
3   Be able to identify antecedents of conflict and the contextual aspects relating to how conflict originates in sport enterprises;
4   Learn the various ways conflicts can be resolved or managed in sport enterprises; and
5   Understand the different types of misbehaviour, and how misbehaviour can be managed in sport enterprises.

WHAT IS CONFLICT?

Conflict is defined as a clash between individuals arising out of a difference in thought process, attitudes, understanding, interests, requirements and even sometimes perceptions. People tend to only see only the observable part of conflict – angry words and actions of opposition

– but this is only a small part of the conflict process (McShane and Glinow 2008). Although conflict can result in heated arguments, physical abuse, changes in relationships and a loss of organizational harmony, it is not always destructive. Whether conflict is functional or dysfunctional it tends to bring about group cohesion and the identification of leaders. The extent to which conflict is beneficial depends, to a large extent, on how it is managed. When conflict, however, becomes dysfunctional to the organization it needs to be resolved. 'Dispute resolution' is a term that refers to a number of processes that can be used to resolve a conflict

TRANSITIONS IN CONFLICT THOUGHT

The early approach to conflict assumed that all conflict was bad. Conflict was viewed negatively and it was used synonymously with such terms such as 'violence', 'destruction' and 'irrationality' to reinforce its negative connotation. Conflict, by definition, was harmful and was to be avoided. The traditional view was consistent with attitudes that prevailed about group behaviour in the 1930s and 1940s. Conflict was seen as a dysfunctional outcome resulting from poor communication, lack of openness and trust between people, and the failure of managers to be responsive to the needs and aspirations of their employees. The view that all conflict is bad certainly offers a simple approach to looking at the behaviour of people who create conflict. Since all conflict is to be avoided, we need merely direct our attention to the causes of conflict and correct these causes to improve group and organizational performance. Although research studies do not provide strong evidence to dispute that this approach to conflict reduction results in high group performance, many organizations still evaluate conflict situations using this outmoded standard. A managed-conflict or human relation view of conflict suggests that conflict is a natural and inevitable process in organizations. The interactionist view encourages conflict on the grounds that a harmonious, peaceful, tranquil and cooperative group is prone to becoming static, apathetic and non-responsive to the need for change and innovation. The major contribution of the interactionist view therefore is encouraging group leaders to maintain an ongoing minimum level of conflict, enough to keep the group viable, self-critical and creative. The interactionist view does not purpose that all conflicts are good. Rather, some conflicts support the goals of the group and improve its performance: these are functional constructive forms of conflict. In addition, there are conflicts that hinder group performance: these are dysfunctional or destructive forms of conflict (Robins *et al.* 2014).

To capture the conflict process Robins *et al.* (2014) conceptualized a 'Conflict Process Model' that comprises five stages. These stages are depicted in Figure 18.1.

Stage 1 is characterized by 'potential opposition or incompatibility' that can arise through antecedent conditions created by poor communication practices, that lead to misunderstandings, structural issues that create ambiguity or goal incompatibility, or personal variables as a result of different individual value systems or personality types. Stage 2 involves 'cognition and personalization', which can either lead to 'perceived conflict' (where one or more individuals or parties recognize conditions or opportunities for conflict are emerging) or 'felt conflict' (anxiety, frustration, hostility or tenseness created through emotional involvement in the conflict). Stage 3 is 'intentions', and this is where decisions are made to act in a particular way. Decisions are considered on a scale of dimensions ranging from

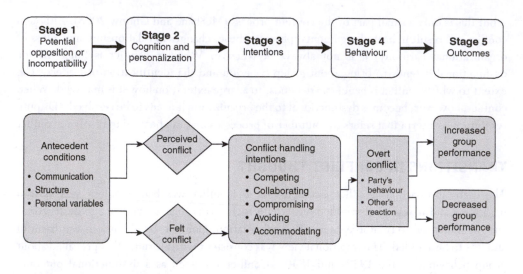

Figure 18.1 Conflict process

Source: Robins *et al.* (2014).

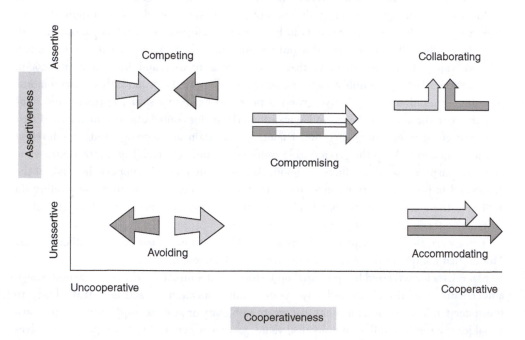

Figure 18.2 Conflict-management grid

Source: Robins *et al.* (2014).

cooperation (where there is an attempt to satisfy the concerns of the other party) through to assertiveness (where self-interest is considered in the sense of satisfying your own concerns).

Figure 18.2 identifies the dimensions and highlights conflict-handling intentions. 'Competing' refers to the desire to satisfy your own interests, regardless of the interests of others. 'Collaborating' is where the desires of all parties involved in the conflict are taken into account. 'Avoiding' is where the conflict is suppressed. 'Accommodating' is where one party involved in the conflict will place the opponents interests above their own. Finally, 'Compromising' is where each party is willing to sacrifice something.

Behaviour is Stage 4, and this is where conflict management comes into play. As conflict is not always seen as dysfunctional, techniques are used to achieve the desired level of conflict. This can vary from creating minor disagreements and misunderstandings to overt efforts to destroy the other party. Conflict-management techniques such as compromise, using independent adjudicators and appointing a devil's advocate are employed to find a solution. The final stage in the process is 'Outcomes'. The outcomes can be functional in that they improve group performance and the quality of decision-making. However, they can also be dysfunctional in that conflict produces group ineffectiveness and leads to the development of discontent. Part of this process involves creating functional conflict (low or moderate levels of conflict), as functional conflict has positive outcomes. This can be achieved through rewarding dissent and punishing those that avoid conflict.

CONTEXTUAL FACTORS OF CONFLICT

Sources of conflict in organizations can be the result of differences in people, personalities, values and goals. These can be produced by: 'age' – as we grow older our goals and value systems may change; 'gender' – women are more orientated to preserving relationships and achieve better outcomes than men when treating negotiations like problem-solving; and 'culture' – the way we negotiate stems from our cultural background. Organizations that are looking to cut costs may scale back on resources such as equipment, access to vehicles or reduce the spending limit on expense accounts. Employees may feel they are competing against each other for resources, which can create friction. Organizations that do not communicate effectively can create conflict; for example, providing unclear instructions to employees can create ambiguity and uncertainty, which can lead to conflict between management and employees.

CONFLICT RESOLUTION

Conflict-resolution approaches can be dependent on the outcome the organization is seeking. This can vary from win-win orientation to win-lose orientation. A problem-solving (win-win orientation) approach (also known as 'confronting') involves the conflicting parties meeting face to face and collaborating to reach an agreement that satisfies the concerns of both parties. This style involves open and direct communication, which should lead the way to solving the problem. Problem-solving should be used when both parties need to win, decrease costs and create a common power base, and skills are complementary, time is sufficient, trust is present and learning is the ultimate goal.

Forcing (win-lose orientation), also known as 'competing', 'controlling' or 'dominating', occurs when one party goes all out to win its position, while ignoring the needs and concerns of the other party. As the intensity of a conflict increases, the tendency for a forced conflict is more likely. This results in a win-lose situation, where one party wins at the expense of the other party. Forcing should be used when a 'do or die' situation is present. In these cases, stakes are high, important principles are at stake, the relationship among the parties is not important and a quick decision must be made.

Other approaches to conflict resolution include 'avoiding', 'yielding' and 'compromising'. Avoiding is also described as withdrawal style. This approach is viewed as postponing an issue for later, or withdrawing from the situation altogether. It is regarded as a temporary solution because the problem and conflict continue to reoccur over and over again. Avoiding should be used when you cannot win, stakes are low or high, but you are not prepared, there is a need to gain time or maintain neutrality or reputation, the problem will go away or you can win by delaying. Yielding is withdrawing to let the other party win. It can be very effective when there is recognition that the issue is much more important to the other party than to you, or where you want to gain allies. If the yield approach is used it is important to do so on the right issues, and before you become too committed to your own approach. Compromising, also described as a 'give and take' style, is when conflicting parties bargain to reach a mutually acceptable solution. Both parties give up something in order to reach a decision, and leave with some degree of satisfaction. Compromising should be used when both parties need to win, there is a deadlock, time is not sufficient, there is a desire to maintain the relationship among the involved parties, if you do not compromise there will be no positive outcome, and the stakes are moderate.

Finally, conflict resolution can involve third-party interventions. Mediation is an informal and non-aggressive forum for conflict resolution in which a third-party representative, known as a mediator, listens to both sides of the disagreement in a casual setting. Negotiation is distinguished from mediation in that it does not involve the use of a third party. Negotiation is the most common form of self-help for conflict management in the workplace. This is why negotiation training is an effective option for conflict management in the workplace. Well-trained individuals are better able to resolve their own conflicts through negotiation, and thus avoid the need for other options. Interest-based negotiating focuses on the interests of the parties. The participants state their interests, explore the interests of the other party and seek to problem-solve by inventing options that will satisfy both parties' interests. This form of negotiation is focused on the problem at hand and not on victory over the other party. Lastly, arbitration is a private and informal adjudicatory process similar to a court. The Arbitrator makes a decision that is legally binding and enforceable upon the parties. The hearing is much less formal in procedure than a court, but each party has the right to present proof and arguments as in a court of law. In arbitration the disputants give up the power to create their own solution and place resolution of their problem in the hands of the Arbitrator.

MANAGING MISBEHAVIOUR

The seriousness of athlete misbehaviour (e.g. abuse of women, excessive alcohol consumption, recreational drug use, match-fixing and gambling) and the unsatisfactory way it is often handled by sport administrators, has resulted in athlete misbehaviour receiving considerable publicity, and has incited community debate on appropriate athlete behaviour. Misbehaviour is damaging to the business of sport, harming not only the public image of the athlete, but also the reputation of the associated sport, league, club and sponsors. Athlete misbehaviour is not only an issue for elite sport; community-level sport also suffers from player misbehaviour on and off the field. Inappropriate behaviour, such as physical violence, racial comments and socially degrading activities, pervades community-level sport, damaging sport participation and life-long engagement in sporting activities (Fields *et al.* 2010). Sport managers also often face problem

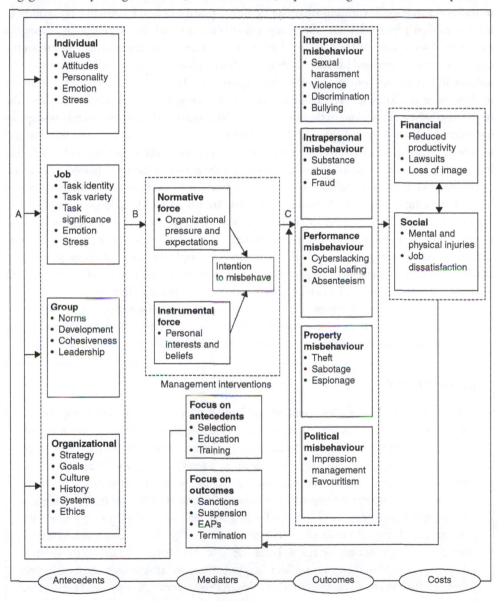

Figure 18.3 Model of organizational misbehaviour

Source: Managing Misbehaviour (n.d.)

behaviours in the work setting that must be solved to prevent additional negative consequences. It is therefore necessary that sport organizations understand how to manage misbehaviour, and that sport managers are responsible for identifying, solving and correcting problems.

Figure 18.3 identifies four types of antecedents to misbehaviour: (1) individual; (2) job; (3) group; and (4) organizational. An example is when an individual believes they are being treated unfairly by management; this may act as the impetus for the individual to misbehave. If others within the organization believe that the person has been treated unfairly they also may decide to misbehave. Intentional work misbehaviour by an individual can lead to negative consequences for the person (dissatisfaction), the group (dissatisfaction) and the organization, owing to increased absenteeism. At the core of the model is the intention to misbehave. This means the behaviour is purposeful and can have detrimental effects (financially and socially) not only on the individual, but also on colleagues within the organization. This purposeful action that leads to misbehaviour mediates the relationship between the antecedents of misbehaviour and the outcomes that are expressions of the misbehaviour. Normative and instrumental forces shape an individual's intention to misbehaviour. Normative forces relate to how the individual is meant to behave, whereas instrumental forces relate to the personal interests, actions and beliefs that influence an individual's intention to misbehave, and the nature of the misbehaviour they chose to exhibit. Examples of misbehaviours (outcomes) are varied, and Figure 18.2 identifies five of these. For example, the 2015 Volkswagen scandal, known as the 'diesel dupe', could lead to significant financial costs to the organization (compensation), cost to management (loss of career) and cost to employees (loss of jobs owing to a reduction in production), as well as substantial social costs (anxiety and depression among employees over potential job losses). Finally, managers engage in management interventions to prevent, restrict or respond to misbehaviour. Managers can focus on careful screening and refusal to hire risky individuals, or shift from prevention to deterrence by focusing on sanctions, suspensions or terminations. These intervention practices offer managers different opportunities to reduce the incidence, consequences or costs of misbehaviour (Managing Misbehavior 2016).

CASE STUDY

Sport seems to be a place where conflicts and disputes occur frequently, especially when its intensity and diversity increase as sport becomes more professionalized and internationalized. The Olympic Games has been at the centre of many conflicts relating to racial discrimination (Jesse Owens), religious conflict (1972 Munich Games) and gender bias (leadership appointments). The Olympic Games has also endured through numerous wars.

To peaceful principles the International Olympic Committee (IOC) has been encouraging each Olympic Games host city to embrace the meaning and spirit of the Olympic Truce in the planning and staging of the Games. The tradition of the Olympic Truce dates back to the ninth century BC, in Ancient Greece. A Truce was announced before and during the Olympic Games to ensure the host city was not attacked, so athletes and spectators could travel safely to the Games and return peacefully to their respective countries. During the Truce period (lasting up to three months), wars were suspended, armies were prohibited from threatening the Games, legal disputes were stopped and the death penalty was forbidden.

In 1992, as an idea to protect the interests of the athletes and sport in general the IOC revived this concept. It was hoped that countries would be inspired by Truce to use sport or culture to promote conflict resolution, reconciliation and peace. Countries carried out initiatives in line with the principles of Truce: for example, during the Opening Ceremony of the 2000 Sydney Games, South- and North-Korean delegations walked in the stadium together, under the same flag. It was the first Olympic Games event where the two divided countries walked side by side. In the 2004 Athens Games, the Olympic Truce was promoted through the Olympic Flame Relay events. During the 2006 Turin Winter Games, athletes and officials showed support for the Olympic Truce by signing one of the three walls situated in the three Olympic Villages (Turin, Sestriere and Bardonecchia). During the 2010 Vancouver Winter Games, Truce projects were carried out as an open invitation for people to 'Make Your Peace', that asked individuals to create everyday peace at home, schools, work and in the community.

In 2015, on behalf of Olympic Movement and Brazil, the Rio 2016 Organizing Committee for the Olympic and Paralympic Games, led by its President, Carlos Nuzman, presented the Olympic Truce Resolution, entitled *Building a Peaceful and Better World through Sport and the Olympic Ideal*, to the United Nations General Assembly. At the Assembly, IOC President Bach appealed for help from member nations to identify top-level athletes, who were currently refugees. Despite having no national team to belong to, no flag to march behind, no national anthem to be played, these refugee athletes were welcomed to the Olympic Games with the Olympic Flag and with the Olympic Anthem.

Source: adapted from: www.olympic.org/olympic-truce and www.rio2016.com/en/
news/180-countries-co-sponsor-rio-2016-olympic-truce-at-un-general-assembly

Questions

1   Research the Jessie Owens incident of the Berlin Olympic Games and discuss how the IOC might have addressed this issue differently.
2   Why is it important for countries to promote the idea of 'Olympic Truce'?
3   Is the Olympic Truce just idealism or can its principles play a role in conflict resolution more broadly?
4   Sport is a place where conflict can occur and yet it can play a role in facilitating peace. Discuss this paradox and the reasons for it.
5   Name, discuss and contrast three views on conflict.
6   What is the difference between functional and dysfunctional conflict?
7   In what situations might conflict be beneficial to the group? Provide an example that is applicable to a sporting organization.
8   Discuss how a sport manager might create dysfunctional conflict in their department, as well as functional conflict.
9   Identify any misbehaviours that are likely to damage the image and the reputation of a sport organization.

Case exercise

Go to the Sport for Development webpage (www.sportanddev.org). Explore the page and identify the different projects in which the organization is involved. What role does the organization see for sport in peace-building and conflict resolution? Can you provide examples of how sport is used in peace-building and conflict resolution?

SUMMARY

This chapter discussed organizational conflict. Three viewpoints to conflict were introduced: (1) traditional; (2) managed conflict; and (3) interactionist. The chapter then detailed the 'Conflict Process Model' that posturizes the intentions of conflict. Next, the sources of conflict were examined, with a discussion of contextual factors such as age, culture and gender, leading to a discussion of conflict resolution. The chapter concluded with a discussion on organizational misbehaviour and its management.

WEBSITE

MindTools.com (n.d.) *Conflict Resolution: Using an Interest Based Relational Approach.* Available from: www.mindtools.com/pages/article/newLDR_81.htm. See this site for understanding approaches to conflict resolution.

REFERENCES AND BIBLIOGRAPHY

Afzalur Rahim, M. (2001). *Managing conflict in organizations.* London: Quorum Books.
Fields, S., Collins, C. and Comstock, R. (2010). Violence in youth sports: Hazing, brawling and foul play. *British Medical Journal*, 44, p.32.
Managing Misbehavior (n.d.). Retrieved from www.mheducation.com.
Olympic Truce. *Peace and the Olympic Games.* Source: adapted from: www.olympic.org/olympic-truce and www.rio2016.com/en/news/180-countries-co-sponsor-rio-2016-olympic-truce-at-un-general-assembly.
Robins, S.P., Judge, T.A., Millet, B. and Boyle, M. (2014). *Organisational behavior* (7th edn). Frenchs Forest, NSW, Australia: Pearson.

Part F

Power, control and change

Chapter 19

Power and politics

OVERVIEW

This chapter examines the concepts of power, politics and influence, and how they shape decision-making processes in sport enterprises. A distinction is made between hard coercive power, on the one hand, and soft influence-based power on the other. This leads into a discussion of the distribution of power in sport enterprises, and the strengths and weaknesses of centralized power arrangements and diffused power relations.

LEARNING OBJECTIVES

Having reflected closely on the theory and cases contained in this chapter, readers will be able to:

1   Explain how power is secured, and how it can be used to achieve personal, group and organizational goals;
2   Identify the centres of power in sport enterprises;
3   Explain the difference between hard and soft power;
4   Explain the difference between formal power and informal power; and
5   Identify and the strengths and weakness of centralized power arrangements, on the one hand, and diffused power settings on the other.

MAKING THINGS HAPPEN

Managers are always having to 'take staff with them', to ensure they are enthusiastically committed to the organization's mission, vision and goals. There are different ways of doing this, and unsurprisingly, there are hard ways and there are soft ways. In some cases, staff may have to be pushed and prodded, but in other instances, they may well be already 'out in front' and, with some gentle reassurance, energetically take the initiative. But, no matter what the situation, and no matter what the service being delivered, managers are expected to 'set the tone', and, one way or another, make sure staff are working towards the core organizational goals, and making things happen without too much fuss, dissent, disruption or trauma.

The capacity to make things happen and to secure the compliance of others in making it happen, is all about power. It is sometimes claimed that power is essentially about coercing people to act in ways you want them to. In other words, if they do not comply with your instructions they will be punished in one form or another. The punishment can be mild or it can be severe. Mild punishments include public shaming, whereas severe punishments can involve demotion, a fall in pay or dismissal. However, power is more than the ability to make threats and take away privileges.

DOES REAL POWER ONLY COME OUT OF THE BARREL OF A GUN?

Power does, in many instances, come from the capacity to punish, but it is far more complex than the above question implies. There are, as it turns out, a number of crucial questions to ask when looking at power in the sport enterprise workplace. First, what is it? Second, how can it be secured? And third, how can it be wielded or applied?

First and foremost, power is all about the capacity to influence others, mobilize resources, 'get one's way', overcome opposition and even resist people in authority in some cases. And as for securing and accumulating power, it comes out of many sources, including one's position in the hierarchy, the knowledge one has, one's personal presence and social standing, one's level of expertise, one's capacity to reward or punish and finally, one's persuasive abilities. In order to come to grips with the notion of power, and to better understand its application in sport enterprises, it is well worth exploring French and Raven's model of the five sources of power. Their model was constructed in 1959, but has stood the test of time. French and Raven's model of power can be explained in terms of five sources. Three of these sources come from one's position in the organization, while the other two arise from one's personal qualities.

POSITIONAL POWER SOURCES

Legitimate power

A prime minister has power and so does a monarch. Prince Charles is powerful, but is limited when contrasted with the influence exerted by his mother Queen Elizabeth II. The CEO of a bank has power and so do a doctor, a lawyer, a leisure-centre manager, a sports coach and an aerobics instructor. People holding these formal, official positions – or job titles – typically have power. Social hierarchies, cultural norms and organizational structure all provide the basis for legitimate power. This type of power, however, can be unpredictable and unstable. If you lose the title or position, legitimate power can instantly disappear, since others were influenced by the position and not you alone. Also, your scope of power is limited to situations that others believe you have a right to control; that is, you have legitimacy, but it is also situational. If a fire officer tells people to stay away from a burning building, they'll probably listen, but if he tries to make people stay away from a fight outside a sports stadium, people may well ignore him.

Reward power

People in power are often able to give out rewards. In organizational settings, promotions, pay rises, desirable assignments, training opportunities and even simple compliments like a pat on the back or a certificate of recognition, can be used to reward employees. If others expect that you'll reward them for doing what you want, there's a high probability that they'll do it. The problem with this basis of power is that you may not have as much control over rewards as you would like. Supervisors, for instance, don't have complete control over salary increases, and managers often can't control staff promotion opportunities. Even a CEO needs permission from the Board of Directors for some actions. So when you use up available rewards, or the rewards don't have enough perceived value to others, your power weakens. One of the frustrations of using rewards is that they often need to be bigger each time if they're to have the same motivational impact. Additionally, if rewards are given frequently, people can become satiated, and as a result, they lose their effectiveness.

Coercive power

This source of power is blunt, but is often very effective and it comes at a cost. It is frequently problematic and can be subject to abuse when managers become wrapped up in their own self-importance and need to not only be in charge, but also to be seen to be in charge. What's more, it can cause dysfunctional behaviour and dissatisfaction in the workplace. Threats and punishment are common tools of coercion. Implying or threatening that someone will be fired, demoted, denied privileges or given undesirable assignments are all examples of using coercive power. In sport, the threat of demotion to a lower grade of competition is especially threatening. Whereas your position may give you the capability to coerce others, it doesn't automatically mean that you have the will or the justification to do so. As a last resort, you may sometimes need to punish people, with public humiliation and the threat of dismissal being prime examples. However, extensive use of coercive power is rarely appropriate in any organizational setting. It is the worst thing to apply to volunteers, since they can just walk away and not return. It then becomes your loss and your problem.

Relying on the above power types – the positional sources of power – will only get people so far. It might work in the short term, but it can often result in a very cold, technocratic, impoverished style of leadership. To be a really effective manager, or true leader, you need a more robust source of power than the one supplied by a formal title, an ability to reward or the capability to punish. So, what else is there? Well, there are two additional important sources of power that go under the heading of 'personal sources of power'.

PERSONAL POWER SOURCES

Expert power

When you have knowledge and skills that enable you to understand a situation, suggest solutions, use solid judgement and generally impact on others, people will probably listen to you. When you demonstrate expertise, people tend to trust you and respect what you say. As a subject-matter expert, your ideas will have more value and others will look to you for leadership in that area. What's more, you can take your confidence, decisiveness and reputation for rational thinking and expand them to other subjects and issues. This is a good way to build and maintain expert power. It doesn't require positional power, so you can use it to go beyond that. This is one of the best ways to improve your management authority, your leadership skill and generally shape the conduct of others in positive ways.

Referent power

This is sometimes thought of as charisma, charm, admiration or appeal. Referent power comes from one person liking and respecting another, and identifying strongly with that person in some way. Celebrities have referent power, which is why they can influence everything from what people buy to who they elect to political office. In a workplace, a person with charm – which means a rich supply of emotional labour – can interact with other staff more effectively, make others feel more comfortable and confident, and in general have a significant amount of influence over the motivation and morale of others. Referent power brings with it big responsibilities, since it can be abused quite easily. Someone who is likeable but lacks integrity and honesty, may rise to power and use that power to hurt and alienate people, as well as gain personal advantage. Relying on referent power alone is therefore not a good strategy for a leader who wants longevity and respect. Referent power is common in sport enterprises, where charisma and forceful personalities can take up lots of organizational space. When combined with other sources of power, it can help you achieve very effective outcomes.

MANAGING POWER

The above discussion begs the question of what can or should be done with power when one has it. Ideally, power should be used to make things happen, and to get people to commit themselves to a task or programme. In this sense power is needed to actually deliver a range of services to people, to run an event, hire more staff, or even take away points from an affiliated or member club that breaks the rules. So, power is not just about getting others to obey your instructions, it is also about using your influence to achieve a good outcome for your association, club or team.

But power can also create problems when used indiscriminately, or without thinking, through the implications of its use. A short-run decision to impose rigid controls on wages despite a legitimate claim for a pay rise may be effective in the short run, but be a disaster in the long run. Power can also lead to conflict, since a person with legitimate or hierarchical power – for instance, the CEO – may have to deal with the influence exerted by another senior staff member, like the Chief Legal Officer, for example. In sport this is likely to happen when looking at some copyright, branding, intellectual property, restrictive trade practice or salary cap issues. Whose view then becomes the catalyst for action? Negotiation and mediation then become critical skills for securing agreement on one or more of the above vexing issues.

Thus, power is a crucial tool for sport enterprise managers. It can be used to constrain, exclude, dispossess and even repress, but it can also be used to enable, incentivize, initiate and motivate. And, to repeat, power comes from a number of sources, which include one's:

- Position in the social or organizational hierarchy;
- Knowledge;
- Personal presence and social standing;
- Level of expertise;
- Capacity to reward or punish; and
- Persuasive abilities.

The other crucial aspect of power is that it is integral to effective leadership. At the same time, good leadership involves the selective use of power. For example, power can be coercive, which means that threats, sanctions and penalties are used to get people to do what you would like them to do. However, good and effective leadership is not usually coercive, since it is all about taking people with you and inspiring people to act under your watch. So, good leadership means that people are prepared to follow you because they think you are right, and because you are so inspirational that whatever you suggest is the only reasonable thing to do. Good leaders also have followers who are prepared to commit themselves to the leader's directions. Additionally, good leaders often involve the followers in the decision-making process, which leads to a spread of power to others.

POWER AND POLITICS

Power and politics come together when sport enterprise managers deal with stakeholders, be they staff demanding an improvement in health and safety standards, suppliers seeking an exclusive purchasing arrangement, or a business firm seeking a partnership agreement. It is rare that one side has complete power over the other, and thus negotiation may be required to reach a mutually satisfactory outcome. This issue is covered in more detail in Chapter 20. Additionally, power is often very situational, which means that whereas you may have a fair bit of clout in one negotiation situation, you may not have any in another. Your sport club may be able to secure a good sponsor because of your strong community profile, but you may not be able to secure the best recruits because other clubs have more financial resources. Also, your level of power is often influenced by perceptions, and you can consequently diminish the power of another when you refuse to acknowledge it. Furthermore, although your actual power may be minimal, creating a perception of power enables you to command more influence over the negotiation's outcome.

However, sport enterprise managers with a strong power base need to be cautious about throwing their weight around unnecessarily. It can damage business relationships and diminish the reputation of the enterprise. It should also be remembered that the balance of power can shift back and forth during the course of any stakeholder negotiation, and that as a result, power should be used prudently to secure an agreement. The heavy use of coercive power, for instance, might secure compliance, but it is unlikely to deliver a comfortable or stable agreement.

CASE STUDY

In every organization and every sporting enterprise, there will be some people with significant amounts of power and influence and other people with very little power and influence. This begs the following questions. First, what is it that allows some individuals to build up a strong base of power and influence? Second, is it appropriate to have a skewed distribution of influence, or should it be spread equally across the organization? The short answer is that power has many sources and, especially in sport enterprises, power is inevitably spread unequally. This unequal spread of power means that things get done with a minimum of fuss, but it also means that this power can be abused and used to deliver benefits for a select few, rather than the whole.

Take, for example, the recent experiences of a large national governing body for elite swimming associations and clubs. Having just gone through a massive restructuring process in response to poor international performances, it was ready to reassert itself and rebuild the nation's international swimming capability in elite international competitions. The senior management positions were reviewed and new appointments were made for not only the CEO's position, but also for four core operating departments. These operating departments were:

- Administration and financial services;
- Marketing, public relations (PR) and corporate partnerships;
- Team management; and
- Coaching and conditioning.

Veronica Vortex was the new CEO. She was an inexperienced manager, but had enormous experience as a competitive swimmer, having won three gold medals in two Olympic Games. Her appointment was an experiment in part, since her management qualities were relatively underdeveloped. However, she was highly articulate and had highly developed social skills. She was well-liked by everybody and rarely had a harsh word to say, even when under severe stress.

The new management appointment for Marketing, PR and Corporate Partnerships was Wayne Workhorse. Wayne was very experienced, but unlike Veronica had little empathy for anyone he viewed as inferior. He also believed that the key to any successful organization, especially when it came to the sport sector, was the capacity to build partnerships with not only Government and its agencies, but also with the corporate sector. Wayne consistently argued the case for additional staff on the grounds that image was everything, and that the stronger the brand, the more successful the organizational outcome. Wayne was also committed to maximizing spending on the grounds that the more resources you could accumulate, the more successful you would be.

This view was shared by Gavin Goodluck, the manager of the Coaching and Conditioning department, who believed that swimmers were only as good as the coaches supervising them. He also argued that you only got good coaches if you paid them good money. Gavin, like

Wayne, was very experienced, having spent five years coaching the USA national swimming squad to many international successes. Gavin had a very strong background in sports science and used this significant base of expertise to shape the training and conditioning programmes of the national swimming team.

The manager of the Administration and Financial Services was Neville Noshow. Neville, was an experienced accountant and was highly competent. His budgeting skills were legendary and he had a commitment to controlling spending and operating within strict financial constraints. But, unlike Wayne and Gavin, he adopted a very low profile and, additionally unlike them, had minimal charismatic leadership qualities. Neville was conscientious and consultative, but he rarely left his office. He thus occupied minimal organizational space, so to speak.

Beryl Backstroke was the team manager. Like Neville, she was highly competent but generally felt more comfortable taking rather than giving orders.

Questions

1   In reflecting on this case, what types of power appear to be important to each of the five people described above?
2   Who do you think is the most powerful of the five staff? Why?
3   Who is the least powerful? Why?
4   How would you describe the distribution of power and influence in this organization?
5   When thinking about the politics of this sporting enterprise, which of the five staff is most likely to use their power base to act in their own special interest?
6   If you were asked to provide advice on the distribution of power among the senior management team of this national governing body for swimming, how might you reorganize the distribution of power to ensure the optimal performance of the sport enterprise? Remember, sport enterprises, like any other organization, need to develop their sporting aspirations against the need to be financially sustainable.

Case exercise

Take a look at the website for the International Cricket Council (ICC); the international governing body for cricket (www.icc-cricket.com). Pay particular attention to the organizational chart and the additional discussion on the roles of the different functional divisions, and the responsibilities of the senior management team. Then, see what you can find out about the background, professional experience and qualifications of the senior management team. So, who wields power and what underpins it? And what has enactment of this power achieved for the ICC?

SUMMARY

This chapter examined the concepts of power, politics and influence, and how they shape the decision-making process in sport enterprises. A distinction was made between hard coercive power on the one hand, and soft influence-based power on the other. This provided the lead into a discussion of the distribution of power in organizations, and the strengths and weaknesses of centralized power arrangements and diffused power relations. The chapter ended with a discussion of the relationship between power and politics, and the tension between politics as a means to promote oneself and politics as a means to promote the interests of the enterprise.

WEBSITE

Bolander, J. (2011). *How to deal with organizational politics.* Available from: www.thedailymba. com/2011/02/28/how-to-deal-with-organizational-politics/. See this site for additional information on the dynamics of organizational politics.

REFERENCES AND BIBLIOGRAPHY

Buchanan, D. and Badham, R. (2008). *Power, politics, and organizational change.* Los Angeles, CA: Sage.

French, J. and Raven, B. (1959). The bases of social power. In D. Cartwright (ed.) *Studies in social power,* (pp.150–167). Ann Arbor, MI: Institute for Social Research.

Ivancevich, J., Konopaske, R. and Matteson, M. (2014). *Organizational behavior and management* (10th edn). New York: McGraw-Hill/Irwin.

Pfeffer, J. (1992). *Managing with power: Politics and influence in organizations.* Boston, MA: Harvard Business School Press.

Robbins, S. and Judge, T. (2012). *Essentials of organizational behaviour* (15th edn). Upper Saddle River, NJ: Prentice Hall.

Chapter 20

Bargaining and negotiation

OVERVIEW

This chapter examines the ways in which bargaining and negotiation can be used to both resolve disputes and problems, and enhance the overall performance of sport enterprises. The symbolic and commercial logic behind the negotiation process is examined, together with the complex psychological and interpersonal conduct that underpins the interaction of the participants.

LEARNING OBJECTIVES

After engaging critically with this chapter, students will be able to:

1   Understand the theory and principles that underpin bargaining and negotiation processes;
2   Identify the range of sport enterprise operations that involve bargaining and negotiation;
3   Explain what is meant by a zero-sum game view of bargaining and negotiation;
4   Explain what is meant by a win-win view of bargaining and negotiation; and
5   Design a sport enterprise-based bargaining and negotiation model that allows for a win-win outcome.

WHY NEGOTIATE?

In simple terms, negotiation is a discussion between two or more disputants who are trying to work out a solution to problems of mutual concern. This intergroup process can occur at a personal level, as well as at a corporate (intra-organizational) or international (diplomatic) level. Negotiations typically take place because the parties wish to create something new that neither could do on their own, or to resolve a problem or dispute between them. The parties acknowledge that there is some conflict of interest between them and think they can use some form of influence to get a better deal, rather than simply taking what the other side will give them voluntarily. They prefer to search for agreement rather than fight openly, give in or break off a previously beneficial relationship.

When parties negotiate, they usually expect some level of give and take. Although they have interlocking goals that they cannot accomplish independently, they do not usually want or need exactly the same thing. This interdependence can be either win-lose or win-win in nature, and the type of negotiation that is appropriate will vary accordingly. Disputants may want to force the other side to comply with their demands, modify the opposing position and move towards compromise, or invent a solution that meets the objectives of all sides.

Mutual adjustment is a core feature of negotiation processes. Both parties know that they can influence the other's outcomes and that the other side can influence theirs. The effective negotiator attempts to understand how people will adjust and readjust their positions during negotiations, based on what the other party does and is expected to do. The parties have to exchange information and make an effort to influence each other. As negotiations evolve, each side proposes changes to the other party's position and makes changes to its own. This process of give and take and making concessions is necessary if a settlement is to be reached. If one party makes several proposals that are rejected, and the other party makes no alternate proposal, the first party may break off negotiations. Parties typically will not want to concede too much if they do not sense that those with whom they are negotiating are willing to compromise.

NEGOTIATING PRINCIPLES

Negotiation can take many forms. A good starting point is to distinguish between positional bargaining – which is competitive – and interest-based 'principled negotiation' – which is primarily cooperative. But they also make the distinction among soft, hard and principled negotiation, the latter of which is neither soft, nor hard, but based on cooperative principles which look out for oneself as well as one's opponent. The factors that determine whether an individual will approach a conflict cooperatively or competitively are first, the nature of the dispute, and second, the goals each side seeks to achieve. Often the two sides' goals are linked together or interdependent. The parties' interaction will be shaped by whether this interdependence is positive or negative.

Goals with positive interdependence are tied together in such a way that the chance of one side attaining its goal is increased by the other side attaining its goal. Positively interdependent goals normally result in cooperative approaches to negotiation, because any participant can attain their goal if, and only if, the others with whom they are linked can attain their goals. On the other hand, negative interdependence means the chance of one side attaining its goal is decreased by the other's success. Negatively interdependent goals force competitive situations, because the only way for one side to achieve its goals and 'win' is for the other side to 'lose'.

Typically, negotiations also involve either creating or claiming value. First, the negotiators work cooperatively to create value; that is, 'enlarge the pie'. But, then they must use competitive processes to claim value; that is, 'divide up the pie'. However, a tension exists between creating and claiming value. This is because the competitive strategies used to claim value tend to undermine cooperation, whereas a cooperative approach makes one vulnerable to competitive bargaining tactics. The tension that exists between cooperation and competition in negotiation is known as 'the Negotiator's Dilemma', which assumes that:

- If both sides cooperate, they will both have good outcomes;
- If one cooperates and the other competes, the cooperator will get a terrible outcome and the competitor will get a great outcome;
- If both compete, they will both have mediocre outcomes;
- In the face of uncertainty about what strategy the other side will adopt, each side's best choice is to compete;
- However, if they both compete, both sides end up worse off.

In real life, parties can communicate and commit themselves to a cooperative approach. They can also adopt norms of fair and cooperative behaviour and focus on their future relationship. This fosters a cooperative approach between both parties and helps them to find joint gains.

PLANNING FOR NEGOTIATIONS

Effective planning is crucial to meeting negotiation objectives. If the parties are to reach a stable agreement, specific events must take place before the parties ever come to the table. The following nine-point plan provides a succinct operational template for a negotiation process that is both efficient and effective.

1   Parties must frame the problem and recognize that they have a common problem, which they share an interest in solving. Frames are the conceptions that parties have of the situation and its risks. They allow the parties to begin to develop a shared definition of the issues involved and the process needed to resolve them. When the frames of both parties match, they are more likely to focus on common issues and have a common definition of the situation. However, when the frames do not match, communication between the parties is likely to be more difficult. Unless the different outlooks on the problem begin to overlap, it is unlikely that negotiations will be successful. If negotiators understand what frame they are operating from and what frame the other is operating from, they may be able to shift the conversation and develop common definitions. The way in which parties define the problem can shape the rest of the planning process.

2   In the early stages of framing, negotiators must also determine their goals, anticipate what they want to achieve, and prepare for the negotiation process. They must define the issues to be discussed and analyse the conflict situation. In many cases, negotiators can appeal to research, or consult experts to help them develop a complete list of the issues at stake. Next, parties should assemble all the issues that have been defined into a comprehensive list. The combined list of issues and priorities from each side determines the negotiation agenda.

3   Negotiators may negotiate the list of issues to be discussed in advance. Consultation between negotiators prior to actual negotiation allows them to agree on the agenda of issues to be discussed, as well as the location of the negotiations, the time and duration

of the sessions, the parties to be involved in the negotiations, and techniques to pursue if negotiation fails. Negotiators should also agree on principles that will guide the drafting of a settlement, the procedures to be used in negotiations and the formula by which a general agreement is to be reached. Discussions about these procedural issues are often crucial for the success of substantive negotiations. If parties cannot agree on negotiation procedures and proposed items for the agenda, they may decide to abandon negotiations.

4   After assembling issues on an agenda, the negotiators must prioritize their goals and evaluate the possible trade-offs among them. Negotiators must be aware of their goals and positions and must identify the concerns, desires and fears that underlie their substantive goals. They must determine which issues are most important, as well as whether the various issues are linked or separate. In addition, negotiators should be aware of the underlying interests and goals of the other side. As the linkages between parties' goals often define the issue to be settled, these goals must be determined carefully. If one party wants more than the other party is capable or willing to give, the disputants must either change their goals or end the negotiation.

5   Once they have determined the relative importance of the issues, parties need to decide the order in which issues should be discussed. Many sequencing options are possible: going from easy to hard, hard to easy, or tackling everything together. Different situations suggest different answers to that question, and different negotiators and mediators prefer one approach over the others.

6   Negotiators will set specific targets with respect to the key issues on the agenda. Parties should try to figure out the best resolution they can expect, what counts as a fair and reasonable deal and what is a minimally acceptable deal. They should also be aware of the strongest points in their position and recognize the strongest points in the other side's position. This enables parties to be aware of the range of possible outcomes and to be flexible in what they will accept. It also improves the likelihood that they will arrive at a mutually satisfactory outcome.

7   Since negotiations typically involve more than one issue, it is helpful for negotiators to anticipate different ways of packaging issues. They can balance the issues they regard as most important by being more flexible about items they deem less important. They should also decide which items they can abandon and use as leverage to get what they really want, with respect to the most important issues.

8   Planning for negotiation also involves the development of supporting arguments. Negotiators must be able to present supporting facts and arguments, anticipate how the other side will respond to these arguments, and respond to the other party's claims with counter-arguments. This includes locating facts to support one's point of view, determining what sorts of arguments have been given in similar negotiations in the past, anticipating the arguments the other side is likely to make, and presenting facts in the most convincing way possible.

9   Planning involves assessing the other party's priorities and interests, and trying to get a better idea of what that party is likely to want. Negotiators should gather background information about the other party's current needs, resources and interests. This can be done through preliminary consultations with those who have done business with the other party in the past. In addition, negotiators need to understand the other party's

objectives. Professional negotiators will often exchange information about targets or initial proposals before negotiations begin. Negotiators should be aware of the other party's negotiation style and reputation, as well as the strategy and tactics they commonly use. They should investigate that party's past behaviour in related settings, determine their organizational position, and find out who they admire and whose advice carries weight. An individual's past negotiation behaviour is a good indication of how they will behave in the future. Negotiators should understand the other party's alternatives. If the other negotiator has strong alternatives, they will probably be willing to set high objectives and be willing to push hard for these objectives during negotiation.

OBSTACLES TO NEGOTIATION

In difficult-to-manage conflicts, removing the obstacles to negotiation is a critical first step in moving towards negotiated agreements. Sometimes people fail to negotiate because they do not recognize that they are in a bargaining position. They may fail to identify a good opportunity for negotiation, and may use other options that do not allow them to manage their problems as effectively. Or, they may recognize the need for bargaining, but may bargain poorly because they do not fully understand the process and lack good negotiating skills.

In cases of intractable conflict, parties often will not recognize each other, talk with each other nor commit themselves to the process of negotiation. They may even feel committed, as a matter of principle, not to negotiate with an adversary. In such cases, getting parties to participate in negotiations is a very challenging process. In addition, both parties must be ready to negotiate if the process is to succeed. If efforts to negotiate are initiated too early, before both sides are ready, they are likely to fail. Then the conflict may not be open to negotiation again for a long time.

Before they negotiate, parties must be aware of their alternatives to a negotiated settlement. They must believe that a negotiated solution would be preferable to continuing the current situation, that a fair settlement can be reached and that the balance of forces permits such an agreement. This is underpinned by the belief that there is a way out of the problem, and also that a mutually beneficial outcome is waiting to be secured. Weaker parties must feel assured that they will not be overpowered in a negotiation, and parties must trust that their needs and interests will be considered fairly in the negotiation process.

In many cases, conflicts become ripe for negotiation when both sides realize that they cannot get what they want through a power struggle, and that they have reached a damaging stalemate. If the parties believe that their ideal solution is not available and that foreseeable settlement is better than the other available alternatives, the parties have a zone of possible agreement (ZOPA). This means that a potential agreement exists that would benefit both sides more than their alternatives would.

However, it may take some time to determine whether a ZOPA exists. The parties must first explore their various interests, options and alternatives. If the disputants can identify their ZOPA, there is a good chance that they will come to an agreement. But if they cannot, negotiation is very unlikely to succeed. In addition, each side must believe that the other side is willing to compromise. If the parties regard each other with suspicion and mistrust, they may conclude that the other side is not committed to the negotiation process and may withdraw.

225

When there is little trust between the negotiators, making concessions is not easy. First, there is the dilemma of honesty. On one hand, telling the other party everything about your situation may give that person an opportunity to take advantage of you. However, not telling the other person anything may lead to a stalemate. The dilemma of trust concerns how much you should believe of what the other party tells you. If you believe everything a person says, then they could take advantage of you. But if you believe nothing the other person says, then reaching an agreement will be very difficult. The search for an optimal solution is aided greatly if parties trust each other and believe that they are being treated honestly and fairly.

In many cases, the negotiators' relationship becomes entangled with the substantive issues under discussion. Any misunderstanding that arises between them will reinforce their prejudices and arouse their emotions. When conflict escalates, negotiations may take on an atmosphere of anger, frustration, distrust and hostility. If parties believe that the fulfilment of their basic needs is threatened, they may begin to blame each other and may break off communication. As the issue becomes more personalized, perceived differences are magnified and cooperation becomes unlikely. If each side becomes locked into its initial position and attempts to force the other side to comply with various demands, this hostility may prevent negotiators from reaching agreement or making headway towards a settlement.

To combat perceptual bias and hostility, negotiators should attempt to gain a better understanding of the other party's perspective, and try to see the situation as the other side sees it. In some cases, parties can discuss each other's perceptions, making a point to refrain from blaming the other. In addition, they can look for opportunities to act in a manner that is inconsistent with the other side's perceptions. Such de-escalating gestures can help to combat the negative stereotypes that may interfere with fruitful negotiations. In ideal circumstances, negotiators also establish personal relationships that facilitate effective communication. This helps negotiators to focus on commonalities and find points of common interest.

Finally, if the 'right' people are not involved in negotiations, the process is not likely to succeed. First, all of the interested and affected parties – that is, the key stakeholders – must be represented. Second, negotiators must truly represent and have the trust of those they are representing. If a party is left out of the process, they may become angry and argue that their interests have not been taken into account. Agreements can be successfully implemented only if the relevant parties and interests have been represented in the negotiations, in part because parties that participate in the negotiation process have a greater stake in the outcome. Similarly, if constituents do not recognize a negotiator as their legitimate representative, they may try to block implementation of the agreement. Negotiators must therefore be sure to consult with their constituents and ensure that they deal adequately with constituents' concerns.

These concerns are related to the 'scale-up' problem of getting constituency groups to embrace the agreements that negotiators create. In many cases, participation in the negotiation process helps negotiators to recognize the legitimacy of the other side's interests, positions and needs. This transformative experience may lead negotiators to develop a sense of respect for the adversary, which their constituents do not share. As a result, negotiators may make concessions that their constituents do not approve of, and they may be unable to get the constituents to agree to the final settlement. This can lead to the last-minute breakdown of negotiated agreements.

NEGOTIATING TACTICS

Although collaborative negotiation is becoming the norm, negotiators are bound to meet other negotiators who have succeeded through hard bargaining methods. Their view is based on the somewhat anachronistic idea that 'all's fair in love and war' and that negotiating is no different. In this highly combative setting the best defence is to build a sound working knowledge of the tactics they use. These tactics include the following.

Extreme demands

Hard bargainers may take an unreasonable opening position, hoping to force others to lower their expectations. The sheer weight of such demands – 'We need a 25 per cent increase in the broadcast rights fees' or 'This player's worth half that much to us' – pushes an unprepared negotiator to make concessions. When faced with an extreme demand, restate it in terms that are more acceptable to you: 'So, you really want us to consider a 25 per cent increase?' or 'And you seriously believe the player's worth less than these other clearly inferior players?' You can reinforce your expectations by stating that you want to reach a fair agreement that satisfies everyone's interests and that such an agreement is necessary 'if we're going to effectively work together'.

Play acting

Some negotiators will try to intimidate those on the other side of the bargaining table by swearing, screaming, pounding the table and generally behaving like a bully. They may also try to make others feel guilty by accusing them of secrecy and threatening conduct. Research shows, however, that low-intensity, unemotional messages produce the greatest attitude shift in bargainers of equal power. Intense language and dramatic actions can be persuasive, but can also be superficial and banal. An effective response to strident self-promotion from those on the opposite side of the bargaining is to either say nothing and allow them to continue, or wait for the moment to pass, then restate your point and ask the other side to clarify more slowly or expand on their concerns. You can also ask if there are additional objections that account for the intense feelings and request a recess until things can be discussed calmly. If, on the other hand, you're intimidated or make too many concessions, you've allowed the other side to control your response.

Limited authority

This method surfaces through statements like 'It's not up to me' or 'The decision will be made upstairs'. The other side will often give you a settlement option, hoping that you'll accept it or make a more favourable counter-offer. You can deal with this tactic by clarifying early on whether the other person is really the decision-maker. You can also ask how decisions of this type have been handled in the past so you can spot contradictions in how your deal's being handled. If limited authority is a ploy, the other side will often 'find' the lost authority. But if a lack of power is genuine, get a commitment to meet with the true decision-maker.

Take it or leave it

This negotiating technique is often couched in terms that imply that someone else stands ready to make the deal if you don't. This tactic immediately undercuts the instigators' feelings of power and lowers their level of expectation. Know your cost and benefit limits, and remember that a bad deal for you is probably bad for your rivals too. Restate the benefits of your deal and note that the other party's offer would be unprofitable and unacceptable as it stands. To be effective against this strategy, however, you must be willing to walk away.

Good guy/bad guy tactic

With this type of tactic the other side brings in a person you haven't met before (the bad guy) to tear your offer to shreds, make unreasonable demands and stalk out of the room. Later, the original negotiator – the good guy – presents a more reasonable proposition that looks good by comparison. The idea is to force the other bargainers to make concessions that the good guy can offer to the bad guy for approval. The instigators need to be both cautious and resilient in this type of situation. One useful response is to re-examine the pre-negotiation plan, but don't make any immediate concessions.

SECURING THE BEST DEAL FOR ALL

Negotiators and deal-makers strive to sort out grievances, resolve conflict, and secure agreements effectively. For the most part a problem-centred, consultative mindset works best. It's especially easy to appreciate when you consider the different ways that negotiations may work out. Take, for example, the following scenarios.

Win-lose

When negotiations produce a winner and a loser, one side goes away feeling it's been 'had' or 'dudded'. Win-lose strategies, which have long dominated the bargaining arena, are traditionally compared to gamesmanship. But games assume that both sides are rational, informed bargainers with 'cast-iron' goals, who negotiate in a social vacuum. Another problem here is that a winner in week 1 may become a loser in week 2.

Lose-lose

This result is more common than many think. Both parties settle for less than they want because they believe it's the best they can get in the time available. Although compromise may be the best practical result in some deals, where time and convenience is at a premium, a problem-solving 'spirit' can often uncover superior solutions.

Win-win

This is the ideal, but it only happens with goodwill and effort. However, it also works best simply because both sides pursue solutions that satisfy everyone's needs. It starts with the mindset that by working together in a spirit of collaboration, both parties can achieve their goals without a massive compromise.

Win-win negotiating just doesn't happen. There are a number of prerequisites to win-win negotiating. In the first place, win-win negotiating challenges both sides to adopt a non-competitive attitude, mutual understanding of each other's needs and goals, a special set of negotiating skills and a certain amount of cooperation. And, if you look closely enough, you will always find points of agreement. Problem-solving comes into play when each side's needs don't seem to yield to the same satisfiers. Each round of win-win negotiating should start with mirror statements, which let each party reflect an understanding of the other's concerns, as well as the nature of the conflict. ('Let me get this straight ... you only want to pay US$500 for the rental of this very attractive indoor recreational space, but you also expect us to provide – that is, throw in – full night-time security for no additional cost to you...? Mate, that is a big ask!') Once you've agreed on the conflict itself, you can join forces to resolve it in a way that meets everyone's needs.

At the same time, it has to be conceded that win-win situations aren't always possible. When the situation won't yield to problem-solving techniques, you'll have to resort to compromise. Nevertheless, your efforts haven't been wasted. Honest attempts to try to learn what the other person wants and to satisfy those wants are bound to create a climate of goodwill and a strong bridge to future negotiations. This can only be a good thing.

CASE STUDY

A key theme running through this chapter is the gains that come from achieving negotiating agreements where both parties believe they have achieved a positive outcome. There is not only the warm glow that comes from securing a material reward, but also from claiming a psychological benefit: when confidence and morale are high, then so too are job satisfaction and productivity. Take, for example, the following case.

The management of a major leisure centre had a dispute with employees about overtime scheduling and evening working hours. Centre staff didn't want to be locked into spur-of-the-moment overtime assignments, yet management needed to be sure that the centre would be fully staffed and all listed programmes would be offered. After attacking the problem (instead of each other), both sides discovered an excellent win-win solution. Supervisors prepared a rotation list, and as staff names approached the top, they could expect an overtime call. Staff could also 'trade' hours among themselves as long as the Centre Manager was made aware of what was happening, and this resulted in a full array of programmes. In the spirit of no-lose negotiation, the parties collaborated to produce a unique answer to a unique problem, and neither side lost.

Questions

1 What is the problem here?
2 Is this case an example of cooperative or competitive negotiation?
3 Was the outcome a good one?
4 Would an immediate pay rise be a better solution to the problem?

Case exercise

Have a look at the American National Football League website (www.nfl.com/). Pay particular attention to its latest broadcasting rights agreement. Then seek out any media commentary on the lead up to the final agreement. Having reflected on the content of these documents, explain how you think the negotiations were conducted, how the final agreement concluded, and to what extent each part had gained from the agreement.

SUMMARY

This chapter examined the ways in which bargaining and negotiation can be used to both resolve disputes and problems and enhance the overall performance of sport enterprises. The symbolic and commercial logic behind the negotiation process was examined, together with the complex psychological and interpersonal conduct that underpins the interaction of the participants. This chapter also discussed the idea of zero-sum games, explained what is meant by a win-win view of bargaining and negotiation, and enabled students to design a sport enterprise-based bargaining and negotiation model that allows for a win-win outcome.

WEBSITE

Fletcher, M. (2015). *Show me the money! How to negotiate like a sports agent.* Available from: www.cnbc.com/2015/10/16/show-me-the-money-how-to-negotiate-like-a-sports-agent-commentary.html. See this site for advice on how sport agents negotiate contracts.

REFERENCES AND BIBLIOGRAPHY

Steele, P. and Beasor, T. (1999). *Business negotiation: a practical handbook.* Aldershot, UK: Gower.

Voss, C. and Raz, T. (2016). *Never split the difference: Negotiating as if your life depended on it.* New York: HarperCollins.

Chapter 21

Change and realignment

OVERVIEW

This chapter examines the ways in which sport enterprises can best accommodate the changes taking place in the broader society, especially as they relate to the interpersonal conduct of staff, volunteers, players and members. Special attention is given to the impact of technological change, the demand for greater cultural and social diversity within sport, and the push to remove dysfunctional stereotyping and discrimination.

LEARNING OBJECTIVES

Having engaged critically with this chapter readers will be able to:

1   Identify the external factors that are requiring sport enterprises to re-examine their current structure, values, policies and day-to-day operations;
2   Specify the implications of these outside pressures for the interpersonal conduct of staff, volunteers, players and members; and
3   Explain how change-programmes can be implemented that can best deal with the issues of technological change, cultural and social diversity within sport, and dysfunctional stereotyping and discrimination.

CHANGE IS THE NEW NORMAL

Organizations – including sport enterprises – are surrounded by a highly turbulent environment that often induces dramatic changes. The accelerated pace of change has transformed how work is organized and performed. Change has thus become an inherent and integral part of organizational life.

In particular, electronic technology, especially desk-top and personal computers, have changed the ways in which people communicate and messages are framed. In any office up to the 1990s, it was taken for granted that letters, notes, briefing papers and reports would be completed by a secretary or typist. The author, usually a male manager, would compose the document, and an assistant would type up the handwritten material. This was a very hierarchical, rigid, sexist and often inefficient arrangement. It was made totally redundant, though, when the World Wide Web — the Internet, if you like — and desk-top computers became part of the office landscape. Subsequently, managers were expected not only to compose their own written work, but also to type it up. This also meant that secretaries and typists were forced to retrain as personal assistants and administrative officers.

This is just one example of organizational change. In practice, organizational change can take on a multitude of forms. Anything that involves departures from the status quo, or challenges traditional ways of doing things will deliver organizational change. In short, if we alter something about the way things are done in organizations, whether it is habits, customs, attitudes, structures, systems or processes, we are practising organizational change.

More generally, economic, technological and political changes have undermined traditional ways of doing things, a number of which have important implications for organizational life, especially in the world of sport. They include globalization, diversification and the growing tensions between technical factors, which include organizational structures and computer hardware, and the social, which involve the interpersonal relations between staff and other stakeholders. These tensions present opportunities as well as threats and, if not managed well, will result in dysfunctional relations and problematic organizational outcomes. Some of these broad contextual changes are discussed below.

Globalization

Organizations operate in a global economy characterized by intense competition, and at the same time, greater economic interdependence and collaboration. More products and services are consumed outside of their country of origin than ever before, as globalization brings about greater convergence in terms of consumer tastes and preferences. Yet at the same time, in the midst of greater convergence, there is the opposite force of divergence at work, where companies have to adapt their corporate and business strategies, marketing plans and production efforts to local domestic markets. Another consequence of globalization is greater mobility in international capital and labour markets. This creates a global marketplace where there is more opportunity, because there are more suppliers, products and customers. However, there is also more competition, as local companies have to compete with foreign companies for customers. Sport has been caught up in this web of globalization.

The many dichotomies of modern economies and industrialized societies — competition versus collaboration, market forces versus State intervention, and global actions versus local solutions — are losing their sharp edges as contradictory forces appear to converge and reinforce each other in organizations across the globe. Companies that compete fiercely in some markets form strategic alliances in others; Government guidance and regulation are required to make markets work effectively; and 'think globally, act locally' has been adopted as a business strategy to deal with the challenges of doing business in the globalized economy. As organizations transform themselves to stay competitive, they will need to confront and resolve these dichotomies.

Globalization also impacts on the fates of people living and working in different parts of the world. Thus local events have significant global impacts, and vice versa. For instance, 11 September 2001 — when terrorists destroyed the World Trade Center in New York City — has been called the 'day that changed the world'. This catastrophic event heightened security concerns across the planet and changed the expectations for people in organizations, and the role of organizations themselves. The threat of terrorism continues to be a major concern worldwide, and has led to a major focus on workplace security, as employees experience a heightened sense of vulnerability. Major sporting events are especially vulnerable to terrorist threats, and mega events like the Olympic Games spend hundreds of billions of dollars on protecting both athletes and spectators from attack.

Diversity

Globalization is impacting how organizations compete with each other. In combination with changing demographics, globalization is causing a rapid increase in diversity within organizations. As noted in Chapter 1, never before have people been required to work together with colleagues and customers from so many different cultures and countries. In addition, this diversity means that society is moving away from 'mass society' to 'mosaic society'. Organizations reflect this mosaic society in their more diverse workforce (in terms of not only race, ethnic or culture, but also in terms of age, sexual orientation and other demographic variables). More than ever, people have to interact and communicate with others who come from diverse backgrounds. This in turn has meant that employees need new relational skills to succeed. An emerging stream of research in international management has called these new relational skills 'cultural intelligence'. Cultural intelligence is defined as the ability to adapt effectively across different national, organizational and professional cultures. More managers take up global work assignments in industries around the world. They learn how to work with people who not only think and communicate differently, but also do things differently. Managers will need to develop their cultural intelligence to manage greater diversity in organizations. The world population is growing at a high rate in developing countries, while remaining stable or decreasing in the developed world. The result will be income inequities and economic opportunity leading to increased immigration and migration within and between nations. More temporary workers will be used for specific tasks, and there will be a greater demand for highly skilled workers.

The ageing workforce population in advanced industrial nations like the USA, Germany, the United Kingdom, Canada and Australia means not only more retirees, but also additional gaps in the availability of experienced workers. Around 20 per cent of these nations are 55 years old or older, which suggests an ageing workforce. At the same time, retirees often want to keep a foot in the workplace door, and recent reports suggest that more than 70 per cent of baby boomers — that is, people born between 1946 and 1955 — envision working part-time after retirement. This will be a burden for young wage-earners, but good for diversity.

People of different ethnic and cultural backgrounds possess different attitudes, values and norms. Increasing cultural diversity in both public and private-sector organizations focuses attention on the distinctions between ethnic and cultural groups in their attitudes and performance at work. This greater focus can result in a tension between finding similarities and accentuating differences in the face of greater diversity in organizations.

This development has led to a debate between those who believe in the value of diversity (the heterogenists) and those who do not want core specialist capabilities diluted (the homogenists). Heterogenists contend that diverse or heterogeneous groups in organizations have performance advantages over homogeneous groups, whereas the homogenists take the opposing view; that homogeneous groups are more advantageous than heterogeneous or diverse groups in organizations. According to the heterogenists, organizations with greater diversity have an advantage in attracting and retaining the best available human talent. The exceptional capabilities of women and minorities offer a rich labour pool for organizations to tap into. When organizations attract, retain and promote maximum utilization of people from diverse cultural backgrounds, they gain competitive advantage and sustain the highest quality of human resources. Again, this is an important issue for sport enterprises to address.

On balance, organizations with greater diversity can understand and penetrate wider and enhanced markets. Not only do these organizations embrace a diverse workforce internally, but also they are better suited to serve a diverse external clientele. Organizations with greater diversity also display higher creativity and innovation. Especially in research-oriented and high technology organizations, the array of talents provided by a gender and ethnically diverse organization becomes invaluable. Heterogeneous or diverse groups display better problem-solving ability as they are more capable of avoiding the consequences of group-think, compared to highly cohesive and homogeneous groups that are more susceptible to conformity.

On the other hand, greater organizational diversity has its drawbacks. With the benefits of diversity come organizational costs. Too much diversity can lead to dysfunctional outcomes. Diversity increases ambiguity, complexity and confusion. Organizations with greater diversity may have difficulty reaching consensus and implementing solutions. In many organizations, diversity can produce negative dynamics such as ethnocentrism, stereotyping and cultural clashes.

The homogenists argue that homogeneous groups often outperform culturally diverse groups, especially where there is a serious communication problem. Cross-cultural training is necessary to enable culturally diverse groups to live up to their potential and overcome communication difficulties. The diversity movement, according to the homogenists, has the potential to polarize different social groups and harm productivity, while breeding cynicism and resentment, heightening intergroup frictions and tensions, and lowering productivity; just the opposite of what managing diversity is intended to accomplish. The challenge therefore is for management to manage the tension produced by heterogeneity versus homogeneity. If properly managed, sport enterprises can reap the benefits of greater diversity.

TECHNICAL CHANGE VERSUS SOCIAL CHANGE

As already noted, technology can provide enormous opportunities for organization leaders and rank-and-file employees alike. On the other hand, the implementation brings many problems, and many staff will be traumatized by these changers. Not surprisingly then, resistance to change will often be very strong. This problem brings into strong relief the tension that exists between an organization's technical systems and its social systems.

The technical subsystem comprises the devices, tools and techniques needed to transform inputs into outputs, in a way which enhances the economic performance of the organization.

The social system comprises the employees (at all levels) and the knowledge, skills, attitudes, values and needs they bring to the work environment, as well as the reward system and authority structures that exist in the organization. Later some authorities broadened the definitions to encompass the wider reach of the organization by including customers, suppliers and the rules and regulations, formal and informal, which govern the relations of the organization to society at large. This became known as the 'environmental subsystem'. The cornerstone of the 'sociotechnical approach', as the work of these researchers was named, was that the fit was achieved by a design process aimed at the joint optimization of the subsystems: any organizational system will maximize performance only if the interdependency of these subsystems is explicitly recognized. Hence any design or redesign must seek out the impact each subsystem has on the other, and design must aim to achieve superior results by ensuring that all the subsystems are working in harmony.

As noted in the early section of this book, organizational development is concerned mainly with the social component of organizational life. And, as also noted in the early part of the book, sport – because of its emphasis on interpersonal relations and public performance – is especially sensitive to social change and the problems that follow.

CHANGE-MANAGEMENT PRINCIPLES

In order for change to be successful and permanent, the change process must be both understood by members of the organization and agreed to. Moreover, the types of changes, and what and how to change, must also be revealed and explained very clearly.

A number of change-related issues need to be addressed if change is to be undertaken successfully. They are briefly explored below.

1   *Change does not equal progress*: It is important not to confuse change, which is simply an act of making things different, and progress, which implies positive and inexorable advancement. The point is that change is not valuable in and of itself, particularly when frequent and apparently arbitrary changes in procedures and systems are often indications of unstable and incompetent management. Progress should be the outcome of thoughtful change-management, but that is not always the case.

2   *Change has its own dynamic*: There is no turning back once a change programme has begun.

3   *Change can be traumatic*: It is a human disposition to experience discomfort as a result of change. This discomfort is particularly acute when people feel that change is being forced upon them.

4   *Change is easier to implement when it clear, precise, uncomplicated and contained*: Small changes are more likely to be accepted than big changes, particularly when they can be easily understood and assimilated into current work processes and systems. Unfortunately, organizations become overzealous and attempt to make radical changes rapidly. Although sometimes this is appropriate, most often change is better approached incrementally.

5   *Change can only be considered successful when it results in added value*: No change may be considered effective unless its end is the creation of 'something' better.

235

MAKING CHANGE HAPPEN

Once the decision-makers within a sport organization recognize that substantial change is needed as soon as possible, they are faced with the daunting prospect of deciding where to start. Research has found that the following four factors should be addressed in order to undertake a change-management strategy.

1   *Confirm that there is significant dissatisfaction with organization*: The bottom line here is that change will not and cannot take place until the people who constitute the organization – its board or owners, managers, employees, volunteers and members/ customers – are dissatisfied with the current situation. In many situations this is a massive hurdle, particularly as sporting clubs often tend to be 'stuck' in their traditional operations, functions and structures, like pylons in concrete. Thus, the board's or owners' first and overriding concern is to create widespread dissatisfaction with the status quo. How this is best accomplished is situation-dependent, but generally will require enormous effort in communicating with employees and customers, either in person or via market research. Ideally, a single term should be sufficient to describe this prerequisite for successful organizational change. Serious discomfort immediately comes to mind at this point. In other words, there must be a critical mass of information combined with an impending sense of 'doom' that collectively justify breaking the status quo.

2   *Create and maintain a shared vision of the future*: Once dissatisfaction is widespread, there must be a common view of how the organization should look instead. In technical terms, this means that a shared vision for the future must be held by everyone. Again, this usually must be created and underpinned by purposeful and energetic leadership, as it rarely occurs naturally. Moreover, the vision, once created, must be communicated with the rest of the organization.

3   *Ensure that organizations have the ability to make the change journey*: In order for change to be successful, even if the first two factors are in place, there must be systems that will support change in a practical, day-to-day manner. Thus, the architects of the change programme must identify the skills, roles and processes that must be undertaken, and provide the appropriate education and training to bolster these systems. In real terms, this means that the average employee has to know exactly what they are going to do differently on Monday morning, compared to the Friday before the change occurred. Change cannot proceed unless the infrastructure is there to uphold it.

4   *Provide the space for leaders to take 'actionable' first steps*: The organization's leaders must take the first steps, demonstrating overtly that the change process has actually begun. These actions must be direct and clearly related to the resolution of the difficulties faced. The initial step in the change-management process must establish a sense of urgency along with the element of dissatisfaction. Although it may seem that dissatisfaction with the status quo may be sufficient to overcome the organizational inertia associated with ingrained and traditional practices, the reality is that most employees are going to be preoccupied with their own processes, activities, agendas and political imperatives. Thus, getting a change programme to gather momentum

necessitates aggressive and proactive effort and commitment. The key to organizational transformation, therefore, lies with the management leadership's ability to empower others to act on the vision, and once they have established new policies, practices and procedures, to anchor them to the organization's culture.

ROLE OF A CHANGE-MANAGEMENT TEAM

The most effective method of facilitating the change process is to set up a change-management project team. This is essential to provide guide-rails for employees who have been 'empowered', but do not know what to do. The change-management team therefore, has both authority over the change process and accountability for its success, allowing for responsive and decisive action when necessary. The change-management teams have eight primary responsibilities:

1   *Establish context and provide guidance*: Ensures that the change process remains consistent with the vision, and that all employees are aware of that vision.
2   *Stimulate communication*: Establish alternative and non-traditional informal communication networks that work top-down and bottom-up.
3   *Provide appropriate resources*: Change is rarely inexpensive. The change-management team must make sure the organization 'puts its money where its mouth is'.
4   *Coordinate projects*: Task and project groups must work synchronously to ensure that every component of the organization is working towards the vision.
5   *Ensure congruence of messages, activities, policies and behaviours*: The change team must be vigilant in eliminating anything that is inconsistent with the vision.
6   *Provide opportunities for joint creation*: In other words, the change-management team is responsible for ensuring that everyone is involved in the change process, and that it proceeds as a partnership rather than through one-way orders.
7   *Anticipate, identify and address people problems*: Change is not easy on people; it will undoubtedly lead to stress and discomfort. It is therefore vital that someone on the change-management team be skilled in diagnosing, anticipating and addressing human-relations issues.
8   *Prepare and maintain the critical mass*: For the change process to be a success, the organization requires a minimum number of 'converts' among the staff. It is the job of the change-management team to 'win' or 'recruit' these pivotal staff members.

UNDERSTANDING CULTURE'S ROLE IN CHANGE

Having discussed the factors that must be in place for change to be successful, the question arises as to what happens when any one of the earlier four factors (see earlier section 'Making change happen') cannot be implemented. For example, it is easy to say that large-scale dissatisfaction exists and must be attended to, but sometimes it will seem impossible: core parts of the organization will not only resist change, but will also vehemently deny that change will improve performance. In some extreme cases they may go so far as to advocate a return to past policies and traditional practices. What needs to be understood is that change is mediated by the

237

personality or culture of an organization, like a normative glue that binds the values and assumptions of an individual person to their behaviour. Thus, at a fundamental level, for an organization to change, the culture and people embedded in it must change first. This point was highlighted in Chapter 3. This will free up the organization and enable it to undertake the structural and operational change necessary to move it in the desired new direction.

CASE STUDY

In this day and age, when political and economic turbulence is everywhere, organizational change is inevitable. As noted in Chapter 1, the forces for change are considerable. At the same time, change is frequently resisted, especially among employees who believe they will be disadvantaged by subsequent reorganization. Change can also be invigorating, since it can bring with it more intensive professional training, the broadening of a skill base and extensive opportunities for innovation. Over the last 40 years sport has been an exemplar of the change-management process. This has to do with many important issues ranging from changes in systems of governance, the implementation of policies to do with performance-enhancing drug use, the building of corporate and community partnerships in order to sustain its development, and in recent times, the reassessment of its policies on violence, harassment, bullying, sexual discrimination and violence against women.

The global fitness sector is a good case study of the importance of managing organizational change effectively. Take, for example, the Hyperactive Gym and Health Club (HGHC). HGHC has gone through both challenging and profitable times. However, over the last two years its membership rates had declined, and its brand image was weak and lacked the capacity to attract members. The HGHC manager Marvin Musclebound had just undertaken an in-depth reconnaissance of the health and fitness industry and its strengths and weaknesses. In the process of this investigation, he uncovered a number of societal trends that were likely to impact on the industry in general and HGHC in particular. Marvin identified the following trends and associated changes in community values, attitudes and behaviours.

- The demographics of the community in which HGHC was located had changed dramatically over the last few years. It was no longer dominated by married couples with teenage children, but had effectively been taken over by young childless people between the age of 20 and 40.
- This upwardly mobile and socially aware demographic cohort, often euphemistically known as 'hipsters', had an eclectic range of interests. Whereas music and the arts were high on their agenda, they also had a commitment to the concept of body improvement. This involved more than the occasional Botox injection. They also focused on keeping fit and looking good.
- This young mainly childless demographic cohort was, on average, fairly affluent and used their spending and leisure activities to create a youthful social identity.
- While long on cash they believed they were short on time. The idea of spending an afternoon, or worse, a full day, to play sport to keep fit and secure friendships was viewed as an extremely poor use of resources. This demographic cohort also had a quite

specific preference for exercise and fitness programmes that were low-impact, time-efficient and had the capacity to ensure an attractive body shape. Exercising to build strength and increase endurance were no longer the main priorities. This demographic group also built its life around flexible working and leisure hours. The idea of a 9–5 workday was relatively unimportant and the idea of exercising in the early morning and late afternoon was just one of many options.

■ This demographic group had increasing levels of pet ownership in which so-called urban-scaled designer dogs were the most popular. Additionally, pets were no longer indoor ornaments, but were also included in their public leisure activities.

It was clear to Marvin that, unless HGHC changed the way it did business, it would be unable to sustain itself into the future. He devised a radically new strategic plan that completely reorganized the structure and programme delivery of the centre. He replaced most of the aerobic programmes with a range of low-intensity, low-resistance exercise programmes that involved extensive stretching, with an emphasis on building up the strength and mobility of the body's core, which includes lower-back, abdominals and hips. He also implemented flexible opening hours in which the facility was open 24 hours, 7 days a week. As a result, staff were also required to be highly adaptable and available on demand. Overall, though they were only required for a few core hours, whereas staff were not available for around 60 per cent of the opening hours, Marvin was committed to ensuring that when they were on-deck so to speak, they would be able to provide the best professional advice possible. This demand required a radical overhaul of the minimum qualifications and skill requirements for staff. Marvin put in place an extensive retraining programme that was mandatory for all people employed at the centre. In addition, Marvin took the equally radical step of eliminating all permanent employment and employing only casual staff. But, as a trade-off, he increased the casual rate of pay by 20 per cent.

Marvin conceded that these initiatives constituted a massive organizational change programme. He also understood that there would be strong resistance to most of these proposals. However, he also had a plan to minimize the resistance through a sensibly organized arrangement, whereby current staff were invited to provide advice on how the programme could be implemented with the least stress and trauma to those affected by the changes. Marvin was cautiously optimistic that he could make it happen, and in the longer term deliver an operation that was both profitable and attractive to the local community.

Questions

1 What were the main external pressures impacting on HGHC?
2 Would it have been appropriate and even strategically smart to ignore these societal trends and continue as it was, under the assumption that these trends were little more than fads and would not last for long?
3 Of the many societal trends listed in the case, which two were clearly so important that they needed to be responded to?

4   If you were a staff member of HGHC, how would you respond to Marvin's initiatives?

5   Would it have been rational for staff to resist the change and even undermine Marvin's initiatives?

6   Would it have been appropriate to provide counselling for affected staff and provide both financial and psychological support to assist the adjustment process?

7   Alternatively, would it have been better for Marvin to take the hardest of lines and propose that if staff could not accommodate the change, they should leave forthwith?

Case exercise

Take a look at the Formula 1 Grand Prix website (www.formula1.com/). Pay particular attention to the scale of its operations, and the types of jobs involved in delivering the event as it moves around the world. Having addressed the strengths, weaknesses, threats and opportunities for this complex global sports circuit, think about the changes that need to be made to ensure a sustainable future. Finally, consider the possible strategies for making change happen, while also protecting the interests of officials, paid staff, volunteers and other stakeholders.

SUMMARY

In this chapter we looked at the issues that emerge when undertaking a programme of change-management. We discussed the external and internal factors forcing sport enterprises to re-examine their current structure, values and policies. We then identified the problems – especially psychological and interpersonal ones – that arise, and the implications they have for the subsequent conduct of staff, volunteers, players and members. We also explained how change-programmes can deal effectively with the issues of technological change, cultural and social diversity within sport, and dysfunctional stereotyping and discrimination.

WEBSITE

Goldsmith, W. (n.d.). *Ten reasons why change is so hard to introduce in sport*. Available from: www.wgcoaching.com/ten-reasons-why-change-is-so-hard-to-introduce-in-sport/. See this site for additional information on the difficulties of making changer happen in sport organizations.

REFERENCES AND BIBLIOGRAPHY

Bridges, W. (2009). *Managing transitions: Making the most of change* (3rd edn). Philadelphia, PA: Da Capo Lifelong.

Hellriegel, D. and Slocum, J. (2011). *Organizational behaviour*, Chapter 20 (13th edn). Mason, OH: South-Western Cengage Learning.

McShane, S. and Von Glinow, M. (2014). *Organizational behavior: Emerging knowledge, global reality* (7th edn). New York: McGraw Hill Education.

Senior, B. and Swailes, S. (2010). *Organizational change* (4th edn). Harlow, UK: Pearson Education.

Skinner, J., Stewart, B. and Edwards, A. (1999). Amateurism to professionalism: Modelling organizational change in sporting organizations. *Sport Management Review*, 2(2), pp.173–192.

Slack, T. and Parent, M. (2006). *Understanding sport organizations: The application of organization theory* (2nd edn). Champaign, IL: Human Kinetics.

Index

Page numbers in *italics* denote figures, those in **bold** denote tables.